The Hare Krishna Book of
Vegetarian Cooking

The Hare Krishna Book of Vegetarian Cooking

Ādirāja Dāsa

THE BHAKTIVEDANTA BOOK TRUST
LOS ANGELES • STOCKHOLM • MUMBAI • SYDNEY

If you are interested in knowing more about Vedic cooking
or philosophy, you are invited by
the International Society for Krishna Consciousness (ISKCON)
to visit one of its centers (see address list in back of book),
contact the author (see biography), or correspond
with the publisher at one of the following addresses.

The Bhaktivedanta Book Trust
P.O. Box 34074
Los Angeles, California 90034, USA
Phone: 1-800-927-4152 (inside USA); 1-310-837-5283 (outside USA)
Fax: 1-310-837-1056
e-mail: bbt.usa@krishna.com; web: www.krishna.com

The Bhaktivedanta Book Trust
PO Box 380
Riverstone, NSW 2765, Australia
Phone: +1-61-2-9627-6306; Fax: +1-61-2-9627-6052
e-mail: bbt.wp@krishna.com

ISKCON Reader Services
P.O. Box 730, Watford, WD25 8ZE, United Kingdom
E-mail: readerservices@pamho.net
www.iskcon.org.uk

Paintings by B.G. Sharma
Photographs by Roger Anney with the author
Illustrations by Subash David
Design by Thomas Keppel

ISBN-13: 978-0-90-267707-4; ISBN-10: 0-902677-07-1

Current printing, 2023: 5,000

Printed in China

This book is dedicated to our spiritual master,
His Divine Grace A.C. Bhaktivedanta Swami Prabhupāda,
who devoted his life to elevating humanity by
spreading Vedic culture all over the world.

Acknowledgements

I wish to express my thanks to everyone who offered criticism and help for the preparation of this book. This book has come together by the grace of Lord Kṛṣṇa and my spiritual master, His Divine Grace A. C. Bhaktivedanta Swami Prabhupāda, and with the help of devotees who, despite their own engagements and projects, found the time to assist in whatever way they could. In particular, I would like to thank Umāpati Dāsa for his invaluable help in editing the book and for his advice and dedication; His Holiness Jayādvaita Swami for his expert advice and his polishing of the final manuscript; Taponidhi Dāsa for composing and designing the book; Vilāsinī Dāsī for proofreading and indexing; Satyarāja Dāsa for his research; Mukhyā Dāsī, Kiśorī Dāsī, and Kāntī Dāsī for eagerly sharing their culinary secrets; Ānandinī Dāsī and Āhāradā Dāsī for enthusiastically and diligently kitchen-testing all the recipes; and my wife, Mahāmedhā Dāsī, for putting family considerations aside in order to help in many ways.

Special thanks to Boutique Girard Willi and Kishori Boutique, in Paris, for their loan of Indian accessories for the photographs.

Editor's Note

Most of the italicized words in this book are listed in the glossary, with the pronunciation shown in the Sanskrit pronunciation guide. The people referred to in this book with Sanskrit names are initiated members of the Hare Kṛṣṇa movement.

Contents

Preface

THIS is no ordinary cookbook. You could say it's more a way of life. I have always believed that we are what we eat. This book of basically Indian recipes supports that philosophy, answers many questions, and offers a viable alternative for so many people who, like myself, were never entirely convinced of the virtues of eating meat. I did not realize it at the time, but that small doubt was the beginning of a whole new way of looking at everything.

I had never been completely happy about being a meat eater. Even being brought up on a farm did not condition me to it. Rather, it made it harder. I could not blind myself to the facts. They were there, part of my life every day. I could never come to terms with the knowledge that those beautiful little calves I had watched being born and had later stroked as they came to nuzzle my hand would end up on my plate. That the should unnecessarily die in fear and pain seemed appalling; and with a third of the world starving, it did not make sense at all to give animals grain that could nourish people. A field of grain that can feed two cows can feed sixty-four people.

It is very easy to label vegetarians mere sentimentalists and health nuts, but we are al aware that there is so much more involved than that. The question concerns us all, on moral, health, economic, and religious grounds.

Still, it was a difficult choice to make, and a difficult path to follow on many respects. The alternatives to meat-eating seemed rather boring and, what's worse, fattening. I imagined that it would require huge amounts of will power.

Then there was the family aspect. Keeping my hungry, active young children fully satisfied and happy at mealtimes was a headache. And, of course, there was the question of nutrition: I was naturally concerned with their getting enough protein. So I gathered a few good vegetarian recipes, which I trotted out again and again, with monotonous regularity. Sure enough, the ever present baked potato was the cause of many a mealtime mutiny. Indeed, I even began to think that if I ever had to look another bean in the face, I would not be answerable for my actions!

I was beginning to despair and lose heart, but help was at hand. You will find it in this book of interesting, varied, and wholesome recipes. It shows how easy it can be to maintain a delicious and balanced diet without ever touching flesh of any kind. Added to this, the recipes are simple and easy to prepare. The days when one's plate looked bare if bereft of meat are a thing of the past.

Of course, underlying all this is the philosophy, the attitude towards eating. You are what you eat. The how and why of it is inextricably tied up with the most fundamental questions of belief and feeling about life, about the true value of life—all life, not simply human.

I first tasted this food at one of the Hare Kṛṣṇa temples in this country. It was absolutely delicious, and made even more so by having been prepared by devotees with pure hearts, and offered with love to God.

Here then is a cookbook with a philosophy behind it. Even if you only enjoy making the recipes, that's good. But if you want to, it can change your life.

Hare Kṛṣṇa!

BEE HOLM

Hayley Mills
May 1984
Hampton, England

Introduction

THIS is a practical cookbook, designed to help you prepare authentic Indian meals in your own home and to acquaint you with the tradition behind India's great vegetarian cuisine. It explains not only the techniques of Vedic, or classical Indian vegetarian cooking, but also the Vedic art of eating, which nourishes both the soul and the body and mind.

The first four chapters discuss Vedic philosophy and vegetarianism with corroborations from classical and modern science, religion, and ethics.

The next three chapters talk about the meal itself: the utensils used for cooking, dishes that go well together, and everything else you might need to know about preparing, serving, and eating an Indian meal.

Then come 130 kitchen-tested recipes. Although this is only a fraction of the thousands of possibilities offered by the Vedic culinary tradition, these recipes, chosen for their diversity as well as their ease of preparation, give an idea of the vastness of Vedic cooking. The recipes were contributed by the best cooks in the Hare Kṛṣṇa movement, some of whom were taught by Śrīla Prabhupāda himself.

The appendixes include a glossary, conversion tables, advice on where to get essential ingredients, and addresses of Hare Kṛṣṇa centers, where you can sample the recipes in this book.

To be fully appreciated, Vedic cooking must be understood in the context of Vedic culture. The word *Vedic* comes from the Sanskrit word *veda*, meaning "absolute knowledge." The ancient

Sanskrit scriptures of India are known as the Vedic scriptures, or the *Vedas,* because they present knowledge of the Absolute. The Vedic culture of ancient India, based on these scriptures, is still followed by many people today.

According to the *Vedas,* a human being is meant to realize his true identity as an eternal servant of God. This Vedic understanding begins with the knowledge that we are not our temporary material bodies but the eternal spiritual souls within our bodies. Because we mistake ourselves for material beings, we suffer, though by constitution we are eternal, full of knowledge, and blissful. The process of reviving our original, joyful consciousness and awakening our dormant love for God is called *bhakti-yoga,* or Kṛṣṇa consciousness.

The name "Kṛṣṇa" has a special significance. Even though there is one God, people call Him by different names, each name describing an aspect of His personality. But there is a name given in the *Vedas* that expresses the sum total of God's infinite characteristics. That all-encompassing name is Kṛṣṇa, which means "infinitely attractive."

The *Vedas* are a treasure-house of knowledge about Kṛṣṇa and our eternal relationship with Him. They differ from the other scriptures of the world in that they describe God's personal features in great detail in order to awaken our love for Him, and the ways in which we can express this love in everything we do. This is India's gift to the world: a culture that unites all fields of human endeavor with the spiritual perfection often thought to be the exclusive property of recluse meditators. Indeed, in Vedic culture Kṛṣṇa consciousness permeates every aspect of life: not only art, music, architecture, and literature, but cooking and eating as well.

What distinguishes Vedic cooking from other types of cooking is the cook's spiritual consciousness, his awareness that he is preparing an offering for God. In most religious systems, people ask God to give them their daily bread, but the devotee of Kṛṣṇa offers the daily bread to God as an expression of love for Him. And God reciprocates. In the *Bhagavad-gītā,* one of the Vedic scriptures, Lord Kṛṣṇa says that He accepts a vegetarian offering, be it no more than a leaf or a fruit, or a glass of water, if it is presented with devotion, and out of His inconceivable mercy He spiritualizes the offering by personally tasting it. What was ordinary food then becomes *kṛṣṇa-prasādam,* the mercy of Lord Kṛṣṇa. And what would have been ordinary eating becomes worship, a loving exchange with the Lord.

The effect of eating *prasādam* is different from that of eating food cooked merely for profit, for the pleasure of the tongue, or even for survival. We think about a lot of things when we cook, but pleasing God isn't usually one of them. And when food is cooked without God consciousness, the materialistic thoughts of the cook subtly affect whoever eats it. But when we eat *prasādam,* food cooked with devotion to God and offered to Him in love, our hearts become purified. Mukunda Gosvāmī, one of the present spiritual masters of the Hare Kṛṣṇa movement, has said, "If you eat ordinary food, you simply develop lusty desires to enjoy this material world; if you eat *prasādam,* you increase your love of God with every mouthful."

Naturally, we don't expect all of our readers to switch over completely to Indian-style cooking. Although you may think that Vedic cooking is exclusively Indian, the principle of offering food to Kṛṣṇa is transcendental to worldly designations. A recipe does not have to come from India, as long as the ingredients and procedures follow the Vedic principles. For example, in Italy where most of our devotees and friends are still very fond of their native cuisine, almost every Indian meal includes a serving of pasta. The style of cooking is not so important as the devotion to Kṛṣṇa that goes into it.

The term "Indian cooking" when used in this book refers to Vedic cooking, not to any of the "chicken-curry" schools of Indian cuisine. Meat-eating was practically nonexistent in the ancient Vedic culture. It was introduced into India by foreign conquerors, especially the Moguls, who came via Persia in the sixteenth century; the Portuguese, who ruled Goa for four centuries; and finally the British colonialists. But despite centuries of domination by meat-eaters, India is still the home of vast numbers of vegetarians.

India is traditionally vegetarian (meat-eaters are called "nonvegetarians") because her timeless Vedic culture teaches that all life is sacred, and to kill innocent creatures unnecessarily is a gross violation of the laws of God. All forms of plant and animal life are bound by nature's laws to follow their instinct in selecting what they eat; but man, with his advanced intelligence, can consider higher spiritual principles in choosing his food. In his writings

Śrīla Prabhupāda explains, "Although the law [of nature] states the human being must subsist on another living being, there is the law of good sense also, for the human being is meant to obey the laws of the scriptures. This isn't possible for animals."

The *Vedas* define a true vegetarian as one who eats no meat, fish, or eggs. Those who abstain from meat but eat eggs or fish are not considered true vegetarians because they are eating flesh, even though it may be hidden, as in eggs, under a calcium coating. One who becomes a vegetarian only to avoid killing may see no reason to refuse unfertilized eggs, but if we take the Vedic view that all flesh is unfit for human consumption, it makes sense to shun eggs, which, fertilized or not, are nothing but the assembled materials for the bodies of chickens. Kṛṣṇa's devotees are strict vegetarians in the Vedic sense of the word: they eat no meat, fish, or eggs.

Some vegetarians, called vegans, abstain not only from meat, fish, and eggs but also from milk and milk products, because of moral concern about abuse of cows in the dairy industry. The devotees of Kṛṣṇa also condemn animal abuse, but rather than abstain from milk, which the *Vedas* consider essential for human beings, they show their compassion in a positive way by teaching the Vedic principle of cow protection, and, as far as possible, drinking milk only from Hare Kṛṣṇa dairy farms, where the cows are loved and protected.

Many people become vegetarian but then later, because of a lack of taste and conviction, fall back into former eating habits. How many more people would consider giving up meat-eating if they knew of an alternative diet which was tastier and scientifically perfect. We hope that the magic touch of Ancient India found in this book will inspire you to see that for health, taste, and spiritual advancement, there is no better way of eating than to eat vegetarian food offered to Kṛṣṇa. It's not only easy, it's absolutely enjoyable. And once you experience the satisfaction of eating food prepared with the consciousness of pleasing Lord Kṛṣṇa, you will know what we mean when we say you have acquired a higher taste.

Vegetarianism, then, from the Vedic point of view, is part of something larger, the natural way of eating for those who want to make the most of their human life. In whatever way we follow the Vedic teachings, whether we become perfect spiritualists or simply purify our eating habits, we become happier and lessen the suffering in the world around us. "Whatever you do, whatever you eat, whatever you offer or give away, and whatever austerities you perform—do that as an offering to Me." (Kṛṣṇa speaking to Arjuna, His dear devotee, in the *Bhagavad-gītā:* 9.27)

"Whatever you do, whatever you eat, whatever you offer or give away, and whatever austerities you perform—do that as an offering to Me." (Kṛṣṇa speaking to Arjuna, His dear devotee, in the *Bhagavad-gītā*: 9.27)

Vegetarianism: A Means to a Higher End

THE word *vegetarian,* coined by the founders of the British Vegetarian Society in 1842, comes from the Latin word *vegetus,* meaning "whole, sound, fresh, or lively," as in *homo vegetus*—a mentally and physically vigorous person. The original meaning of the word implies a balanced philosophical and moral sense of life, a lot more than just a diet of vegetables and fruits.

Most vegetarians are people who have understood that to contribute towards a more peaceful society we must first solve the problem of violence in our own hearts. So it's not surprising that thousands of people from all walks of life have, in their search for truth, become vegetarian. Vegetarianism is an essential step towards a better society, and people who take the time to consider its advantages will be in the company of such thinkers as Pythagoras, Socrates, Plato, Clement of Alexandria, Plutarch, King Asoka, Leonardo da Vinci, Montaigne, Akbar, John Milton, Sir Isaac Newton, Emanuel Swedenborg, Voltaire, Benjamin Franklin, Jean Jacques Rousseau, Lamartine, Percy Bysshe Shelley, Ralph Waldo Emerson, Henry David Thoreau, Leo Tolstoy, George Bernard Shaw, Rabindranath Tagore, Mahatma Gandhi, Albert Schweitzer, and Albert Einstein.

Let's examine some of the advantages of becoming vegetarian.

Health and Nutrition

Can a vegetarian diet improve or restore health? Can it prevent certain diseases?

Advocates of vegetarianism have said yes for many years, although they didn't have much support from modern science until recently. Now, medical researchers have discovered evidence of a link between meat-eating and such killers as heart disease and cancer, so they're giving vegetarianism another look.

Since the 1960s, scientists have suspected that a meat-based diet is somehow related to the development of arteriosclerosis and heart disease. As early as 1961, the *Journal of the American Medical Association* said: "Ninety to ninety-seven percent of heart disease can be prevented by a vegetarian diet."[1] Since that time, several well-organized studies have scientifically shown that after tobacco and alcohol, the consumption of meat is the greatest single cause of mortality in Western Europe, the United States, Australia, and other affluent areas of the world.[2]

The human body is unable to deal with excessive amounts of animal fat and cholesterol.[3] A poll of 214 scientists doing research on arteriosclerosis in 23 countries showed almost total agreement that there is a link between diet, serum cholesterol levels, and heart disease.[4] When a person eats more cholesterol than the body needs (as he usually does with a meat-centered diet), the excess cholesterol gradually becomes a problem. It accumulates on the inner walls of the arteries, constricts the flow of blood to the heart, and can lead to high blood pressure, heart disease, and strokes.

On the other hand, scientists at the University of Milan and Maggiore Hospital have shown that vegetable protein may act to keep cholesterol levels low. In a report to the British medical journal *The Lancet,* D.C.R. Sirtori concluded that people with the type of high cholesterol associated with heart disease "may benefit from a diet in which protein comes only from vegetables."[5]

What about cancer? Research over the past twenty years strongly suggests a link between meat-eating and cancer of the colon, rectum, breast, and uterus. These types of cancer are rare among those who eat little or no meat, such as Seventh-Day Adventists, Japanese, and Indians, but they are prevalent among meat-eating populations.[6]

Another article in *The Lancet* reported, "People living in the areas with a high recorded incidence of carcinoma of the colon tend to live on diets containing large amounts of fat and animal protein; whereas those who live in areas with a low incidence live on largely vegetarian diets with little fat or animal matter."[7]

Rollo Russell, in his *Notes on the Causation of Cancer,* says, "I have found of twenty-five nations eating flesh largely, nineteen had a high cancer rate and only one had a low rate, and that of thirty five nations eating little or no flesh, none had a high rate."[8]

Why do meat-eaters seem more prone to these diseases? One reason given by biologists and nutritionists is that man's intestinal tract is simply not suited for digesting meat. Flesh-eating animals have short intestinal tracts (three times the length of the animal's body), to pass rapidly decaying toxin-producing meat out of the body quickly. Since plant foods decay more slowly than meat, plant-eaters have intestines at least six times the length of the body. Man has the long intestinal tract of a herbivore, so if he eats meat, toxins can overload the kidneys and lead to gout, arthritis, rheumatism, and even cancer.

And then there are the chemicals added to meat. As soon as an animal is slaughtered, its flesh begins to putrefy, and after several days it turns a sickly gray-green. The meat industry masks this discoloration by adding nitrites, nitrates, and other preservatives to give the meat a bright red color. But research has now shown many of these preservatives to be carcinogenic.[9] And what makes the problem worse is the massive amounts of chemicals fed to livestock. Gary and Steven Null, in their book, *Poisons in your Body,* show us something that ought to make anyone think twice before buying another steak or ham. "The animals are kept alive and fattened by continuous administration of tranquilizers, hormones, antibiotics, and 2,700 other drugs. The process starts even before birth and continues long after death. Although these drugs will still be present in the meat when you eat it, the law does not require that they be listed on the package."[10]

Because of findings like this, the American National Academy of Sciences reported in 1983 that "people may be able to prevent many common types of cancer by eating less fatty meats and more vegetables and grains."[11]

But wait a minute! Weren't human beings designed to be meat-eaters? Don't we need animal protein?

The answer to both these questions is no. Although some historians and anthropologists say that man is historically omnivorous, our anatomical equipment—teeth, jaws, and digestive system—favors a fleshless diet. The American Dietetic Association notes that "most of mankind for most of human history has lived on vegetarian or near-vegetarian diets."

And much of the world still lives that way. Even in most industrialized countries, the love affair with meat is less than a hundred years old. It started with the refrigerator car and the twentieth-century consumer society.

But even in the twentieth century, man's body hasn't adapted to eating meat. The prominent Swedish scientist Karl von Linne states, "Man's structure, external and internal, compared with that of the other animals, shows that fruit and succulent vegetables constitute his natural food." The chart on the next page compares the anatomy of man with that of carnivorous and herbivorous animals.

As for the protein question, Dr. Paavo Airola, a leading authority on nutrition and natural biology, has this to say: "The official daily recommendation for protein has gone down from the 150 grams recommended twenty years ago to only 45 grams today. Why? Because reliable worldwide research has shown that we do not need so much protein, that the actual daily need is only 30 to 45 grams. Protein consumed in excess of the actual daily need is not only wasted, but actually causes serious harm to the body and is even causatively related to such killer diseases as cancer and heart disease. In order to obtain 45 grams of protein a day from your diet you do not have to eat meat; you can get it from a 100 percent vegetarian diet of a variety of grains, lentils, nuts, vegetables, and fruits."[12]

Dairy products, grains, beans, and nuts are all concentrated sources of protein. Cheese, peanuts, and lentils, for instance, contain more protein per ounce than hamburger, pork, or porterhouse steak.

Still, nutritionists thought until recently that only meat, fish, eggs, and milk products had complete proteins (containing the eight amino acids not produced in the body), and that all vegetable proteins were incomplete (lacking one or more of these amino acids). But research at the Karolinska Institute in Sweden and the Max Planck Institute in Germany has shown that most vegetables, fruits, seeds, nuts, and grains are excellent sources of complete proteins. In fact, their proteins are easier to assimilate than those of meat—and they don't bring with them any toxins. It's nearly impossible to lack protein if you eat enough natural un-

Meat-eater	Plant-eater	Human Being
has claws	no claws	no claws
no skin pores; perspires through tongue to cool body	perspires through millions of skin pores	perspires through millions of skin pores
sharp, pointed front teeth to tear flesh	no sharp pointed front teeth	no sharp pointed front teeth
salivary glands in the mouth (not needed to predigest grains and fruits)	well-developed salivary glands, needed to predigest grains and fruits	well-developed salivary glands, needed to predigest grains and fruits
acid saliva; no enzyme ptyalin to pre-digest grains	alkaline saliva; much ptyalin to pre-digest grains	alkaline saliva; much ptyalin to pre-digest grains
no flat back molar teeth to grind food	flat back molar teeth to grind food	flat back molar teeth to grind food
much strong hydrochlorid acid in stomach to digest tough animal muscle, bone, etc.	stomach acid ten times less strong than meat eaters	stomach acid ten times less strong than meat eaters
intestinal tract only 3 times body length so radlt decaying meat can pass out of body quickly	intestinal tract 6 times body length fruits do not decay as rapidly so can pass more slowely through body	intestinal tract 6 times body length

Based on a chart by A.D. Andrews, *Fit Food for Men*, (Chicago American Hygiene Society, 1970)

refined food. Remember, the vegetable kingdom is the real source of *all* protein. Vegetarians simply eat it "direct" instead of getting it second-hand from the vegetarian animals.

Too much protein intake even reduces the body's energy. In a series of comparative endurance tests conducted by Dr. Irving Fisher of Yale University, vegetarians performed twice as well as meat-eaters. When Dr. Fisher knocked down the nonvegetarians' protein consumption by twenty percent, their efficiency went up thirty-three percent.[13] Numerous other studies have shown that a proper vegetarian diet provides more nutritional energy than meat. A study by Dr. J. Iotekyo and V. Kipani at Brussels University showed that vegetarians were able to perform physical tests two to three times longer than meat-eaters before tiring out—and the vegetarians fully recovered from fatigue three times more quickly than the meat-eaters.[14]

Economics

Meat feeds few at the expense of many. For the sake of producing meat, grain that could feed people feeds livestock instead. According to information compiled by the United States Department of Agriculture, over ninety percent of all the grain produced in America goes to feed livestock—cows, pigs, sheep, and chickens—that wind up on dinner tables.[15] Yet the process of using grain to produce meat is incredibly wasteful. Figures from the U.S. Department of Agriculture show that for every sixteen pounds of grain fed to cattle, we get back only one pound of meat.[16]

In *Diet for a Small Planet,* Frances Moore Lappé asks us to imagine ourselves sitting down to an eight-ounce steak. "Then imagine the room filled with 45 to 50 people with empty bowls in front of them. For the 'feed cost' of your steak, each of their bowls could be filled with a full cup of cooked cereal grains."[17]

Affluent nations do not only waste their own grains to feed livestock. They also use protein-rich plant foods from poor nations. Dr. Georg Borgstrom, an authority on the geography of food, estimates that one-third of Africa's peanut crop (and peanuts give the same amount of protein as meat) ends up in the stomachs of cattle and poultry in Western Europe.[18]

In underdeveloped countries, a person consumes an average of four hundred pounds of grain a year, most of it by eating it directly. In contrast, says world food authority Lester Brown, the average European or American goes through two thousand pounds a year, by first feeding almost ninety percent of it to animals for meat. The average European or American meat-eater, Brown says, uses five times the food resources of the average Colombian, Indian, or Nigerian.[19]

Facts such as these have led food experts to point out that the world hunger problem is artificial. Even now, we are already producing more than enough food for everyone on the planet—but we are allocating it wastefully.

Harvard nutritionist Jean Mayer estimates that bringing down meat production by only ten percent would release enough grain to feed sixty million people.[20]

Another price we pay for meat-eating is degradation of the environment. The heavily contaminated runoff and sewage from slaughterhouses and feedlots are major sources of pollution of rivers and streams. It is fast becoming apparent that the fresh water resources of this planet are not only becoming contaminated but also depleted, and the meat industry is particularly wasteful. Georg Borgstrom says the production of livestock creates ten times more pollution than residential areas, and three times more than industry.[21]

In their book *Population, Resources, and Environment,* Paul and Anne Ehrlich show that to grow one pound of wheat requires only sixty pounds of water, whereas production of one pound of meat requires anywhere from 2,500 to 6,000 pounds of water.[22]

And in 1973 the *New York Post* uncovered a shocking misuse of this most valuable resource: one large chicken-slaughtering plant in the United States was using one hundred million gallons of water daily, an amount that could supply a city of twenty-five thousand people.[23]

But now let's turn from the world geopolitical situation, and get right down to our own pocketbooks. A spot check of supermarkets in New York in January 1986 showed that sirloin steak cost around four dollars a pound, while ingredients for a delicious, substantial vegetarian meal average less than two dollars a pound. An eight ounce container of cottage cheese costing sixty cents provides sixty percent of the minimum daily requirement of protein. Becoming a vegetarian could potentially save you at least several thousand dollars a year, tens of thousands of dollars over the course of a lifetime. The savings to America's consumers would amount to billions of dollars annually. And the same principle applies to consumers all over the world. Considering all this, it's hard to see how anyone could afford *not* to become a vegetarian.

Ethics

Many people consider the ethical reasons the most important of all for becoming vegetarian. The beginning of ethical vegetarianism is the knowledge that other creatures have feelings, and that their feelings are similar to ours. This knowledge encourages one to extend personal awareness to encompass the suffering of others.

In an essay titled *The Ethics of Vegetarianism,* from the journal of the North American Vegetarian Society, the conception of "humane animal slaughter" is refuted. "Many people nowadays have been lulled into a sense of complacency by the thought that animals are now slaughtered 'humanely', thus presumably removing any possible humanitarian objection to the eating of meat. Unfortunately, nothing could be further from the actual facts of life . . . and death.

"The entire life of a captive 'food animal' is an unnatural one of artificial breeding, vicious castration and/or hormone stimulation, feeding of an abnormal diet for fattening purposes, and eventually long rides in intense discomfort to the ultimate end. The holding pens, the electric prods and tail twisting, the abject terror and fright, all these are still very much a part of the most 'modern' animal raising, shipping, and slaughtering. To accept all this and only oppose the callous brutality of the last few seconds of the animals' life, is to distort the word 'humane'."

The truth of animal slaughter is not at all pleasant—commercial slaughterhouses are like visions of hell. Screaming animals are stunned by hammer blows, electric shock, or concussion guns. They are hoisted into the air by their feet and moved through the factories of death on mechanized conveyor systems. Still alive, their throats are sliced and their flesh is cut off while they bleed to death. Why isn't the mutilation and slaughter of farm animals governed by the same stipulations intended for the welfare of pets and even the laboratory rat?

Many people would no doubt take up vegetarianism if they visited a slaughterhouse, or if they themselves had to kill the animals they ate. Such visits should be compulsory for all meat eaters.

Pythagoras, famous for his contributions to geometry and mathematics, said, "Oh, my fellow men, do not defile your bodies with sinful foods. We have corn, we have apples bending down the branches with their weight, and grapes swelling on the vines. There are sweet-flavored herbs, and vegetables which can be cooked and softened over the fire, nor are you denied milk or thyme-scented honey. The earth affords a lavish supply of riches of innocent foods, and offers you banquets that involve no bloodshed or slaughter; only beasts satisfy their hunger with flesh, and not even all of those, because horses, cattle, and sheep live on grass."

In an essay titled *On Eating Flesh,* the Roman author Plutarch wrote: "Can you really ask what reason Pythagoras had for abstinence from flesh. For my part I rather wonder both by what accident and in what state of mind the first man touched his mouth to gore and brought his lips to the flesh of a dead creature, set forth tables of dead, stale bodies, and ventured to call food and nourishment the parts that had a little before bellowed and cried, moved and lived... It is certainly not lions or wolves that we eat out of self-defense; on the contrary, we ignore these and slaughter harmless, tame creatures without stings or teeth to harm us. For the sake of a little flesh we deprive them of sun, of light, of the duration of life they are entitled to by birth and being."

Plutarch then delivered this challenge to flesh-eaters: "If you declare that you are naturally designed for such a diet, then first kill for yourself what you want to eat. Do it, however, only through your own resources, unaided by cleaver or cudgel or any kind of ax."

The poet Shelly was a committed vegetarian. In his essay A *Vindication of Natural Diet,"* he wrote, "Let the advocate of animal food force himself to a decisive experiment on its fitness, and as Plutarch recommends, tear a living lamb with his teeth and, plunging his head into its vitals, slake his thirst with the steaming blood . . . then, and then only, would he be consistent."

Leo Tolstoy wrote that by killing animals for food, "Man suppresses in himself, unnecessarily, the highest spiritual capacity—that of sympathy and pity towards living creatures like himself—and by violating his own feelings becomes cruel." He also warned, "While our bodies are the living graves of murdered animals, how can we expect any ideal conditions on earth?"

When we lose respect for animal life, we lose respect for human life as well. Twenty-six hundred years ago, Pythagoras said, "Those that kill animals to eat their flesh tend to massacre their own." We're fearful of enemy guns, bombs, and missiles, but can we close our eyes to the pain and fear we ourselves bring about by slaughtering, for human consumption, over 1.6 billion domestic mammals and 22.5 billion poultry a year.[24]

The number of fish killed each year is in the trillions. And what to speak of the tens of millions of animals killed each year in the "torture camps" of medical research laboratories, or slaughtered for their fur, hide, or skin, or hunted for "sport"? Can we deny that this brutality makes us more brutal too?

Leonardo da Vinci wrote, "Truly man is the king of beasts, for his brutality exceeds theirs. We live by the death of others. We are burial places!" He added, "The time will come when men will look upon the murder of animals as they now look upon the murder of men."

Mahatma Gandhi felt that ethical principles are a stronger support for lifelong commitment to a vegetarian diet than reasons of health. "I do feel," he stated, "that spiritual progress does demand at some stage that we should cease to kill our fellow creatures for the satisfaction of our bodily wants." He also said, "The greatness of a nation and its moral progress can be judged by the way its animals are treated."

Religion

All major religious scriptures enjoin man to live without killing unnecessarily. The Old Testament instructs, "Thou shalt not kill." (Exodus 20:13) This is traditionally misinterpreted as referring only to murder. But the original Hebrew is *lo tirtzach,* which clearly translates "Thou shalt not kill." Dr. Reuben Alcalay's *Complete Hebrew/English Dictionary* says that the word *tirtzach,* especially in classical Hebrew usage, refers to "any kind of killing," and not necessarily the murder of a human being.

Although the Old Testament contains some prescriptions for meat-eating, it is clear that the ideal situation is vegetarianism. In Genesis (1:29) we find God Himself proclaiming, "Behold, I have given you every herb-bearing tree, in which the fruit of the tree yielding seed, it unto you shall be for meat." And in later books of the Bible, major prophets condemn meat-eating.

For many Christians, major stumbling blocks are the belief that Christ ate meat and the many references to meat in the New Testament. But close study of the original Greek manuscripts shows that the vast majority of the words translated as "meat" are *trophe, brome,* and other words that simply mean "food" or "eating" in the broadest sense. For example, in the Gospel of St. Luke (8:55) we read that Jesus raised a woman from the dead and "commanded to give her meat." The original Greek word translated as "meat" is *phago,*" which means only "to eat." The Greek word for meat is *kreas* ("flesh"), and it is never used in connection with Christ. Nowhere in the New Testament is there any direct reference to Jesus eating meat. This is in line with Isaiah's famous prophecy about Jesus's appearance, "Behold, a virgin shall conceive, and bear a son, and shall call his name Immanuel. Butter and honey shall he eat, that he may know to refuse the evil and choose the good."

In *Thus Spake Mohammed* (the translation of the *Hadith* by Dr. M. Hafiz Syed), the disciples of the prophet Mohammed ask him, "Verily are there rewards for our doing good to quadrupeds, and giving them water to drink?" Mohammed answers, "There are rewards for benefiting *every* animal."

Lord Buddha is known particularly for His preaching against animal killing. He established *ahiṁsā* (nonviolence) and vegetarianism as fundamental steps on the path to self-awareness and spoke the following two maxims, "Do not butcher the ox that plows thy fields," and "Do not indulge a voracity that involves the slaughter of animals."[25]

The Vedic scriptures of India, which predate Buddhism, also stress nonviolence as the ethical foundation of vegetarianism. "Meat can never be obtained without injury to living creatures," states the *Manu-saṁhitā,* the ancient Indian code of law, "Let one therefore shun the use of meat." In another section, the *Manu-saṁhitā* warns, "Having well considered the disgusting origin of flesh and the cruelty of fettering and slaying of corporeal beings, let one entirely abstain from eating flesh." In the *Mahābhārata* (the epic poem which contains 100,000 verses and is said to be the longest poem in the world), there are many injunctions against killing animals. Some examples: "He who desires to increase the flesh of his own body by eating the flesh of other creatures lives in misery in whatever species he may take his birth.";"Who can be more cruel and selfish than he who augments his flesh by eating the flesh of innocent animals?"; and "Those who desire to possess good memory, beauty, long life with perfect health, and physical, moral and spiritual strength, should abstain from animal food."

All living entities possess a soul. In the *Bhagavad-gītā,* Kṛṣṇa describes the soul as the source of consciousness and the active principle that activates the body of every living being. According to the *Vedas,* a soul in a form lower than human automatically evolves to the next higher species, ultimately arriving at the human form. Only in the human form of life can the soul turn its consciousness towards God and at the time of death be transferred back to the spiritual world. In both the social order and the universal order, a human being must obey laws.

In his *Śrīmad-Bhāgavatam* purports, Śrīla Prabhupāda says, "All living entities have to fulfill a certain duration for being encaged in a particular type of material body. They have to finish the duration allotted in a particular body before being promoted or evolved to another body. Killing an animal or any other living being simply places an impediment in the way of his completing his term of imprisonment in a certain body. One should therefore not kill bodies for one's sense gratification, for this will implicate one in sinful activity." In short, killing an animal interrupts its progressive evolution through the species, and the killer will invariably suffer the reaction for this sinful behavior.

In the *Bhagavad-gītā* (5.18), Kṛṣṇa explains that spiritual perfection begins when one can see the equality of all living beings, "The humble sage, by virtue of true knowledge, sees with equal vision a learned and gentle *brāhmaṇa* (a priest), a cow, an elephant, a dog, and a dog-eater (outcaste)." Kṛṣṇa also instructs us to adopt the principles of spiritual vegetarianism when He states, "Offer Me with love and devotion a fruit, a flower, a leaf, or water, and I will accept it."

Karma

The Sanskrit word *karma* means "action", or more specifically, any material action that brings a reaction that binds us to the material world. Although the idea of *karma* is generally associated with Eastern philosophy, many people in the West are also coming to understand that *karma is* a natural principle, like time or gravity, and no less inescapable. For every action there is a reaction. According to the law of *karma,* if we cause pain and suffering to other living beings, we must endure pain and suffering in return, both individually and collectively. We reap what we sow, in this life and the next, for nature has her own justice. No one can escape the law of *karma,* except those who understand how it works.

To understand how *karma* can cause war, for example, let's take an illustration from the *Vedas.* Sometimes a fire starts in a bamboo forest when the trees rub together. The real cause of the fire, however, is not the trees but the wind that moves them. The trees are only the instruments. In the same way, the principle of *karma* tells us that the United States and the Soviet Union are not the real causes of the friction that exists between them, the friction that may well set off the forest fire of nuclear war. The real cause is the imperceptible wind of *karma* generated by the world's supposedly innocent citizens.

According to the law of *karma,* the neighborhood supermarket or hamburger stand (the local abortion clinic too, but that could be the subject for another book) has more to do with the threat of nuclear war than the White House or the Kremlin. We recoil with horror at the prospects of nuclear war while we permit equally horrifying massacres every day inside the world's automated slaughterhouses.

The person who eats an animal may say that he hasn't killed anything, but when he buys his neatly packaged meat at the supermarket he is paying someone else to kill for him, and both of them bring upon themselves the reactions of *karma.* Can it be anything but hypocritical to march for peace and then go to McDonald's for a hamburger or go home to grill a steak? This is the very duplicity that George Bernard Shaw condemned:

We pray on Sundays that we may have light
To guide our footsteps on the path we tread;
We are sick of war, we don't want to fight,
And yet we gorge ourselves upon the dead.

As Śrīla Prabhupāda says in his explanations of *Bhagavad-gītā,* "Those who kill animals and give them unnecessary pain—as people do in slaughterhouses—will be killed in a similar way in the next life and in many lives to come... In the Judeo-Christian scriptures, it is stated clearly 'Thou shalt not kill.' Nonetheless, giving all kinds of excuses, even the heads of religion indulge in killing animals and, at the same time, try to pass as saintly persons. This mockery and hypocrisy in human society brings about unlimited calamities such as great wars, where masses of people go out onto the battlefields and kill each other. Presently they have discovered the nuclear bomb, which is simply waiting to be used for wholesale destruction." Such are the effects of *karma.*

Those who understand the laws of *karma,* know that peace will not come from marches and petitions, but rather from a campaign to educate people about the consequences of murdering innocent animals (and unborn children). That will go a long way toward preventing any increase in the world's enormous burden of *karma.* To solve the world's problems we need people with purified consciousness to perceive that the real problem is a spiritual one. Sinful people will always exist, but they shouldn't occupy positions of leadership.

One of the most common objections non-vegetarians raise against vegetarianism is that vegetarians still have to kill plants, and that this is also violence. In response it may be pointed out that vegetarian foods such as ripe fruits and many vegetables, nuts, grains, and milk do not require any killing. But even in those cases where a plant's life is taken, because plants have a less evolved consciousness than animals, we can presume that the pain involved is much less than when an animal is slaughtered, what to speak of the suffering a food-animal experiences throughout its life.

It's true vegetarians have to kill some plants, and that is also violence, but we do have to eat something, and the *Vedas* say, *jīvo jīvasya jīvanam:* one living entity is food for another in the struggle for existence. So the problem is not how to avoid killing altogether—an impossible proposal—but how to cause the least suffering to other creatures while meeting the nutritional needs of the body.

The taking of any life, even that of a plant, is certainly sinful, but Kṛṣṇa, the supreme controller, frees us from sin by accepting what we offer. Eating food first offered to the Lord is something like a soldier's killing during wartime. In a war, when the commander orders a man to attack, the obedient soldier who kills the enemy will get a medal. But if the same soldier kills someone on his own, he will be punished. Similarly, when we eat only *prasādam,* we do not commit any sin. This is confirmed in the *Bhagavad-gītā (3.13)* "The devotees of the Lord are released from all kinds of sins because they eat food which is offered first for sacrifice. Others, who prepare food for personal sense enjoyment, eat only sin." This brings us to the central theme of this book: vegetarianism, although essential, is not an end in itself.

Beyond Vegetarianism

Beyond concerns of health, economics, ethics, religion, and even *karma,* vegetarianism has a higher, spiritual dimension that can help us develop our natural appreciation and love of God. Śrīla Prabhupāda tells us in his explanations of *Śrīmad-Bhāgavatam,* "The human being is meant for self-realization, and for that purpose he is not to eat anything that is not first offered to the Lord. The Lord accepts from His devotee all kinds of food preparations made from vegetables, fruits, milk products, and grains. Different varieties of fruits, vegetables, and milk products can be offered to the Lord, and after the Lord accepts the foodstuffs, the devotee can partake of the *prasādam,* by which all suffering in the struggle for existence will be gradually mitigated."

Kṛṣṇa Himself confirmed the divinity of *prasādam* when He appeared in this world as Śrī Caitanya Mahāprabhu 500 years ago: "Everyone has tasted these material substances before, but now, these same ingredients have taken on extraordinary flavors and uncommon fragrances. Just taste them and see the difference. Not to mention the taste, the fragrance alone pleases the mind and makes one forget all other sweetnesses. It is to be understood therefore, that these ordinary ingredients have been touched by the transcendental nectar of Kṛṣṇa's lips and imbued with all of Kṛṣṇa's qualities."

Offered food, traditionally called *prasādam,* "the mercy of God," offers not only the healthy life of a vegetarian, but also God realization; not just food for the starving masses, but spiritual nourishment for everyone. When Kṛṣṇa accepts an offering, He infuses His own divine nature into it. *Prasādam,* therefore, is not different from Kṛṣṇa Himself. Out of His unbounded compassion for the souls entrapped in the material world, Kṛṣṇa comes in the form of *prasādam, so* that simply by eating, we can come to know Him.

Eating *prasādam* nourishes the body spiritually. By eating *prasādam* not only are past sinful reactions in the body vanquished, but the body becomes immunized to the contamination of materialism. Just as an antiseptic vaccine can protect us against an epidemic, eating *prasādam* protects us from the illusion and influence of the materialistic conception of life. Therefore, a person who eats only food offered to Kṛṣṇa, can counteract all the reactions of one's past material activities, and readily progresses in self-realization. Because Kṛṣṇa frees us from the reactions of *karma*, or material activities, we can easily transcend illusion and serve Him in devotion. One who acts without *karma* can dovetail his consciousness with God's and become constantly aware of His personal presence. This is the true benefit of *prasādam*.

One who eats *prasādam is* actually rendering devotional service to the Lord and is sure to receive His blessings. Śrīla Prabhupāda often said that by eating *prasādam* even once we can escape from the cycle of birth and death, and by eating only *prasādam* even the most sinful person can become a saint. The Vedic scriptures speak of many people whose lives were transformed by eating *prasādam*, and any Hare Kṛṣṇa devotee will vouch for the spiritual potency of *prasādam* and the effect it has had on his life. Eating only food offered to Kṛṣṇa is the ultimate perfection of a vegetarian diet. After all, pigeons and monkeys are also vegetarian, so becoming a vegetarian is not in itself the greatest of accomplishments. The *Vedas* inform us that the purpose of human life is to reawaken the soul to its relationship with God, and only when we go beyond vegetarianism to *prasādam* can our eating be helpful in achieving this goal.

Footnotes and References

1) *Journal of the American Medical Association,* Editor: Diet and Stress in vascular disease. JAMA 176: 134–5, 1961

2) Inter-Society Commission for Heart Disease Resources. Report of Inter-Society Commission for Heart Disease Resources: Primary prevention of the arteriosclerotic diseases. Circulation 42: A53–95, December 1970; also Senate Select Committee on Nutrition and Human Needs: Dietary Goals for the United States. U.S. Government Printing Office, Washington, D.C, 20402, 1977.

3) Saturated fats are found primarily, but not exclusively, in foods of animal origin; hydrogenated fats are found in commercially prepared foods; cholesterol is found only in animal products.

4) Kaare R. Norum, "What is the Experts' Opinion on Diet and Coronary Heart Diseases?" *Journal of the Norwegian Medical Association,* 12 February 1977.

5) CR. Sirtori, et. al., "Soybean Protein Diet in the Treatment of Type II Hyperlipoproteinaemia," *The Lancet* 1 (8006): 275–7, (5 February 1977).

6) R.L. Phillips, "Role of Lifestyle and Dietary Habits in Risk of Cancer Among Seventh-Day Adventists," Cancer Research 35:3513, (November 1975); Morton Mintz, "Fat Intake Seen Increasing Cancer Risk," *Washington Post,* 10 September 1976.

7) M.J. Hill, "Bacteria and the Aetiology of Cancer of the Large Bowel," *Lancet,* 1:95–100, 1971.

8) Quoted from *Cancer and Other Diseases from Meat Consumption,* Blanche Leonardo, Ph.D. 1979, p. 12.

9) M. Jacobson, "How Sodium Nitrite Can Affect Your Health," (Washington, D.C.: Center for Science in the public interest, 1973); W. Linjinsky, and S.S. Epstein, "Nitrosamines as Environmental Carcinogens," *Nature,* no. 225 (1970), p. 21–3; Committee on Nitrate Accumulation, National Academy of Sciences, 2101 Constitution Ave., Washington, D.C, 20418, 1972, and the *Lancet,* "Nitrate and Human Cancer," 2 (8032): 281, 6 August 1977.

10) Gary and Steven Null, *Poisons in Your Body,* Arco Press, 1977, p. 52.

11) American Academy of Sciences, *Diet, Nutrition, and Cancer,* National Research Consul, National Academy Press, Washington, June 1982.

12) Dr. Paavo Airola, "Health Forum", *Vegetarian Times,* August 1982, p. 67.

13) Irving Fisher, "The Influence of Flesh Eating on Endurance," *Yale Medical Journal,* 13(5); 205–21 (March 1907).

14) J.L. Buttner, *A Fleshless Diet: Vegetarianism as a rational dietary,* Fredrick A. Stokes Company, New York, 1910, p. 131–2.

15) Frances Moore Lappe, *Diet for a Small Planet,* (New York Ballantine Books, 1975), p. 12.

16) Ibid., p. 10.

17) Ibid., p. 235.

18) Georg Borgstrom cited in Frances Moore Lappe, *Diet for a Small Planet,* p. 25.

19) Lester Brown cited in Vic Sussman, *The Vegetarian Alternative* (Rodale Press, 1978), p. 234.

20) Dr. Jean Mayer cited by the U.S. Senate Select Committee on Nutrition and Human Needs, Dietary Goals for the U.S. (Washington, D.C.: February 1977), p. 44.

21) Georg Borgstrom cited in Frances Moore Lappe, *Diet for a Small Planet,* p. 32.

22) Paul and Anne Ehrlich, *Population, Resources, Environment,* W.H. Freeman and Company, 1970, p. 64.

23) "Food Price Rises," Sylvia Porter, *New York Post,* July 27, 1973.

24) These totals of domestic mammals and poultry slaughtered each year have been compiled by the author from statistics found in the *FAO Production Yearbook 1984,* vol. 38,

Statistics Series No. 61, Food and Agriculture Organization of the United Nations/ Rome, p. 226–47.

The data on livestock slaughtered shown in this yearbook is collected from about 200 countries and territories. Estimates have been made by the FAO for nonreporting countries as well as for countries reporting partial coverage. For the interest of our readers, the FAO statistics given for the number of livestock slaughtered in 1984, of some major species, are as follows: cattle and calfs, 229,249,000; buffalo, 7,269,000; sheep and lamb, 409,500,000; goat, 177,296,000; pig, 765,424,000; horse, 4,032,000; chicken, 21,902,400,000; duck, 234,000,000; and turkey, 372,300,000.

Instead of giving the number of horses and poultry (chickens, ducks, and turkeys) slaughtered in the world each year, the *FAO Production Yearbook* gives the metric tonnage (MT) of horsemeat and poultry meat produced. The world total for 1984 is 504,000 MT and 29,958,000 MT (chickens, 27,378,000 MT; ducks, 390,000 MT; turkeys, 2,190,000 MT) respectively. The author corresponded with the chief of the FAO Basic Date Unit Statistics Division to find that an average of seven horses, 800 chickens, 600 ducks, or 170 turkeys comprise a metric ton of meat. These figures were also confirmed by butchers in Paris.

25) It is interesting to note that the Vedic scriptures consider Buddha an incarnation of Lord Kṛṣṇa. The *Śrīmad-Bhāgavatam* predicted Buddha's appearance in the world, and the great spiritual master Śrīla Jayadeva Gosvāmī later wrote in his prayers to Lord Kṛṣṇa, "O my Lord, a Personality of Godhead, all glories unto You. You compassionately appeared in the form of Lord Buddha to condemn animal sacrifices."

Their Lordships Śrī Śrī Rādhā-Paris-Īśvara, the Rādhā-Kṛṣṇa Deities in the Hare Kṛṣṇa temple in Paris.

A Temple of Krishna in Your Home

GUESTS visiting a temple of Kṛṣṇa for the first time are often puzzled by the ceremonial offering of vegetarian dishes to the form of Kṛṣṇa on the altar—and understandably so. After all, what does the omnipotent, omniscient, omnipresent Lord want with our little plate of rice and vegetables? Has He suddenly become hungry? Hasn't He created countless tons of food? Isn't God self-sufficient? Does Kṛṣṇa really need these offerings of food?

In fact, Kṛṣṇa *does* ask for these offerings, not because He needs our rice and vegetables, but because He wants our devotion. In *Bhagavad-gītā* (9.26) He says, "If one offers Me with love and devotion a leaf, a flower, fruit, or water, I will accept it."

When Kṛṣṇa asks us to offer Him food, we should understand that He is actually inviting us to reawaken our eternal loving relationship with Him. At first we comply in a mood of faith mixed with duty; later, as our realization matures, we do it with affection and love. Just as anybody naturally offers the best he has to his beloved, the devotee offers Kṛṣṇa his wealth, his intelligence, his life, and his vegetarian food.

Kṛṣṇa is the ultimate beloved of everyone, but how can we offer gifts to a beloved we don't yet know? The Vedic tradition can guide us. If you would like to try, but can't follow all the procedures, you can remember that when the great devotee Hanumān and his companions were building a bridge of large, heavy stones for King Rāma, an incarnation of Kṛṣṇa, a little spider also pleased the Lord by carrying the largest pebbles he could.

First, reserve a special place for the offering. It can be a tabletop or an entire room converted into a temple. Make an altar with a picture of Lord Kṛṣṇa on it. On Kṛṣṇa's left you will see Śrīmatī Rādhārāṇī, His eternal consort. She is Kṛṣṇa's pleasure potency, and it is She who awards love of Godhead to the sincere devotee.

If possible, put a photograph of a Kṛṣṇa conscious spiritual master on the altar. The spiritual master accepts the offering of his disciple and offers it to his own spiritual master, who in turn offers it to his spiritual master. In this way the offering ascends through a succession of spiritual masters, until it reaches Lord Kṛṣṇa. The devotees of the Hare Kṛṣṇa movement always have a photograph of Śrīla Prabhupāda, the founder and spiritual master of the International Society for Krishna Consciousness (ISKCON), and if a devotee is a disciple of one of Śrīla Prabhupāda's disciples, he also has a photograph of his own spiritual master.

A Kṛṣṇa conscious spiritual master who is visibly present in the world can personally guide you to perfection in spiritual life. Just before Śrīla Prabhupāda left this material world, he asked some of his senior disciples to become spiritual masters and perpetuate the Vedic tradition. If you would like to find out more about these spiritual masters and how you can meet one of them, you can inquire at any ISKCON center.

From the shopping to the cooking, meditate on pleasing Kṛṣṇa. Look for the freshest and best fruits and vegetables. Shopping in supermarkets requires care. There's more to it than simply avoiding obvious meat, fish, and eggs. Take the time to read every label. And don't assume that products stay the same; they change. Watch out for rennet (made from the lining of a calf's stomach and used to make cheese), gelatin (boiled bones, hooves and horns, used to set foods), and lecithin (if it is not marked "soy lecithin," it may come from eggs). Anything with onions or garlic is unofferable to Kṛṣṇa, because these foods, the *Vedas* say, increase the mode of ignorance. Watch out for animal fat. Many products have it. And if a product has a blank label, don't buy it: the manufacturer doesn't want you to know what's inside.

You can also look into alternatives to supermarket shopping. Many cooperatives have inexpensive produce that is free from chemical fertilizers and pesticides. And, if you have a little space in your yard, why not grow something for Kṛṣṇa yourself?

Now you are ready to cook for Kṛṣṇa. Here's how we do it in our temples:

• The cook thinks about Kṛṣṇa's pleasure, not his own. He thinks, "My Lord has kindly provided me with these ingredients, so let me combine them and cook them in such a way that He will be pleased." Chanting the Hare Kṛṣṇa *mantra* or listening to devotional recordings helps him remember Kṛṣṇa and he avoids mundane talk in the kitchen.

• Cleanliness is next to Godliness. The cook should have a clean body and a clean mind, and wear clean clothes in the kitchen. Hair should be tied back so it stays out of the food and out of the fire. The kitchen and cooking utensils should be spotless, so he takes a minute to sponge off the work areas before beginning to cook. "Kṛṣṇa will accept a very simple offering from a clean kitchen," Śrīla Prabhupāda said, "but He will not accept an elaborate offering from a dirty kitchen."

• *Prasādam* (food already offered) and *bhoga* (food not yet offered) are never mixed. We don't want to offer Kṛṣṇa the same thing twice, so we keep *prasādam* in specific containers so that it won't be accidentally mixed with *bhoga.*

• This may surprise you: the cook never tastes the food before offering it—not even to test it. Kṛṣṇa must be the first to relish it. Experience teaches the cook to judge the correct amounts of seasonings. If something is taken before being offered to the Deity, the entire preparation is polluted and can no longer be offered.

When the meal is ready, it is time to offer it to Kṛṣṇa. In our temples we arrange portions of the food on diningware kept especially for this purpose. (No one else eats from these dishes). The rest of the food stays in the pots until the offering is finished.

Put a small glass of cool water by Kṛṣṇa's plate, along with a spoon and a tiny plate with a little salt and pepper. You might also light one or two sticks of incense to provide a pleasant atmosphere. After putting the plate on the altar, recite the Hare Kṛṣṇa *mantra:*

Hare Kṛṣṇa, Hare Kṛṣṇa, Kṛṣṇa Kṛṣṇa, Hare Hare
Hare Rāma, Hare Rāma, Rāma Rāma, Hare Hare

Recite the *mantra* three times. Then leave the offering on the altar for a few minutes. The Hare Kṛṣṇa *mantra is* a prayer: "My dear Rādhārāṇī and Kṛṣṇa, please engage me in Your devotional service."

The more our consciousness is fixed on pleasing Kṛṣṇa, the more He enjoys the offering. We can offer Kṛṣṇa the best dishes we can but what really attracts Kṛṣṇa is our sincerity. Our love and devotion are the essential ingredients. Lord Kṛṣṇa is also called *Bhāva-grāhi-janārdana,* which means "One whose pleasure is the devotional attitude of His devotee." Once, when Kṛṣṇa was present on earth five thousand years ago, His friend and pure devotee Vidura was offering Him bananas. But Vidura was overcome with devotional ecstasy because of Kṛṣṇa's presence, and was inadvertently discarding the fruits and offering the skins, which Kṛṣṇa ate with relish because they were offered out of love. Another great devotee, Sanātana Gosvāmī, was so poor that he could offer only dry *chapatis* to Kṛṣṇa; but to Kṛṣṇa they tasted like nectar because they were offered with love.

After the offering, remove Kṛṣṇa's plate from the altar and transfer the *prasādam* to a serving plate. Wash Kṛṣṇa's plate and bowls and put them away. Now the *prasādam* can be served. The *prasādam* that comes directly from the Lord's plate is called *mahā-prasādam (mahā* means "great," *prasādam* means "mercy") and is extra special. The person serving should see that everyone gets some *mahā-prasādam.*

The proper mentality for eating *prasādam is* described by Śrīla Prabhupāda in the *Śrī Caitanya-caritāmṛta: "Prasādam is* nondifferent from Kṛṣṇa. Therefore, instead of eating *prasādam,* one should honor it. When taking *prasādam,* one should not consider the food to be ordinary preparations. *Prasādam* means favor. One should consider *prasādam* a favor of Kṛṣṇa. Kṛṣṇa is very kind. In this material world we are all attached to tasting various types of food. Therefore, Kṛṣṇa eats many nice varieties of food and offers the food back to the devotees, so that not only are one's demands for various tastes satisfied, but by eating *prasādam* one makes advancement in spiritual life. Therefore, we should never consider ordinary food on an equal level with *prasādam."*

In other words, if while eating *prasādam* one thinks of it as a manifestation of Kṛṣṇa's mercy, he is considered to have actually *stopped* eating; now his eating has become honoring. By thus honoring Kṛṣṇa, who has come in the form of *prasādam,* one pleases Kṛṣṇa, and when Kṛṣṇa is pleased His devotee is pleased.

This is real yoga, linking with the Supreme Lord. The simple process of offering food makes us aware of an essential teaching of the *Vedas:* everything comes from Kṛṣṇa, and everything should be offered back to Him for His pleasure.

So every day when you cook, cook for Kṛṣṇa and offer the food to Him. Before long, your home will start to feel like a temple, and you'll be well on your way back to Godhead.

If you are new to offering your food to Kṛṣṇa, we suggest the recitation of the Hare Kṛṣṇa *mantra* as the easiest method. However, if you like, you can recite the same prayers that the devotees use. Acknowledging that it is through the mercy of the spiritual master and Lord Caitanya that Kṛṣṇa accepts our offering, every devotee recites three times the *praṇāma mantra* to his own spiritual master (you can use the *praṇāma mantra* of any of the present ISKCON spiritual masters) and the following two prayers in glorification of Śrī Caitanya Mahāprabhu and Lord Kṛṣṇa.

namo-mahā-vadānyāya kṛṣṇa-prema-pradāya te
kṛṣṇāya kṛṣṇa-caitanya-nāmne gaura-tviṣe namaḥ

"O most munificent incarnation! You are Kṛṣṇa Himself appearing as Śrī Kṛṣṇa Caitanya Mahāprabhu. You have assumed the golden color of Śrīmatī Rādhārāṇī, and You are widely distributing pure love of Kṛṣṇa. We offer our respectful obeisances unto You."

namo brahmaṇya-devāya go-brāhmaṇa-hitāya ca
jagad-dhitāya kṛṣṇāya govindāya namo namaḥ

"I offer my respectful obeisances to the Supreme Absolute Truth, Kṛṣṇa, who is the well-wisher of the cows and the *brāhmaṇas,* as well as the living entities in general. I offer my repeated obeisances to Govinda, who is the pleasure reservoir for all the senses."

Śrīla Prabhupāda, the founder and spiritual master of the International Society for Krishna Consciousness, giving *prasādam* to his disciples and guests.

Vegetarianism and the Hare Krishna Movement

BHAKTI-YOGA, the science of devotion to Kṛṣṇa, has been faithfully handed down through the ages for the spiritual health of humanity. The Vedic culture considers a person who caters to the whims of the body and mind, neglecting the needs of the soul, to be infected with the disease of materialism. As doctors prescribe a medicine and a special diet for a disease, the Vedic sages recommend the chanting of Kṛṣṇa's holy names as the medicine for the materialistic disease, and *prasādam* as the diet. The Vedic scriptures have predicted that this remedy for human suffering will reach every town and village in the world.

Eager to hasten the fulfillment of this prediction, His Divine Grace A.C. Bhaktivedanta Swami Prabhupāda, following in the footsteps of his great spiritual predecessors, dedicated his life to spreading Kṛṣṇa consciousness. In 1965, he left India for the United States to introduce Kṛṣṇa consciousness to the people of the West, as his own spiritual master, His Divine Grace Bhaktisiddhanta Sarasvatī, had requested of him many years earlier. Śrīla Prabhupāda was undaunted by his advanced age and the many other obstacles that faced him. Relying fully on the mercy of Lord Kṛṣṇa, he started what was to become a worldwide movement, in the form of the International Society for Krishna Consciousness (ISKCON). Between 1965, when Śrīla Prabhupāda came to America from India, and 1977, when he passed away from this world, he conveyed the fullness of spiritual life through his lectures, letters, books, and tape recordings, as well as his personal example. He established more than one hundred temples, translated nearly eighty volumes of transcendental literature, and initiated almost five thousand disciples.

Śrīla Prabhupāda was motivated by a sense of urgency, because he could see that the world needed India's great spiritual culture, which was rapidly disappearing. In India he saw that leaders who had neither faith in the Vedic teachings nor knowledge of how to apply them were trying to solve essentially spiritual problems with material solutions. He saw the young generation of Indian people turning away from their sublime spiritual heritage in favor of Western materialism, at the same time that many people in the West, disillusioned with materialism, were looking for a new life with a higher set of values.

Śrīla Prabhupāda was keenly aware of the problems of both India and the West, and he offered a sensible solution. He compared India, which still has some spiritual vision, but lacks widespread technology, to a lame man; and the Western countries, which excel in technology but lack spiritual vision, to a blind man. If the seeing lame man sits on the shoulders of the walking blind man, they become like one man who sees and walks. The International Society for Krishna Consciousness is this seeing and walking man, using the best of both India and the West to revive Vedic culture in India and spread it to the rest of the world.

Kṛṣṇa consciousness, Śrīla Prabhupāda would often say, is not something dry. And *prasādam* was one way he proved his assertion. He showed his disciples how to cook many kinds of vegetarian dishes, how to offer them to Kṛṣṇa, the Supreme Lord, and how to relish the sanctified food as Kṛṣṇa's mercy. Śrīla Prabhupāda was always pleased to see his disciples eating only Kṛṣṇa's *prasādam.* Many times he personally cooked the *prasādam* and served his disciples with his own hand.

In Volume Two of *Prabhupāda Nectar,* His Holiness Satsvarūpa dāsa Gosvāmī describes the mood in which Śrīla Prabhupāda gave out *prasādam.* "He liked to give *prasādam* from his hand, and everyone liked to receive it. It was not just food, but the blessings of *bhakti,* the essence of devotional service. Śrīla Prabhupāda gave out *prasādam* happily, calmly, and without discrimination. When he gave to children, they liked the sweet taste of it, in the form of a cookie or sweetmeat, yet also they liked it as a special treat from Prabhupāda, who sat on the *vyāsāsana* [seat of the spiritual master] leaning forward to them. Women liked it because they got a rare chance to come forward and extend their hand before Prabhupāda. They felt satisfied and chaste. And stalwart men came forward like expectant children, sometimes pushing one another just to get the mercy from Prabhupāda. To Prabhupāda it was serious and important, and he would personally supervise to make sure that a big plate was always ready for him to distribute... Although now *prasādam* distribution in the Kṛṣṇa consciousness movement is done on a huge scale, as Prabhupāda desired, it all started from his own hand, as he gave it out one-to-one."

Śrīla Prabhupāda taught that giving *prasādam* to others is an important part of the Kṛṣṇa conscious way of life. A spiritual movement is useless without free distribution of sanctified foods, Śrīla Prabhupāda said. He wanted free *prasādam* to be part of every Hare Kṛṣṇa function. Indeed, with full faith in the spiritual potency of *prasādam* to elevate humanity to God consciousness, Śrīla Prabhupāda wanted the whole world to taste *kṛṣṇa-prasādam.*

The doors are open to the public every day at each of the two hundred Hare Kṛṣṇa temples and thirty-five farm communities around the world, where anyone can take free *kṛṣṇa-prasādam.* On Sunday, each center invites the public for a sumptuous multi-course "love feast," a program Śrīla Prabhupāda started in 1966 at the first temple on the Lower East Side of New York City. Every center also has several public festivals a year, such as Ratha-yātrā, the Festival of the Chariots, perhaps the world's oldest spiritual festival. And at each festival, tens of thousands of people see the beautiful form of Kṛṣṇa and eat *kṛṣṇa-prasādam.*

In 1979 some devotees in North America created the "Festival of India," a touring cultural program that crisscrosses the United States and Canada every year, holding 40 festivals in 20 major cities. Under six large tents and at numerous booths and display panels, thousands of people experience Vedic culture as it was presented to the West by Śrīla Prabhupāda, through drama, dance, music, diorama exhibits, Vedic literature, and free vegetarian feasts.

The Hare Kṛṣṇa movement also has restaurants in major cities like London, Paris, Milan, Los Angeles, Dallas, and Sydney. As far as possible, the restaurants use ingredients grown on farms run by Kṛṣṇa devotees. The devotees also give courses in cooking *kṛṣṇa-prasādam.* In England, the United States, and Australia, the Hare Kṛṣṇa Vegetarian Club on many of the major campuses, provides a humane alternative to the slaughterhouse-oriented college nutrition courses. And having become acquainted with the Kṛṣṇa conscious philosophy, which encompasses all of the ordinary arguments for vegetarianism, and then goes beyond by giving lucid spiritual arguments, most of the people who participate in these clubs become very resolute vegetarians.

Many people have come to know the devotees of Kṛṣṇa through the public congregational chanting of Kṛṣṇa's holy names. This public chanting, inaugurated in India five hundred years ago, is always accompanied by the distribution of free *prasādam.*

In some countries, the temples sponsor free *prasādam* restaurants. For example, at Mukunda's Drop-In Centre in Sydney, Australia, over one million meals have been given away by the end of 1985.

Another prasādam-distribution program started in 1973, when Śrīla Prabhupāda looked out the window of his room one day in Śrī Māyāpur, India, and saw a young girl searching through some garbage for food. At that moment he resolved that no one within ten kilometers of the Hare Kṛṣṇa temple in Śrī Māyāpur should ever go hungry, and he told this to his disciples. A few days later, looking out the same window, Śrīla Prabhupāda was happy to see his disciples passing out *prasādam* to hundreds of villagers, who sat in long rows eating heartily from round leaf plates. "Continue this forever," Śrīla Prabhupāda told his disciples. "Always distribute *prasādam.*" This was the birth of the ISKCON Food Relief program, which now distributes more than fifteen thousand meals each week, especially in India, Bangladesh and Africa.

A similar project, Hare Kṛṣṇa Food for Life, lives up to its motto "Feeding the Hungry Worldwide" by distributing over twenty thousand plates of *prasādam* every day to needy people in both the Third World and the industrialized countries of the West. The Hare Kṛṣṇa movement is one of the world's leading promoters of a vegetarian diet as a long-range solution to the problem of world hunger. And to relieve the immediate effects of hunger, the devotees of Kṛṣṇa are feeding disaster victims, the homeless, the unemployed, and the hungry through this "Food for Life" program. Working in cooperation with the local officials in different countries, "Food for Life" is often helped with government grants and donations of surplus foodstuffs.

These programs give away more than food, however. Śrīla

Prabhupāda emphasized that simply feeding the hungry was not enough, that it was false charity to feed someone unless you gave him *prasādam* and thereby liberate him from birth and death.

It is not surprising, then, that the Hare Kṛṣṇa movement is often called the "kitchen religion," the movement that combines philosophy with good food. And though some people may not accept the philosophy, hardly anyone says no to the food. In fact, every year more than twenty million people relish *kṛṣṇa-prasādam,* food offered to the Supreme Personality of Godhead, Lord Kṛṣṇa.

We look forward to the time when unlimited amounts of *prasādam* will be distributed all over the world and people everywhere will offer their food to God. Such a revolution in this most universal of human rituals—eating—will certainly cure the materialistic disease of mankind.

Śrī Bhagavān Dhanvantari, the inaugurator of the science of medicine in the universe.

The Science of Eating and Good Health

INDIA is the home not only of vegetarian cooking, but also of the science of healthful living. The scripture known as the *Āyur-veda,* is the oldest known work on biology, hygiene, medicine, and nutrition. This branch of the *Vedas* was revealed thousands of years ago by Śrī Bhagavān Dhanvantari, an incarnation of Kṛṣṇa. "Old" is not the same as "primitive", however, and some of the instructions of the *Āyur-veda* will remind today's reader of modern nutritional teachings or just plain common sense. Other instructions may seem less familiar, but they will bear themselves out if given the chance.

We shouldn't be surprised to see bodily health discussed in spiritual writings. The *Vedas* consider the human body a divine gift, a chance for the imprisoned soul to escape from the cycle of birth and death. The importance of healthful living in spiritual life is also mentioned by Lord Kṛṣṇa in the *Bhagavad-gītā* (6.16–17), "There is no possibility of becoming a yogi, O Arjuna, if one eats too much or eats too little, sleeps too much or does not sleep enough. One who is temperate in his habits of eating, sleeping, working, and recreation can mitigate all material pains by practicing the yoga system."

Proper eating has a double importance. Besides its role in bodily health—over-eating, eating in a disturbed or anxious state of mind, or eating unclean foods causes indigestion, "the parent of all diseases"—proper eating can help the aspiring transcendentalist attain mastery over his senses. "Of all the senses, the tongue is the most difficult to control," says the *Prasāda-sevayā,* a song composed by Śrīla Bhaktivinoda Ṭhākura, one of the spiritual predecessors of Śrīla Prabhupāda, "but Kṛṣṇa has kindly given us this nice *prasādam* to help us control the tongue."

Here are a few guidelines for good eating taken from the *Āyurveda* and other scriptures.

Spiritualize your eating

The *Bhagavad-gītā* (17.8-10) divides foods into three classes: those of the quality of goodness, those of the quality of passion, and those of the quality of ignorance. The most healthful are the foods of goodness. "Foods of the quality of goodness [milk products, grains, fruits, and vegetables] increase the duration of life; purify one's existence; and give strength, health, happiness, and satisfaction. Such foods are sweet, juicy, fatty, and palatable."

Foods that are too bitter, sour, salty, pungent, dry or hot, are of the quality of passion and cause distress. But foods of the quality of ignorance, such as meat, fish, and fowl, described as "putrid, decomposed, and unclean," produce only pain, disease, and bad *karma*. In other words, what you eat affects the quality of your life. There is much needless suffering in the world today, because most people have no other criterion for choosing food than price, and sensual desire.

The purpose of food, however, is not only to increase longevity and bodily strength, but also to purify the mind and consciousness. Therefore the spiritualist offers his food to the Lord before eating. Such offered food clears the way for spiritual progress. There are millions of people in India and around the world who would not consider eating unless their food was offered first to Lord Kṛṣṇa.

Eat at fixed times

As far as possible, take your main meal at the solar midday, when the sun is highest, because that's when your digestive power is strongest. Wait at least three hours after a light meal and five after a heavy meal before eating again. Eating at fixed times without snacking between meals helps make the mind and tongue peaceful.

Eat in a pleasant atmosphere

A cheerful mood helps digestion; a spiritual mood, even more. Eat in pleasant surroundings and center the conversation around spiritual topics. According to the *Kṣema-kutūhala,* a Vedic cookbook from the 2nd century A.D., a pleasant atmosphere and a good mood are as important to proper digestion as the quality of the food.

Look upon your food as Kṛṣṇa's mercy. Food is a divine gift, so cook it, serve it, and eat it in a spirit of joyful reverence.

Combine foods wisely

Foods should be combined for taste, and for efficient digestion and assimilation of nutrients. Rice and other grains go well with vegetables. Milk products such as cheese, yogurt, and buttermilk go well with grains and vegetables, but fresh milk does not go well with vegetables.

The typical Vedic lunch of rice, split-lentil soup, vegetables, and *chapatis is* a perfectly balanced meal.

Avoid combining vegetables with raw fruits. (Fruits are best eaten as a separate meal or with hot milk). Also avoid mixing acidic fruits with alkaline fruits, or milk with fermented milk products.

Share prasādam with others

Śrīla Rūpa Gosvāmī explains in the *Upadeṣāmṛta,* a five-hundred-year-old classic about devotional service, "One of the ways for devotees to express love is to offer *prasādam* and accept *prasādam* from one another." A gift from God is too good a thing to keep to oneself, so the scriptures recommend sharing *prasādam* with others, be they friends or strangers. In ancient India—and many still follow the practice—the householder would open his door at mealtime and call out, *"Prasādam! Prasādam! Prasādam!* If anyone is hungry, let him come and eat!" After welcoming his guests and offering them all the comforts at his disposal, he would feed them to their full satisfaction before taking his own meal. Even if you can't follow this practice, look for occasions to offer *prasādam* to others, and you will appreciate *prasādam* more yourself.

Be clean

Vedic culture places great emphasis on cleanliness, both internal and external. For internal cleanliness, we can cleanse the mind and heart of material contamination by chanting Vedic *mantras,* particularly the Hare Kṛṣṇa *mantra.* External cleanliness includes keeping a high standard of cleanliness when cooking and eating. Naturally this includes the usual good habits of washing the hands before eating, and the hands and mouth after.

Eat moderately

Vitality and strength depend not on how much we eat, but on how much we are able to digest and absorb into our system. The stomach needs working space, so instead of filling it completely, fill it just halfway, by eating only half as much as you think you can, and leave a fourth of the space for liquids and the other fourth for air. You'll help your digestion and get more pleasure from eating.

Moderate eating will also give satisfaction to your mind and harmony to your body. Overeating makes the mind agitated or dull and the body heavy and tired.

Don't pour water on the fire of digestion

Visible flames and invisible combustion are two aspects of what we call "fire". Digestion certainly involves combustion. We often speak of "burning up" fat or calories, and the word "calorie" itself refers to the heat released when food is burned. The *Vedas* inform us that our food is digested by a fire called *jaṭharāgni* (the Fire in the Belly). Therefore, because we often drink with our meals, the effect of liquid on fire becomes an important consideration in the art of eating.

Drinking before the meal tempers the appetite and, consequently, the urge to overeat. Drinking moderately while eating helps the stomach do its job, but drinking afterwards dilutes the gastric juices and reduces the fire of digestion. Wait at least an hour after eating before drinking again, and, if need be, you can drink every hour after that until the next meal.

Don't waste food

The scriptures tell us that for every bit of food wasted in times of plenty, an equal amount will be lacking in times of need. Put on your plate only as much as you can eat, and save any leftovers for the next meal. (To reheat food it is usually necessary to add liquid and simmer in a covered pan. Stir well and frequently).

If for some reason *prasādam* has to be discarded, then feed it to animals, bury it, or put it in a body of water. *Prasādam* is sacred and should never be put in the garbage. Whether cooking or eating, be careful about not wasting food.

Try an occasional fast

It may seem unusual for a cookbook to recommend fasting, but according to the *Āyur-veda,* fasting strengthens both will power and bodily health. An occasional fast gives the digestive system a rest and refreshes the senses, mind, and consciousness.

In most cases, the *Āyur-veda* recommends a water fast. Juice fasting is popular in the West because Western methods encourage long fasts. In *Āyur-vedic* treatment, however, most fasts are short—one to three days. While fasting, one should not drink more water than needed to quench one's thirst. *Jaṭharāgni,* the fire of digestion, being freed from the task of digesting food, is busy incinerating the accumulated wastes in the body, and too much water inhibits the process.

Devotees of Kṛṣṇa observe another kind of fast on *Ekādaśī,* the eleventh day after the full moon and the eleventh day after the new moon, by abstaining from grains, peas, and beans. The *Brahma-vaivarta* scripture says, "One who observes *Ekādaśī* is freed from all kinds of reactions to sinful activities and thereby advances in pious life."

Utensils

PEOPLE new to Indian cooking are often delighted to find that success depends more on creative ingenuity than on specialized equipment. If your kitchen is well-equipped with common utensils—frying pans, saucepans, knives, a slotted spoon, mixing bowls, a grater, a metal strainer, a colander, cutting boards, cheese cloth, a set of measuring spoons, and maybe a scale—you have all you need to cook genuine Indian meals.

You can also use modern appliances such as pressure cookers and food processors in Indian cooking. A pressure cooker is useful for speeding up the *dal* soups and chickpea preparations; a food processor, for mincing ginger and herbs, and for kneading bread dough and *paneer.* (It kneads the *paneer* in just a few seconds. Don't let it run longer, or the *paneer* will fall apart). Microwave ovens are suspected by some scientists of diminishing the nutritive value of food, and so we don't recommend their use.

The functions of most utensils used in Indian cooking can often be performed by their Western counterparts, sometimes more efficiently. A few examples:

• Ordinary pans of fairly heavy metal can replace the brass *dekchi,* a saucepan without handles that is used throughout India. Heavy metal distributes heat evenly and prevents food from burning or scorching. Thin pans made from light metals will develop hot spots to which food invariably sticks. See that your pans have tight-fitting lids. (Food generally cooks quicker with a lid and it saves energy). Avoid using aluminum pans, which chemically taint your foods, nutritive value of food especially those containing milk products and acidic ingredients.

• The versatile electric blender can replace the grinding stone used daily in the Indian kitchen. In addition to powdering spices, a blender will liquefy or puree fruits and vegetables. Get a blender with blades close to the bottom so it will pulverize small quantities.

Another handy machine is an electric coffee grinder. It can grind small quantities of spices or nuts in seconds, and it's inexpensive. If you don't care for "electric cooking," you can get excellent results with a mortar and pestle (and a little elbow grease).

• Wooden spoons and spatulas, though generally not used in India because wood is considered hard to clean, are more practical than metal spoons, which burn your fingers and can affect the taste of the food. Wooden spoons also save wear and tear on pots.

There are, however, some Indian utensils that simplify cooking Indian food. If you can't obtain them, their Western counterparts will do.

• *Karhai.* A deep, rounded pan, with handles on both sides. It can be made of brass, cast-iron, or stainless steel. Because it has a wide top and a concave bottom, it allows you to use a small amount of oil to fry a large amount of food. It is sometimes used for sauteing vegetables. A Chinese wok has the same shape as a *karhai* and makes a good substitute. Both are easily available and reasonably priced. The most useful size is 12 to 15 inches (30 to 35 cm) across. If you can't find either a *karhai* or a wok, you can use a frying pan with deep sides instead.

• *Tava.* A circular, slightly concave, cast-iron frying pan with a handle. It's ideal for making *chapatis, parathas,* and patties. A cast-iron frying pan with a good distribution of heat can replace the *tava*. Even a well-seasoned griddle will do. For making chaunces and dry-roasting spices, you can use a small cast-iron frying pan.

• *Chimti.* A pair of long flat tongs with blunt edges used to turn a *chapati* and hold it over a flame without puncturing it. Any long blunt-edged tongs are just as suitable.

• *Velan.* A solid wooden rolling pin without handles. It's about 12 to 15 inches (30 to 35 cm) long, and it's wide in the middle and gradually tapers off to the ends. It's very handy for rolling Indian breads. If you can't find one, have someone make one for you. Otherwise use whatever rolling pin you have.

• *Masala dibba. A* stainless steel or brass container that holds seven small containers with spices for daily use. A metal lid fits snugly over the top. If this useful item cannot be found, a wooden spice box with glass containers will do the job.

Suggested Menus

FOLLOWING the Vedic custom of a substantial breakfast, an even more substantial lunch, a light dinner, and from time to time an elaborate feast, the suggested menus in this section will give you an idea of which dishes go well together. With the recipes in this book, you'll be able to make a different menu for each day of the month. Feel free, of course, to add preparations to the menus or delete them, as you wish.

• A typical breakfast consists of a main dish of grains and vegetables, a light bread, a little yogurt, and a slice of fresh ginger. A natural herb tea (like ginger tea) will go well with this meal. If you prefer a lighter breakfast, there are many possibilities, such as *puris* and jam, *shrikhand* and *papadams,* vegetable or fruit *pakoras,* a *raita,* or fresh fruit and yogurt.

Scrambled cheese with fried tomatoes
Whole-wheat pancakes
Fried chickpeas and peppers
Salty yogurt drink

Boiled rice, dal, and vegetables
Banana puris
Fried chickpeas in yogurt
Yogurt

Vegetable and dal stew
Steamed dal and yogurt
Coconut chutney
Yogurt

Vegetable semolina
Potato-stuffed pancakes
Spiced chickpeas
Sweet yogurt drink

• The classic Vedic lunch consists of rice, *dal, chapatis,* and a vegetable. To round it out, you can add a salad, chutney, sweet, and beverage. In the summer a little yogurt goes well with lunch.

Plain white rice
Dal and vegetable soup
Chapatis
Green beans in sauce
Tomato chutney or
Spinach and yogurt salad
Fruit fritters
Salty yogurt drink

Lemon rice
Creamy vegetable soup
Chickpea-flour pancakes
Peas, cheese, and tomatoes
Pineapple chutney or
Potato and coconut salad
Indian ice cream
Anise-flavored drink

Rice and yogurt
Tomato and toor dal soup
Chapatis
Eggplant, spinach, and tomato puree
Dal croquettes in yogurt
Date and tamarind chutney
Sweet semolina pudding

Coconut rice
Urad dal with spiced yogurt
Chickpea-flour bread
Cauliflower and potatoes in sauce
Pan-fried seasoned cheese
Creamed vermicelli
Cumin and tamarind drink

• For dinner, a vegetable with a light bread goes well with a savory, chutney, sweet, and beverage. It's not advisable to eat a lot of grain before resting, otherwise the stomach works hard all night. For a snack before retiring, try hot milk and banana *puris.*

Seasoned okra with coconut
Indian crackers
Fried potato patties
Tomato chutney
Crisp fried spirals

Stuffed cabbage leaves
Puris
Lemon rice
Carrot pudding
Anise-flavored milk

Bengali mixed vegetable stew
Flaky whole-wheat bread
Apple chutney
Fruit turnovers
Lemon drink

Vegetable and dal stew
Potato-filled flat bread
Vegetable fritters
Mint chutney
Thick, flavored yogurt

• Śrīla Prabhupāda gave us this standard feast menu: an opulent rice, a wet vegetable, a dry vegetable, a savory, a chutney, *puris*, a *raita*, one or two sweets, a beverage, and *khir.* A sumptuous feast gives many people a chance to experience the opulence of Kṛṣṇa. Śrīla Prabhupāda taught that normally a devotee does not hanker for palatable dishes, and eats only what he needs. Therefore he advised the devotees to eat simple meals during the week, and on Sunday, to enjoy the "love feast" with the temple guests. The number of feast dishes can increase unlimitedly. In our temples, we celebrate auspicious occasions such as the birthday of Lord Kṛṣṇa or the spiritual master with feasts of as many as 108* dishes, or even more.

Mixed vegetable rice
Deep-fried cheese balls in cream sauce
Potatoes au gratin
Spiced carrot croquettes
Mint chutney
Banana puris
Fruit turnovers
Cumin and tamarind drink
Sweet rice

Spicy rice
Vegetable and cheese stew
Fried cauliflower, potatoes and cheese
Dal croquettes in yogurt
Date and tamarind chutney
Puris
Thick, flavored yogurt
Anise-flavored drink
Sweet rice

Plain white rice
Sweet and sour vegetable
Steamed spinach and cheese
Vegetable fritters
Tomato chutney
Puris
Chickpea-flour confections
Lemon drink
Sweet rice

Saffron rice with cheese balls
Spinach balls in tomato sauce
Stuffed vegetables
Vegetable turnovers
Coriander chutney
Masala puris
Fancy Indian cheese sweet
Sweet yogurt drink
Sweet rice

Note: All of the above recipes are listed in the index at the end of the book.

---

* In Vedic culture the number 108 is considered auspicious because there are 108 principal *gopīs* (cowherd girlfriends) of Lord Kṛṣṇa and 108 *Upaniṣads* (part of the Vedic literature).

Preparing and Serving a Vedic Meal

PREPARING food for the pleasure of the Supreme Personality of Godhead is a wonderful way to express creativity. Combining colors, flavors, and textures in various dishes (and not going over your budget) develops the skill of a true artist. Cooking for Kṛṣṇa calls for a personal touch, and the cook should desire not only to feed but also to delight.

Vedic cooking is practical because it means making the best dishes in the shortest time. One who cooks to please the Supreme Lord cooks efficiently, without haste or waste. Śrīla Prabhupāda showed us how to make a complete meal in less than an hour.

Use time to your best advantage by being organized. For example, plan the sequence in which you'll cook the dishes. Start the meal the night before. It takes only a few minutes to start a yogurt culture, make *paneer* and hang it to drain, or put beans to soak. Almost all Indian sweets can be made a day in advance and kept in the refrigerator until needed. Also, on the day the meal is served, you can make and chill the beverage several hours ahead.

If you're new at Indian cooking, it may be useful to arrange all the ingredients before you start, since the cooking will call for your uninterrupted attention. Start with the dishes that need to cook the longest, such as *dal* and cooked chutney. Make the bread dough next so you'll have enough time for it to stand. If you haven't made fresh cheese the night before, you can make it now and press it under a weight. If you're making rice or *halava,* put a pot of water over heat. Now start on the vegetables, savories, and side dishes. If one dish in the menu requires a great deal of preparation, see that others are quick and easy. Cook the breads and savories at the end, so you can serve them hot.

You'll keep your mind clear and reduce the cleaning at the end if you clean as you cook. "Cooking means cleaning," Śrīla Prabhupāda said. Take the time to sponge off working surfaces, and wash pots as you go along. Once you realize that half the pleasure of the cooking is in the cleaning, you'll always leave the kitchen cleaner than it was when you began.

The same care that goes into preparing the meal should go into presenting it. In India, where there is no table setting as in the West, food is generally served in *katoris,* little bowls of silver, brass, or stainless steel, placed on a *thali,* a round, rimmed tray of the same metal. Rice, breads, and other dry foods are served directly on the *thali.* Cooked vegetables, chutneys, *dal,* yogurt, and other liquid or semiliquid foods go in the *katoris.* In the absence of *thalis* and *katoris,* ordinary plates and bowls will do. All the courses are served together, to be eaten in whatever order one likes.

An Indian meal should seduce first the eyes, then the nose, and finally the tongue. The home-cooked bread, the sweets of various shapes and colors, and the soup and vegetables garnished with lemon slices and fresh coriander leaves delight the eyes. The aromas of the seasonings and fresh ingredients please the nose, and the balance of spicy and bland foods pleases the tongue.

If you would like to try eating Indian-style, make a seat on the floor with a carpet, mat, or cushion, and put the *thali* on a low table before you. Indian music (or, better yet, Vaiṣṇava chanting) will create a pleasant atmosphere.

Alcoholic beverages have no place in Vedic dining. The taste of *prasādam* enlivens the soul and purifies the senses; intoxicants have the opposite effect. If intoxicants were at all conducive to elevating our consciousness, true yogis would drink and smoke, but they don't. Alcohol dulls the consciousness and obscures the delicate taste of vegetarian food, so it's better to drink water or one of the beverages from this book. Normally, no tea or coffee is served after an Indian meal. Instead one chews a little anise seed and crushed cardamom to refresh the mouth and please the stomach.

Silverware is optional. Indians eat with the fingers of the right hand (the left hand cleans the body; the right one feeds it). Fingers and Indian food, it seems, were meant for each other. How else could you tear off a piece of *chapati,* wrap it around a bit of sauce-covered vegetable, and convey it to your mouth without losing any on the way? You can, of course, use silverware if you prefer.

A well-prepared meal served hot, on time, and in abundance is an even greater pleasure when the person serving it is eager to please his guest. The person eating the meal may choose to eat moderately, but the person serving the meal should simply be concerned with feeding his guests to their hearts' content. A Vaiṣṇava song glorifying the spiritual master says, "When the spiritual master sees that the devotees are satisfied by eating *kṛṣṇa-prasādam,* then he is satisfied."

We can get a glimpse of this spirit from *Planting the Seed,* Volume Two of the biography of Śrīla Prabhupāda by His Holiness Satsvarūpa dāsa Gosvāmī. Here, a devotee recalls the early days of the Hare Kṛṣṇa movement: "Prabhupāda's open decree that everyone should eat as much *prasādam* as possible created a humorous mood and a family feeling. No one was allowed to sit, picking at his food, nibbling politely. They ate with a gusto Swamiji [Śrīla Prabhupāda] almost insisted upon. If he saw someone not eating heartily, he would call the person's name and smilingly protest, 'Why are you not eating? Take *prasādam.'* And he would laugh. 'When I was coming to your country on the boat,' he said, 'I thought, 'How will the Americans ever eat this food?' And as the boys pushed their plates forward for more, Keith would serve seconds—more rice, *dal, chapatis,* and *sabji."*

Even Lord Kṛṣṇa Himself, in His incarnation 500 years ago as Śrī Caitanya Mahāprabhu, derived great pleasure from serving *prasādam* to His devotees. The *Śrī Caitanya-caritāmṛta,* the Bengali devotional classic about the pastimes of this most magnanimous incarnation of Godhead says: "Śrī Caitanya Mahāprabhu was not accustomed to taking *prasādam* in small quantities. He therefore put on each plate what at least five men could eat. Everyone was filled up to the neck because Śrī Caitanya Mahāprabhu kept telling the distributors, 'Give them more! Give them more!'" And since Lord Caitanya was the omniscient Lord Himself, He astonished everyone by knowing exactly what each person wanted. In this way He fed all the devotees until they were fully satisfied.

You and your guests will also be fully satisfied. Whether you sit on the floor or at a table, whether you eat with your fingers or with silverware, whether you serve or are served, whether you have a meal of one dish or 130, you'll find your home-cooked Indian meal a true feast for the senses, the mind, and the soul.

Recipes

• The recipes in this book make portions for four to six people.
• Each recipe lists the ingredients in the order of their use.
• For British, Canadian, and Australian users, there are conversion tables in the appendix on page 297.
• The cup measurement in this book is one which holds 8 fl oz (236.6 ml) of water, 4 oz (100 g) of flour, 7 oz (200 g) of *mung dal,* 6 oz (175 g) of rice, 5 oz (150 g) of semolina or farina, 7 oz (200 g) of granulated sugar.
• All cup and spoon measures given in the recipes are level.
• Two of the most common ingredients in the recipes—ghee (clarified butter) and *paneer* (homemade cheese)—are described in the section on milk products, beginning on page 88.. To know how much milk you need to make a specific amount of *paneer,* see the chart on page 95.
• Many recipes give the choice between *ghee* and vegetable oil. If you use vegetable oil, use mixed vegetable oil, or peanut oil, corn oil, sunflower oil, safflower oil, or mustard oil. Olive oil is not recommended, because its strong flavor overpowers the subtle taste of the spices.
• The term "thick cream" refers to ordinary sweet cream, which is called heavy cream in the U.S. and single cream in the U.K.
• As a rule, allow ½ tsp of salt to 1 lb (450 g) of vegetables, and ½ tsp to 1 cup (250 ml) of water. Remember that it's easier to add salt later than to remove it.
• The approximate sizes for cut pieces of food are:

cubed— ½–1 inch (1 – 2½ cm) across
diced — ¼ inch (5 mm) across
minced — ⅛ inch (3 mm) across.

• Don't be discouraged if anything goes wrong. Even the best cooks have failures; success comes with practice.
• Most recipes end with suggestions for serving. The suggested combinations of dishes are only guidelines—you'll undoubtedly want to experiment with others. There's one suggestion, however, that goes with every recipe and every combination: offer the food first to Lord Kṛṣṇa.

When offering food to Kṛṣṇa, remember . . .

• The offering actually begins in the kitchen, so don't taste the food during the cooking. Let Kṛṣṇa be the first to enjoy.
• When the cooking is finished, place a generous portion on a plate for Kṛṣṇa. If possible, reserve a set of plates and bowls for His exclusive use.
• Set the plate before a picture of Kṛṣṇa.
• In a devotional mood, ask Kṛṣṇa to accept your offering. You can do this by reciting three times the Hare Kṛṣṇa mantra:

Hare Kṛṣṇa, Hare Kṛṣṇa, Kṛṣṇa Kṛṣṇa, Hare Hare
Hare Rāma, Hare Rāma, Rāma Rāma, Hare Hare

• Afterward, remove the food from the offering plate. This food and any food remaining in the cooking pots may now be served.

See the section A Temple of Kṛṣṇa in Your Home *for more details.*

ROSE WATER
MADE IN INDIA
MDH
Amchoor
POWDER

Spices and Herbs

1 Asafoetida *(hing)*
2 Cardamom *(elaichi)*
3 Cayenne pepper *(pesa hui lal mirch)*
4 Chilies, fresh *(hari mirch)*
5 Chilies, whole, dried *(sabut lal mirch)*
6 Cinnamon *(dalchini)*
7 Cloves *(laung)*
8 Coriander, fresh *(hara dhania)*
9 Coriander seeds, whole and ground *(dhania, sabut* and *pesa)*
10 Cumin seeds, whole and ground *(safed jeera, sabut* and *pesa)*
11 Curry leaves *(kari patti)*
12 Fennel *(sauf)*
13 Fenugreek *(methi)*
14 Ginger, fresh *(adrak)*
15 Kalinji seets *(kalinji)*
16 Mango powder *(amchur)*
17 Mint leaves *(pudina ki patti)*
18 Mustard seeds, black *(rai)*
19 Nutmeg *(jaiphal)*
20 Rose-water *(gulab jal)*
21 Saffron *(kesar)*
22 Tamarind *(imli)*
23 Turmeric *(haldi)*

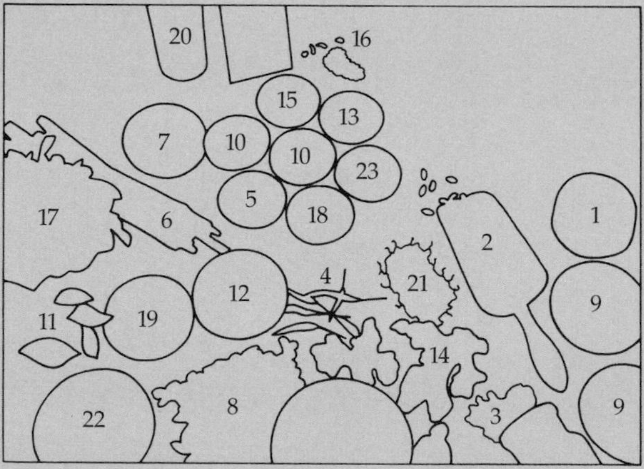

THE heart of Indian cooking is the seasoning—the wise use of the spices, herbs, and seasonings. Spices are roots, barks, or seeds, used whole, crushed, or powdered. Herbs are fresh leaves or flowers. Seasonings include such natural ingredients as salt, citric juices, nuts, and rose-water.

The imaginative use of selected aromatic spices and herbs to bring out the dormant flavors of a dish gives Indian cooking its unique character. It is not heavy spicing but delicate spicing that is responsible for the appetizing nuances of subtle taste and aroma. The extent to which a dish need be spiced is not rigid; it's a matter of personal taste. Although Indian food is always spiced (a dish may call for one spice or more than ten), it doesn't have to be hot. The hotness in Indian food comes from chilies, and you can use as many or as few as you want. You can even leave them out entirely, and your food will still be tasty and authentically Indian.

Spices and herbs, the "jewels of Indian cooking," make the meal not only tasty but also more digestible. Most spices have medicinal properties. Turmeric, for example, is a diuretic; cayenne pepper, a gastric stimulant; and fresh ginger, a tonic. The science of using spices to accentuate the taste of foods and maintain good health goes back thousands of years, to the *Āyur-veda* and *Artha-śāstra* scriptures.

A thousand years ago, Baber the Great, the founder of the Mogul Empire in India, paid a high tribute to the role of spices in Indian cooking. "If my countrymen had had the Indians' knowledge of spices," he wrote in his memoirs, the *Babernama,* "I would have conquered the whole world."

The magic of spicing is in the *masala,* the blend. The cook who knows how to blend spices and herbs can transform everyday foods into an unlimited variety of succulent dishes, each with its own taste. Even the humble potato will reveal a surprising variety of flavors, brought out by the *masalas* with which it is cooked.

How to make masalas

The technique of browning spices in hot *ghee* or oil to release their flavors and aromas is unique to Indian cooking. In making a *masala* sometimes you use whole spices, sometimes powdered spices, but most often a combination of both. First assemble the spices near the stove. Then heat just enough *ghee* or vegetable oil to keep the spices and other ingredients from sticking to the pan (generally 1 – 2 tablespoons). Make it extremely hot but not burning. Then drop the spices into the *ghee*. They immediately begin to swell, pop, brown, or change in some other way. Then just at the precise moment, when the spices are browned and ready, pour them over the dish you're cooking, or put what you're cooking into the seasonings to saute or simmer.

Since different spices take different times to brown, yet must finish all at once, a sense of timing is of paramount importance. For example, a recipe may call for cumin seeds, fenugreek seeds, grated fresh ginger, ground coriander, and powdered asafoetida. Since the cumin and fenugreek seeds both take about 30 seconds to brown, add them together to the hot *ghee* or oil first. Then ten seconds later, add the grated ginger, which takes about 20 seconds. The ground coriander takes about 5 seconds to brown, so toss it in 15 seconds later, and finally, add the asafoetida. And there you've got it!

When you add a dish you're cooking to a *masala,* stir it at first to coat the ingredients with the spices and to prevent the spices from overcooking on the bottom of the pan. In recipes that call for ground spices only, the *ghee* or vegetable oil should be only moderately hot, so that the spices will brown without burning. And aside from the *masala,* herbs and seasonings generally go in during the cooking, or at the end.

With just a little experience in preparing *masalas,* you'll become familiar with the flavor and aroma of each spice. With strong spices such as cloves, cayenne pepper, and asafoetida you'll use very small quantities. For mild spices, such as cumin seeds and ground coriander, you'll use more.

Some *masala* blends, such as *panch masala* and *garam masala,* can be prepared in advance. You can make enough to last several weeks or even months. *Panch masala,* a mixture of five whole spices, is used mostly in cooking vegetables. *Garam masala,* literally "hot spices" (to warm the body), is actually a mixture of ground sweet spices. It's added to a dish at the end of cooking, sometimes just before serving.

Here is one recipe for *panch masala* and one for *garam masala:*

Panch masala:

- 2 tbs cumin seeds
- 2 tbs black cumin seeds or kalinji seeds
- 2 tbs black mustard seeds
- 2 tbs anise or fennel seeds
- 1 tbs fenugreek seeds

Mix all the spices and store them in an airtight jar in a cool, dry, dark place. Shake the jar before each use to make sure the spices are evenly distributed.

Garam masala:

- 4 tbs coriander seeds
- 2 tbs cumin seeds
- 2 tbs black pepper corns
- 2 tsp cardamom seeds
- 1 tsp whole cloves
- 2 cinnamon sticks, 2 inches (5 cm) long

Dry-roast each of the spices separately in a heavy cast-iron frying pan. After putting each spice into the pan, shake the pan until the spice turns a shade or two darker and gives off a freshly roasted aroma. When all the spices have been roasted, grind them together to a fine powder in an electric coffee grinder. Put the ground *masala* into a glass jar with a tight lid, and keep it in a cool place. Made with good-quality spices and kept in an airtight container, *garam masala* will keep its taste and aroma for several months.

For another *garam masala* mixture, dry-roast and grind the same amounts of cardamom, cloves, and cinnamon as in the previous recipe, then add half a nutmeg kernel, finely grated.

• Before using whole spices, especially those you buy in large quantity, pick through them to eliminate any small stems or stones.

• Keep all your spices in tightly sealed jars or cans in a cool, dry place away from direct sunlight. To avoid spoilage from constantly dipping into the big jars, keep spices for daily use in small bottles. Be sure to label all jars and containers.
• Many recipes call for ground spices. Rather than purchase powdered spices, which soon lose their flavor, it's always better to buy whole spices and grind them yourself as you need them. In India it's done on a grinding stone, but an electric coffee grinder is excellent for this work. The aroma and taste of freshly ground spices is incomparable.
• Avoid commercially made curry powder or gourmet powders. Often made with inferior spices, these flavorless curry blends lend a wearisome uniformity to your cooking. In India they're practically unknown. It is far better to make fresh spice blends of your own.
• Sometimes a recipe requires a *masala* paste. You can make this by grinding together the specified spices and a few drops of water with a mortar and pestle. Then fry the paste in *ghee* or oil for a minute or so to bring out its flavor before adding the other ingredients.
• Before beginning to cook, read the recipe carefully. Gather the spices you need near the stove. There may be no time later to stop and hunt for a spice. Something on the stove may burn if you do.
• Sometimes you can use one spice as a substitute for another you don't have. Often you can even leave out the unavailable spice and the dish will still turn out fine. The recipes indicate some possible substitutes and deletions. Experience will also help you.
• Even though dried herbs are often twice as pungent as fresh ones, use fresh herbs whenever possible. Instructions for growing and storing your own coriander and fenugreek are given here.

Since it's the spices and seasonings, judiciously blended, that give Indian food its distinctive character, it's worth while to examine them one by one and become acquainted with their qualities and uses.

ASAFOETIDA *(hing):* This aromatic resin, from the root of *Ferula asafoetida,* is used in small pinches for its distinctive taste and medicinal properties. Asafoetida is so effective in preventing flatulence that it can cure horses of indigestion. It's available as a resin or as a fine powder. The resin form is the purer of the two, but you have to grate it when you need it. Powdered asafoetida is mixed with white flour, but it's more convenient to use. Add a pinch or a fraction of a teaspoon to hot *ghee* or vegetable oil for a second or two before adding the other ingredients. If you can't find asafoetida or don't want to use it, your recipes will be all right without it.

CARDAMOM *(elaichi):* The pale green seed pods of this member of the ginger family, *Elettaria cardamomum,* are used to flavor sweets, or are chewed as a breath sweetener and digestive. White cardamom pods, which are nothing other than bleached green ones, are more easily available, but have less flavor. When cooking with whole pods, remove them before serving, or push them to the side of the plate. They're not meant to be eaten whole. When a recipe calls only for the black, pungent seeds, remove them from the pods and pulverize them with a mortar and pestle or with a rolling pin. Ground cardamom seeds are used in *garam masala.*

CAYENNE PEPPER *(pesa hui lal mirch):* Cayenne powder, made from dried red chilies, is often called red chili powder. This is the spice that makes Indian food hot. Use it according to your taste.

CHILIES, fresh *(hari mirch)*: These bright red or green seed pods of *Capsicum annum* are found in both Asian groceries and in supermarkets. The flat, round, white seeds on the inside give hotness to food. If you want flavor without hotness, make a slit in the pod and remove the seeds with the tip of a small knife. Wash your hands carefully with soap and warm water after handling chilies, because their volatile oils irritate the skin. Store them unwashed, wrapped in newspaper, in the refrigerator. Discard any that go bad.

CHILIES, whole, dried *(sabut lal mirch):* Dried red chili) pods are used extensively in Indian cooking, for hotness and flavor. When crushed chilies are called for, grind them with a mortar and pestle or break them into tiny bits with your fingers. Remember to wash your hands after touching them. If you don't like chilies you can use fewer than called for or eliminate them entirely from the recipe.

CINNAMON *(dalchini):* True cinnamon comes from the inner bark of an evergreen tree, *Cinnamomum zeylanicum,* native to Śrī Lanka and the West Indies. Look for the thin sun-dried bark sheaths sold packed one inside the other. When using whole cinnamon sticks in chutneys or rice dishes, remove the sticks before serving the meal. Rather than buy ground cinnamon, buy whole sticks to dry-roast and grind as needed. The strong-flavored, slightly bitter cinnamon commonly sold in the market, *Cinnamomum cassia,* comes in single thick pieces or in powdered form. It is a poor substitute for the other, which has a delicate, sweet taste.

CLOVES *(laung):* This dried flower bud of the tropical tree *Myrtus caryophyllus* has always been the basis of the spice trade. The word *clove* comes from the Latin *clavius* meaning "nail", which describes its shape. Clove oil is antiseptic and strongly aromatic. It is said that the custom of "chewing the clove" when addressing the emperor started in China. During the reign of Queen Elizabeth I, it was the custom of courtiers to chew cloves in the Queen's presence. Cloves can be used as a blood purifier, a digestive aid, and a local analgesic for toothache. Dry-roasted and ground, they are an essential ingredient in *garam masala.* Buy cloves that are well formed and plump, not shrivelled and dusty.

CORIANDER, fresh *(hara dhania):* The fresh leaves of *Coriandrum sativum* are as widely used in India as parsley is in the West—not merely as a garnish though, but as an essential flavoring. Sometimes called cilantro or Chinese parsley, fresh coriander is worth looking for. Its delicate taste is unique. You can substitute parsley if coriander isn't available, but the flavor won't be the same. Fresh coriander is generally sold in bunches. To store it, put its roots or cut stalks into a small vase of water, insert the vase into a plastic bag, and keep it in the refrigerator. They will keep for more than a week. Wash it just before using it. Use the leaves and the upper portions of the stalks, chopped.

If you have difficulty buying fresh coriander (or fresh fenugreek), you can easily grow it yourself. Scatter some coriander seeds in a small patch of the garden, cover them with a thin layer of soil, and water them every day. They will germinate in 18 to 20 days and grow rapidly. Pick the stalks when they are about 6 inches (15 cm) high and before the plants go to seed.

CORIANDER SEEDS, whole and ground *(dhania, sabut and pesa):*

Coriander seeds are round, beige, and highly aromatic. A most important spice in Indian cooking, they are becoming increasingly popular in the West. In 1983, the United States and England each imported over three million tons of coriander seeds. The oils in coriander seeds help assimilate starchy foods and root vegetables. Generally ground before use, coriander seeds impart a fresh, springtime aroma to foods. To get the most flavor, buy the seeds whole and grind them in small quantities with an electric grinder.

CUMIN SEEDS, whole and ground *(safed jeera, sabut and pesa):* The seeds of white cumin, *Cuminum cyminum,* are an essential ingredient in preparing vegetable curries, rices, savories, and *dal.* Although ground cumin is available in all supermarkets, it's better to grind your own. When a recipe calls for roasted cumin, fry the amount of seeds you want in a preheated frying pan. Shake the pan until the seeds darken a little and become fragrant. If you need roasted and ground cumin seeds, put the roasted seeds into an electric coffee grinder and grind them fine. If you don't have a coffee grinder, use a mortar and pestle, or simply crush the seeds with the back of a spoon.

Kala jeera, or black cumin seeds *(Cuminum nigrum),* smaller and darker than the white ones, have a more bitter taste and a sharper smell.

CURRY LEAVES *(kari patti):* The fresh leaves from the Kari tree of Southwest Asia, *Murraya koenigri,* are used mainly as an aromatic and flavoring for curries and soups. Dried leaves are more easily available but less aromatic than fresh ones. When starting a curry or *masala,* put the fresh or dried leaves into the oil to fry until crisp.

FENNEL *(sauf):* Sometimes known as "sweet cumin," the long, pale-green seeds of *Foeniculum vulgare* look like cumin but taste like anise seed or liquorice. Fennel seeds are sometimes used in curries. Dry-roasted, they're an effective breath sweetener. If you can't find them, substitute an equal amount of anise seeds.

FENUGREEK *(methi):* The leaves and tender stalks of *Trigonella fenumgraecum* are a popular vegetable in India. Its squarish, rather flat, brownish-beige seeds are essential in many vegetable curries and savories. In India, women eat fenugreek seeds with jaggery (unrefined palm sugar) after childbirth, to strengthen the back, increase bodily force, and stimulate the flow of breast milk. Fenugreek seeds have a slightly bitter flavor so don't exceed the recommended quantities, and avoid burning them, which makes them more bitter. Fenugreek, like coriander, is easy to grow (see page 80).

GINGER, fresh *(adrak):* This light-brown knobby rhizome of *Zingiber officinalis* is used extensively in all forms of Indian cooking. Choose fresh ginger that is plump and not shrivelled, that has firm flesh, and that is only slightly fibrous. Before you chop, grate, slice, or grind ginger into a paste, scrape off its potato-like skin with a sharp knife. To grate ginger, use the fine holes of a metal grater. Powdered ginger can't be substituted for fresh, because the flavor is different. Dried ginger *(sonth),* more pungent than fresh ginger, must be soaked before use. (One teaspoon of dried ginger equals one tablespoon of chopped fresh ginger). Ginger is used medicinally for colic and dyspepsia. Eaten in small quantities it cures stomachache, and ginger tea is an excellent remedy for colds.

KALINJI SEEDS *(kalinji):* These are the black, teardrop-shaped seeds of the onion plant *Nigella indica*. They impart a faint onion flavor and are used in vegetable dishes and *pakora* batter. Although often confused with black cumin seeds, the two have nothing in common. If they're unavailable, simply leave them out of the recipe.

MANGO POWDER *(amchur):* The raw fruits of the mango tree, *Mangifera indica,* are cut into strips, then dried, ground, and used as a souring and flavoring agent in vegetable curries. Mango powder is used as freely in North Indian cooking as lemon is in Western cooking to give food a tangy and sour taste. It burns easily, so use it with care.

MINT LEAVES *(pudina ki patti):* The two most common mints are spearmint *(Mentha spicata)* and peppermint *(Mentha piperita)*. Aside from adding color as a garnish, mint leaves lend a refreshing taste to beverages. They can also be used to make mint chutney. Mint stimulates the digestive tract and will allay nausea and vomiting. You can easily grow the plants at home in practically any soil, either in sun or in partial shade. Dried mint loses its color but keeps its flavor fairly well.

MUSTARD SEEDS, black *(rai):* Indian cooking wouldn't be the same without the seeds of *Brassica juncea*. Black mustard seeds are round, tiny (smaller than the yellow variety), and not really black but a dark reddish brown. They are pungent, nut-flavored, and nutritious, and they add texture and eye appeal to a dish. The frying of mustard seeds is one of the highlights of preparing *masalas*. You scatter seeds into a small amount of smoking hot ghee or oil, and a few seconds later they crackle and pop—and jump out of the pan unless you cover it quickly.

NUTMEG *(jaiphal):* Nutmeg is the kernel of the seed of the tropical tree *Myristica fragrans*. Buy whole kernels that are round, compact, oily-looking, and heavy. They may be dark, or white from the lime used to repel insects. Grated nutmeg is used in small amounts (sometimes with other spices) to flavor puddings, sweets, and vegetable dishes. It's best to grate nutmeg straight into the dish; once grated it rapidly loses its flavor. Store whole or powdered nutmeg in a tightly closed container.

ROSE-WATER *(gulab-jul):* Rose-water is the diluted essence of rose petals extracted by steam distillation. It's a widely used flavoring in Indian sweets and rice dishes. You can use a measuring spoon for rose-water, but if you cook with rose essence or concentrate be careful not to use too much. Count the drops.

SAFFRON *(kesar):* Saffron is known as "the king of spices." It's the dried stigma of the saffron crocus, *Crocus sativus,* which is cultivated in Kashmir, Spain, and Portugal. Each crocus flower has only three saffron threads, so one pound of saffron takes the hand-plucked threads of about seventy thousand flowers. Saffron is expensive, but a little goes a long way. Beware of cheap saffron or "bastard saffron." It looks similar and gives a saffron color, but it has none of the authentic fragrance.

Saffron has a pleasant delicate flavor and imparts a rich yellow color to whatever it's mixed with. It's used for flavoring and coloring sweets, rice dishes, and beverages. To extract the flavor and bright orange color from the saffron threads, dry-roast them slightly and then crumble them and steep them in a tablespoon or so of warm milk. Then pour the milk into the dish to be flavored. Saffron is also available in powdered form, which is twice as strong as the threads.

TAMARIND *(imli):* This sour, acid-tasting seasoning comes from the large broad bean pod of a tropical tree, *Tamarindus indica*. The brown flesh (sometimes with the dark shiny seeds) is scraped from the pods, dried, and sold in packets.

To use, remove the seeds and tear or chop the pulp into small pieces. Boil the pieces in a small amount of water for about 10 minutes, or until the pieces of pulp soften and fall apart. (Use about one cup [250 ml] of water to 8 oz [225 g] of tamarind). Then force as much of the pulp as possible through a strainer. Keep the liquid and discard the fibrous residue left in the strainer. If tamarind is unavailable, you can simulate its flavor somewhat by a mixture of lemon juice and brown sugar.

TURMERIC *(haldi):* A member of the ginger family *(Curcuma longa)*, turmeric is a rhizome that varies in color from dark orange to reddish-brown, but when dried and ground into powder it is always bright yellow. It is used in small amounts to give a warm, pungent flavor to vegetables, soups, and savories, or simply to add color to rice dishes. Ground turmeric keeps its coloring properties for a long time but loses its aroma quickly. One ounce is enough to keep at home unless you live on spicy rice and curries. Turmeric stains, so be careful with your clothes. It also burns easily, so cook it with care. Turmeric is used in *Ayur-vedic* medicine as a diuretic, blood purifier, and intestinal stimulant.

Milk Products

1 Ghee *(Clarified butter)* 92
2 Paneer *(Homemade cheese)* 94
3 Dahi *(Yogurt)* 96

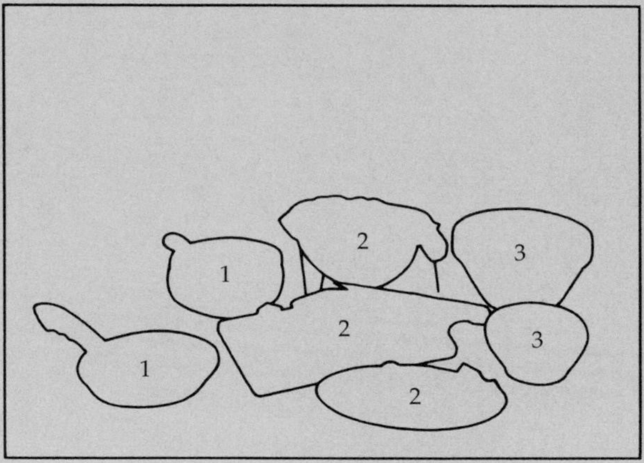

BOTH modern textbooks and the ancient *Vedas* praise milk as a miracle food because it contains all the nutrients needed for good health. The Vedic scriptures add that milk develops the fine cerebral tissues needed for understanding Kṛṣṇa consciousness. In the Vedic age, many yogis lived only on milk, which was so abundant that householders gave it away freely. Because milk nourishes man both physically and spiritually, Vedic culture considers it the most important of all foods, essential to a civilized society.

The importance of milk indicates the importance of protecting cows. Like human beings, a cow is happy when she feels protected. A cow that can suckle her calf and trust her owner not to kill her when she runs dry is happy, and naturally gives sweeter, more abundant milk. The *Śrīmad-Bhāgavatam* tells us that under the protection of the saintly king Yudhiṣṭhira, the cows were so happy that their large udders filled to overflowing and they wet the ground with creamy milk. Another great Vedic king, Mahārāja Parīkṣit, astonished to find someone trying to kill a cow in his kingdom, immediately arrested the culprit and punished him.

Because people drink the cow's milk, the *Vedas* consider the cow one of the mothers of human society. "The blood of the cow is very nutritious," Śrīla Prabhupāda said, "but civilized men utilize it in the form of milk." The bull, who helps produce grains by tilling the fields, is considered the father of human society. The interdependence of man and the bull and cow is a perfect example of the harmony of nature, as ordained by Kṛṣṇa Himself. Furthermore, both these animals are considered valuable because from them come *pañca-gavya,* five pure substances, namely milk, yogurt, ghee, cow dung and cow urine. All these substances are required in Vedic ceremonies. Even the cows dung and urine are antiseptic and fit for sacrificial offerings and medicine. Thus, in *Bhagavad-gītā* Kṛṣṇa personally speaks of *go-rakṣā,* cow protection. Unfortunately, in our "advanced" civilization, people neglect spiritual knowledge and promote cow-killing on a massive scale. "It is to be understood then," writes Śrīla Prabhupāda, "that human society is advancing in the wrong direction and is clearing the path to its own condemnation."

In the matter of protecting cows, some meat-eaters will protest, but in answer to them we say that since Kṛṣṇa gives stress to cow protection, those who are inclined to eat meat, despite all reasonable arguments to the contrary, should eat the flesh of less important animals like hogs, poultry, or fish, but they should not kill cows. The Vedas state that anyone implicated in the killing of a cow will have to take as many rebirths in the material world as there are hairs on the back of the cow. And the Vedas are not the only scriptures to condemn cow-killing. In the Bible (66:3) Isaiah declares, "He that killeth an ox is as he that killeth a man."

On the whole, meat-eating is not completely forbidden in Vedic culture: a particular class of people is allowed to eat meat according to various circumstances and injunctions. Killing cows, however, is strictly forbidden to everyone. Śrīla Prabhupāda proposed that if someone must eat beef, then he should eat the carcasses of cows that die naturally. After an initial period of apparent scarcity, there will be plenty of carcasses to go around.

The most important reason for protecting cows is that Kṛṣṇa loves them. The Vedic scriptures tell us that in Kṛṣṇaloka, Lord Kṛṣṇa's eternal abode in the spiritual sky, there are cows called *surabhi,* which the Lord Himself takes care of. Kṛṣṇa's abode is also called Goloka, or the planet of the cows.

Five thousand years ago, when Lord Kṛṣṇa appeared in this world, He played as a cowherd boy in the North Indian village of Vṛndāvana and showed His affection for cows. His childhood pastimes revolved around His cows and calves, His cowherd friends, and milk products. So Kṛṣṇa is also called Govinda, "one who gives pleasure to the cows," and Gopala, "the friend of the cows. Because in play He pilfered His neighbors' stocks of butter and yogurt, He is called Mākhana-taskara, "the butter thief."

Cow's milk is the source of three essential ingredients in Vedic cooking: *ghee* (clarified butter), *paneer* (fresh cheese), and *dahi* (yogurt). *Ghee* has been an esteemed cooking medium since the Vedic times, when along with grains and cows it was counted among the riches of the household. *Ghee* is the essence of butter and the very best of all cooking mediums. It is made by heating butter very slowly until all the water is driven off and the solids have separated, leaving a clear golden-yellow oil. It has a faintly sweet, delicate, nutlike flavor that lends an irresistible quality to foods cooked in it. And it won't raise the cholesterol level in your blood.

Ghee has other attributes besides its taste. You can heat it to high temperatures and it won't bubble or smoke, because the water (which boils at 212°F/100°C) and the protein solids (which burn at 250°F/125°C) have been removed. *Ghee* is ideal for sauteing, braising, pan-frying, and deep-frying. It will add a new dimension to your cooking.

Cheese as we know it in the West is virtually unknown in India, where people prefer their milk products fresh, rather than aged. *Paneer* is a fresh homemade cheese that has many uses. Drained, it can be added directly to soups and vegetable dishes, or eaten as is. Pressed, it can be made into sweets, or, it can be cut into cubes and used, raw or deep-fried, in vegetable dishes.

Yogurt finds its way into practically every Indian meal. If not served plain in a little bowl (always unsweetened), it's used in preparing some dish. The bland taste of yogurt complements the flavor of spicy dishes, and, mixed with rice and vegetables, it acts as a binder to make it easy to eat with your hands. The *Āyur-veda* suggests that yogurt be eaten with other foods, not alone.

Yogurt gets its healthful qualities from the friendly bacteria in it. Avoid commercially produced yogurt that has been heat-treated, sterilized, or treated with artificial preservatives, sweeteners, and flavors. The processing destroys the bacteria. We hope you will discover how easy and pleasant it is to make your own yogurt.

Ghee

Clarified butter

Making ghee is neither difficult nor complicated, but it does take some time. Bringing out the sweet, nutlike flavor of the melted butter requires long, slow cooking to fully evaporate the water and allow the milk solids to separate and float to the surface leaving clear, amber-colored ghee.

2 to 10 lbs (1 to 5 kg) unsalted butter

Begin by heating the butter in a large heavy saucepan over medium heat until it comes to a boil. When the surface of the butter is covered with a white foam, reduce the heat to as low as possible and simmer uncovered. From time to time remove the solids that accumulate on the surface. Make sure the *ghee* doesn't burn. If *ghee* is cooked over too high a heat or cooked too long, it will darken and give off a pungent odor.

How much time you need for preparing the *ghee* depends on how much you are making (see table below). The finished *ghee* should be golden-colored and clear enough to see through to the bottom of the saucepan. Carefully ladle the *ghee* into a can or crock and allow it to cool uncovered to room temperature. The milk solids skimmed off the surface and the solids remaining in the bottom of the pan can be mixed into cooked vegetables, soups, and grains.

Ghee properly prepared and stored in closed containers in a cool dry place will keep for months.

Preparation and cooking time

Quantity of butter	Cooking Time	Yield of ghee
2 lbs (1 kg)	½ hr	1¾ lbs (800 g)
5 lbs (2.5 kg)	3 hrs	4 ½ lbs (2.2 kg)
10 lbs (5 kg)	5 hrs	9 lbs (4.6 kg)

• There are two types of *ghee: usli ghee* and vegetable *ghee.* When we refer to *ghee* in this book, we always mean *usli ghee,* or genuine *ghee,* which is clarified butter and can be made at home. Vegetable *ghee* is a combination of various vegetable oils and can be bought in large cans. Vegetable *ghee* may be less expensive and lighter, but it can never compare to real *ghee* for flavor.

• *Ghee* is pure butterfat. Since it is has no milk solids to turn rancid, it will keep for months, even without refrigeration.

• All ingredients to be deep-fried should be prepared, shaped, cut, or rolled close at hand, and at room temperature. When using *ghee* to pan-fry spices, gather all the spices first, so that the *ghee* doesn't burn while you're looking for them.

• Before putting *ghee* in a pan for deep-frying, make sure the pan is perfectly dry. Avoid mixing or splashing water into hot *ghee.* The *ghee* will splatter violently.

• The *ghee* may foam when moist vegetables are deep-fried, so leave enough space at the top of the pan to prevent spilling over. You can tell if the *ghee* is hot enough for deep-frying when a morsel of food dropped into it rises immediately to the surface and sizzles. Then lower the heat just enough to keep the ghee from burning.

• If the *ghee* is too hot, it darkens and burns the outside of the food, leaving the inside undercooked; if it's not hot enough, your food will soak up too much *ghee* and become greasy. Cover the surface of the *ghee* with only one layer of food, leaving enough space for the food to move. Too much food put into the *ghee* at one time will lower the temperature.

• To conserve *ghee,* which devotees sometimes call "liquid gold," drain the fried foods in a colander or strainer placed over a pan to catch the drippings. Filter the *ghee* through several layers of paper towels or a fine sieve before using it again, otherwise residues from the previous cooking will burn, discoloring the ghee and altering its flavor.

• For deep-frying, you can use the same *ghee* for several weeks, as long as it isn't burned. If the *ghee* stays dark even after being filtered, or if it gives off a pungent odor, it should be discarded.

Paneer
Homemade cheese

Fresh cheese, called paneer in Hindi, can be eaten by itself or used as an ingredient in recipes. There is no substitute for paneer. It is unique among cheeses for its versatility, its fine taste, and its resistance to melting at high temperatures.

10 cups (2.3 ltr) whole milk
5 tablespoon lemon juice, or 2 tsp citric acid,
or 1¼ cups (300 ml) yogurt, or 2½ cups (600 ml) sour whey

Heat the milk over medium heat in a pot large enough to allow the milk to rise without overflowing. While waiting for the milk to boil, prepare the curdling agent and get a strainer ready by lining it with two layers of cheesecloth and propping it above a receptacle to collect the whey.

When the milk begins to rise, stir in the curdling agent. Almost immediately, the spongelike paneer will separate from the clear, yellow-green whey with a kind of a magical suddenness. If the whey is not clear, add a little more curdling agent and stir again.

After the curds and the whey have separated completely, remove the pot from the heat. Collect the curds in the cheesecloth. Rinse them under cold water for half a minute to make them firmer and to remove any excess curdling agent, which would alter the taste. Then press out the rest of the liquid in one of the following ways:

• If you want firm paneer for making cheese cubes or kneading into a dough, bind the paneer within the cheesecloth and press it with a weight for some time. The longer it is pressed, the firmer it will be. Remove the weight, cut the paneer into the desired shapes, and use as required. Paneer will also become firm if you suspend it in a piece of cheesecloth and leave it to drain.

• If you need soft cheese, simply tighten the cheesecloth around the paneer and squeeze out the water.

Some people refer to fresh curds as *chenna,* and pressed *chenna* as *paneer*. For the purposes of this book, however, the term *paneer* will mean fresh curds, and pressed *paneer* will mean pressed curds. Remember also that the terms *cheese, Indian cheese, curds,* and *paneer* all refer to the same thing, *paneer*. To know approximately how much milk you will need to make specific amounts of *paneer* (drained for a few minutes) or pressed *paneer* (pressed under a weight for ten minutes), see the following table.

Preparation and cooking time: about 30 min

Quantity of milk curdled		**Yield of paneer**		**Yield of pressed paneer**	
cups	**liters**	**oz**	**g**	**oz**	**g**
2½	**600 ml**	**4**	**100**	**3**	**75**
7	**1.7**	**9**	**250**	**7**	**200**
12	**3**	**14**	**400**	**12**	**350**

The following are a few of the most commonly used curdling agents and their characteristics.

• *Lemon juice*. This gives a light, sour taste to cheese. About 1 tablespoon of lemon juice will curdle 2½ cups (600 ml) of milk.

• *Citric acid (sour salt)*. These crystals, obtainable in any pharmacy and most supermarkets, are practical to use and store. For nice, firm curds, bring the milk to a full boil. Begin to add the citric acid, a little at a time, stirring constantly until the milk curdles completely. Then stop and remove the pan from the heat. Too much citric acid will result in mushy curds. About ½ teaspoon of citric acid will curdle 2½ cups (600 ml) of milk.

• *Yogurt*. Some cooks prefer yogurt because it produces a thick, soft cheese. Before adding the yogurt to the boiling milk, dilute it in a small quantity of warm milk. Generally, 4 or 5 tablespoons of yogurt will curdle 2½ cups (600 ml) of milk.

• *Whey*. Whey left over from curdled milk can be used as a curdling agent the next day. Whey becomes sour, and therefore more effective, if kept at room temperature for 2 days or more. Like lemon juice, it imparts a faintly sour taste to the cheese. At least ⅔ cup (150 ml) of sour whey is required to curdle 2½ cups (600 ml) of milk.

Dahi
Yogurt

With a little experience you'll learn how to make yogurt and get good results every time. Keep your equipment clean to guard against incubating unwanted strains of bacteria.

10 cups (2.3 ltr) whole milk
¼ cup (50 ml) plain yogurt

Bring the milk to a boil in a pot and remove from the heat. Now lower the temperature of the milk either by letting it cool by itself or by placing the pot in cold water.

The ideal temperature for the yogurt bacteria is 110 – 115°F (43 – 45°C). If you don't have a thermometer, there is a simple test: the milk should be just hot enough for you to hold your little finger in it, without burning it, for 10 seconds, just long enough to say, "Hare Kṛṣṇa, Hare Kṛṣṇa, Kṛṣṇa Kṛṣṇa, Hare Hare/ Hare Rāma, Hare Rāma, Rāma Rāma, Hare Hare." Mix the yogurt into a cup of the warm milk and stir it back into the pot. On cold days you may need more yogurt to start a culture than on warm days.

The yogurt bacteria need several hours of warmth and quiet to grow. Keep the temperature of the milk constant by wrapping the covered pot in a thick cloth and placing it near a source of heat. Avoid leaving the pot near anything that may cause movement; if possible, make your yogurt at night, when there is the least chance of disturbance. It usually takes from four to eight hours for the yogurt to become firm. Once the yogurt sets, refrigerate it to retard the growth of the bacteria. Otherwise they'll continue to eat the milk sugars in the yogurt and turn it sour in two days.

Preparation and cooking time: 15 min
Setting time: 4 – 8 hrs

Your yogurt should stay good for four to five days. Don't forget to save some as a culture to start your next batch of yogurt. If the starter culture grows weak, replace it with newly bought yogurt.

Because of yogurt's health-giving properties and its many uses in preparing foods, it has an important place in the Vedic diet. The

Āyur-veda speaks in detail of the curative properties of yogurt.

Outside India, yogurt is most popular with the people of Russia and the Balkan countries, who are known for their longevity. The link between a yogurt-rich diet and increased longevity was revealed a hundred years ago by the Russian gerontologist Elie Metchnikoff. His major contribution to science was his auto-intoxication theory, which stated that it is possible for the contents of the colon to enter the bloodstream and thereby poison the entire body. Metchnikoff examined and interviewed many centenarians in Asia and Russia and noted that their diets contained large amounts of yogurt and fermented milk. He concluded that their longevity was due to the bacilli in these products, which replaced the bacteria of putrefaction in the bowel. In the wake of his theory came the first wave of interest in yogurt as a health food. As the consumption of yogurt in the West increases, modern science is discovering more of its remarkable qualities.

A few examples:

• Yogurt produces lactic acid, which destroys the bacteria responsible for the putrefaction of food in the large intestine, one of the main causes of disease and premature aging.

• Because it is pre-digested by its *lactobacillus bulgaris* bacteria, yogurt is assimilated by the body faster than milk.

• Yogurt is rich in proteins, minerals, enzymes, and most known vitamins, including hard-to-get ones like D and B12.

• Yogurt gives the intestinal bacteria their favorite food: lactose. People whose intestinal bacteria have been destroyed by antibiotics are often advised by their doctors to eat yogurt to replenish the bacteria.

• Yogurt has natural antibiotic properties strong enough to kill certain amoebas and such virulent bacteria as staphylococcus, streptococcus, and typhus.

Rice

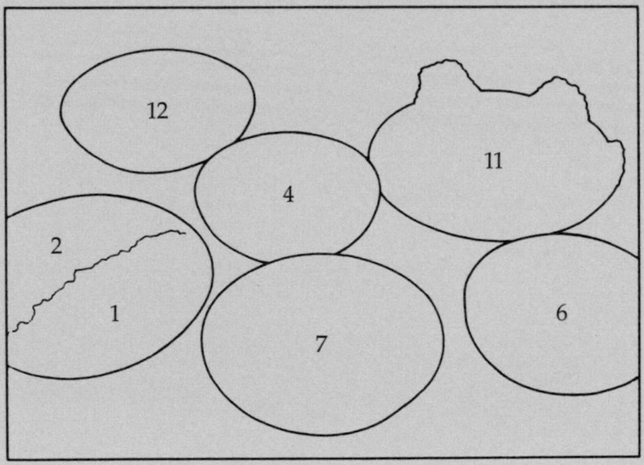
12
11
4
2
1
7
6

RICE is one of the most important ingredients in Vedic cuisine. In India, where most people eat rice at least once a day, we find a seemingly infinite variety of ways to cook it and combine it with other foods.

Cooked with herbs, spices, nuts, raisins, homemade cheese, and vegetables, rice makes a hearty *pulao*. Cooked and seasoned, with yogurt folded into it, it makes a cooling side dish for a hot summer's day. With seasonings, *dal* beans, and vegetables, it becomes a delicious all-in-one meal. Boiled with milk, sugar, and sweet spices, it makes a creamy pudding. You can grind rice into flour, heat it into puffs, or use it in pancakes, dumplings, sweets, and snacks.

Whatever the recipe, the first step is to choose the best rice. In our kitchens, we never use "easy-to-cook," parboiled, precooked, or instant rice, because they're weak in both taste and nutrition. Besides, when you offer food to Kṛṣṇa, it's best to offer what you have cooked yourself.

Different kinds of rice are suited for different dishes. Long-grained rice is the one we use most often, because it has a fluffy consistency. Medium-grained rice works well for combination rice-*dal* dishes such as *khichri* and *sambar*. Short-grained rice is used for milk puddings, and it's sometimes ground to make *dosas*. If you use brown rice, remember that it requires more water and around one hour to cook (45 minutes with a pressure cooker).

There are three excellent varieties of long-grained rices: North Indian Patna, American Carolina, and Dehradum *basmati* (the best of all). The people who harvest, husk, and winnow *basmati* rice have shunned the bleaching, pearling, oiling, and powdering that produce a commercially appealing rice at the expense of flavor and nutrition. *Basmati* rice, nutritious and easy to cook, has a unique nutlike taste and fragrance. You can buy it in most Indian and Middle Eastern grocery stores, or in gourmet food shops.

Most people in the West don't know how to cook rice properly. They use too much water and cook it longer than necessary. The result is generally mushy and unappetizing. But when you follow the recipes in this section, it's easy to cook rice so that each grain comes out firm, separate, and tasty.

Some points worth remembering when cooking rice

- Use about ⅓ cup (60 g) of rice per person.
- With packaged American and European rice, you don't have to pick through it for small stones or other impurities, but with *basmati* rice you must. Empty the rice onto one end of a large platter or cookie sheet and work the rice from one side of the platter to the other, inspecting the grains carefully. Push any stones or other foreign objects to the side.
- Wash the rice to get rid of the dust, chaff, and starchy powder left over from the milling process. Put the rice in a large bowl filled with cold water. Swirl the rice with your hand, and the water will become cloudy with starch. Slowly pour the water away, holding back the grains with your free hand or with a strainer. Repeat this three or four times until the water is reasonably clear.
- Before you cook your rice, try letting it soak for 15 to 30 minutes. Each grain absorbs water and will therefore stick less to the other grains while cooking. Before cooking, put the rice in a colander and let it drain for a few minutes. If you're going to saute the rice, let it drain for at least 10 to 15 minutes.
- Sauteing the rice before you boil, bake, or steam it is another way to keep the grains from becoming soggy. Saute the grains gently in a little ghee, butter, or vegetable oil, stirring constantly to keep them from burning and to make sure every grain is saturated. Continue until some of the grains have become translucent.
- When you cook rice by steaming it, use about 1¾ parts water for each part of rice. If you've soaked the rice beforehand, you can use a little less water for steaming.

• When you steam large quantities of rice, you need less water. For example, for more than 2½ Ibs (1.1 kg) of rice, use about 1½ parts of water for each part of rice. For 5 lbs (2.2 kg), use a little less than 1½ parts water.

• When you add boiling water to the grains, stir a few times to keep them from sticking.

• In most recipes, trapped steam helps cook the rice, so keep the pan covered tightly. Any time you're unsure about the fitting of the lid, interpose a layer of aluminum foil between the lid and the saucepan. When you steam rice, use the lowest heat, without lifting the lid or stirring.

The reason for not stirring rice is that as the rice expands, it forms a network of steam tunnels. If these are disturbed, the rice will cook unevenly with the bottom soggy or burned and the top not done.

• The rice is done when the grains are tender but firm. Uncover the saucepan and allow the rice to cook for 2 to 3 minutes more. This boils off the excess moisture and keeps the grains from sticking together.

• Before you serve the rice, take off any whole spices from the top. Take the rice out of the pan in layers, being careful not to break the grains. Then mix it gently with a fork.

Chawal
Plain white rice

Well-prepared plain white rice is a delicacy. It can complement fancy or spicy dishes, or it can be dressed with garnishes and fried spices. A teaspoon of turmeric in a tablespoon of ghee *can be mixed into the rice to make it yellow. Here are three different ways of making plain white rice.*

2 cups (350 g) basmati or other good-quality long grained white rice
3 1/2 cups (825 ml) water
2 tsp salt
1 or 2 tbs ghee or butter

Steamed Rice

This method of cooking rice is most often used in India. All the water, and whatever flavoring may be added, is absorbed into the rice. You will need a tight-fitting lid to keep the steam from escaping. If too much escapes, the rice will not cook thoroughly.

If you want to flavor the rice, try adding one of the following: a little lemon juice, a tiny pinch of turmeric, a few raw cumin seeds, the skin (not seeds) of a green chili, a piece of fresh ginger.

Wash the rice, soak it for 15 minutes, and let it drain. Put the water and salt to boil in a 3-quart (2-liter) saucepan.

Heat the *ghee* or butter in another saucepan over medium heat and fry the drained rice, stirring for a minute or so to saturate the grains evenly with the ghee. When the grains become translucent, pour the boiling water into the rice. Let the water come to a boil again. Boil rapidly for 1 minute, and stir once to prevent the rice from forming clumps. Cover tightly. Turn the heat to the lowest setting and cook for about 15 to 20 minutes (depending on the type of rice you use) or until the rice has absorbed all the water and is tender and fluffy.

Boiled Rice

Boiling is the quickest way to cook rice. This method is therefore especially useful (but not essential) when the rice is to be mixed with other ingredients. For this method, the rice (washed or unwashed) is boiled in more water than it can absorb, then drained when done.

Bring to a boil 10 cups (2.3 liters) of water with the salt in a heavy-bottomed saucepan. Add the rice and boil briskly for about 10 minutes. To tell if the rice has cooked enough withdraw a grain from the water and squeeze it between the thumb and forefinger. It should mash completely, the center should not be hard. If the center is still hard, boil it for a few more minutes and test again. Drain the rice in a colander, then put it into a serving bowl and dot it with the butter.

Baked Rice

First the rice is boiled on the stove until partially cooked, then finished in the oven. This method of cooking rice is the slowest, but requires the least care and always produces a rice with firm, well-separated grains.

Preheat the oven to 300° F (150° C). Bring to a boil 10 cups (2.3 liters) of water with the salt. Add the rice. Bring to a second boil, and boil briskly for 4 to 6 minutes. Drain the rice in a colander. Now put the rice in an oven-proof dish and dot it with the butter. Some cooks also sprinkle a few drops of milk on the rice at this point.

Cover the dish with aluminum foil and crinkle it around the edges to seal it as thoroughly as possible. The rice has to cook in its own steam. Put the dish in the oven and bake for about 20 minutes. Then check to see if it's done. Each grain should be separate, fluffy, and tender.

Preparation and cooking time

Steamed rice: 20 min

Boiled rice: 15 min

Baked rice: 30 min

Nimbu chawal

Lemon rice

This dish is the ideal rice for a summer picnic. One of the most striking sights at our annual Ratha-yātrā festival in Los Angeles is the "mountain" of lemon rice. Nimbu chawal *is flavored mainly by the lemon so be careful not to exceed the recommended quantities of spices.*

2 cups (350 g) basmati or other good-quality long-grained rice
1 tbs ghee or vegetable oil
½ tsp cumin seeds
1½ tsp black mustard seeds
5 curry leaves (if available)
1 cinnamon stick, 2 inches (5 cm) long
1 green chili, chopped
3 1/2 cups (825 ml) water
2 tsp salt
½ tsp turmeric (optional)
½ cup (125 ml) lemon juice
2 tbs butter
1 lemon, cut into 8 wedges
5 or 6 sprigs of parsley

Wash the rice in cold water and soak it for 15 to 20 minutes. Then leave it in a colander or sieve to drain. Meanwhile, heat the *ghee* or vegetable oil in a saucepan over medium heat and toss in the cumin seeds, black mustard seeds, curry leaves, and cinnamon. When the cumin seeds change color, put in the chopped chili) and then the drained rice.

Stir-fry the rice for 2 to 3 minutes. When the grains begin to turn translucent pour the salted water into the rice and bring it to a boil for a minute. (If you want yellow rice, add the turmeric powder with the water). Cover the pan, turn the heat down, and cook (without stirring) for about 18 minutes or until all the water is absorbed.

Lift the lid and remove the pieces of cinnamon stick. Sprinkle the lemon juice over the rice and dot with the butter.

Continue to cook, uncovered, for 2 or 3 minutes more. Finally, fluff the rice gently with a fork and garnish each serving with a lemon wedge and a sprig of parsley.

Soaking time: 15 to 20 min
Preparation and cooking time: 30 min

Palak chawal
Rice with spinach

Śrīla Prabhupāda's program of chanting, dancing, philosophy, and feasting has had wide success in Kenya. The Kenyans, like the Bengalis, eat plenty of vegetable greens and large amounts of rice, so whenever the Kenyan devotees combine greens and rice in palak chawal, *the feast is a great success.*

2 cups (350 g) basmati or other good-quality long-grained rice
1½ tsp salt
3½ cups (825 ml) water
½ lb (225 g) fresh spinach
1 tbs ghee
1 tsp ground coriander
2 bay leaves
¾ cup (100 g) unsalted peanuts, lightly fried (optional)
1 pinch ground black pepper

Wash the rice thoroughly, soak it for 15 minutes, and let it drain. Put the water and the salt in a pot over high heat. Remove the tough stalks from the spinach, wash the leaves in several changes of water, and drain. Then wilt the leaves by plunging them into boiling water. Put them in a colander and rinse under cold water. Drain and chop them into small pieces.

In a medium-sized saucepan, heat the *ghee* and fry the ground coriander and bay leaves. Add the rice and stir-fry until the grains are coated with *ghee* and become translucent. Add the chopped spinach, stir for a minute, then pour the salted water into the saucepan and bring to a boil.

Cover the pan and cook gently on low heat for 20 minutes. If you use peanuts, put them in without stirring, 5 minutes before the end of cooking. When the rice is completely cooked, add the pepper. Mix the ingredients with a fork before serving.

Preparation and cooking time: 30 to 40 min

Narial chawal
Coconut rice

On Bali, the Indonesian paradise once ruled by Vedic princes, several of the island's best traditional dancers have become devotees of Kṛṣṇa. When the temple puts on a theatrical presentation of the Rāmāyaṇa, a Gamelan orchestra (forty to fifty native musicians with traditional instruments) is customarily hired to provide the background music. But the musicians have become so fond of prasādam, *especially fancy rice dishes like* narial chawal, *that instead of money they simply ask for their travel expenses and as much* prasādam *as they can eat.*

2 cups (350 g) basmati or other good-quality medium or long-grained rice
3½ cups (825 ml) water
1 cup (200 g) sugar
½ tsp finely ground cardamom seeds
2¼ cups (150 g) grated coconut, lightly toasted
½ cup (50 g) pistachio or cashew nuts, toasted
⅓ cup (50 g) raisins
1 tbs butter

Soak the rice for 1 hour and let it drain. In a medium-sized saucepan, bring the water, sugar, and cardamom powder to a boil. Now drop the rice in the boiling water and bring to a second boil. Simmer for 2 to 3 minutes, then turn the heat very low. Cover the pot tightly, cook for 10 minutes, then lift the cover and quickly put in the remaining ingredients. Replace the cover and cook 10 minutes longer or until done. Then remove the cover and allow the rice to cook on the same low heat for 2 to 3 more minutes to allow the steam to evaporate.

Finally, mix the rice gently and serve on a platter with *masala dosas* or *atta dosas* for breakfast or lunch.

Soaking time: 1 hr
Preparation and cooking time: 30 min

Masala bhat
Spicy rice

2 cups (350 g) basmati or other good-quality long-grained white rice
3½ cups (825 ml) water
1 tsp salt
2 tbs ghee or vegetable oil
1 tsp cumin seeds
2 fresh red or green chilies, seeded and sliced
1 tsp ground cinnamon
1 tsp grated fresh ginger
½ tsp ground nutmeg
3 cardamom pods, bruised
2 tbs chopped fresh coriander or parsley leaves
2 tbs butter

Wash the rice well, soak it for 15 minutes; then let it drain for 15 minutes. Put the water and salt in a pot over high heat.

Heat the *ghee* or vegetable oil in a medium-sized saucepan and fry the cumin seeds and chilies. After a few seconds, when the cumin seeds begin to darken, add the cinnamon, ginger, cardamom, and nutmeg. Stir once, add the rice, and continue stirring. In a minute or two the rice should be lightly toasted. Pour the boiling water into the rice, cover, and turn the heat very low. Without lifting the cover or stirring, cook for 15 to 18 minutes or until the rice has absorbed all the water.

Uncover the pot and allow the steam to escape for a few minutes. Discard the cardamom pods and gently mix the butter and the chopped fresh coriander or parsley leaves into the rice with a fork. Serve with any vegetable dish or combination of dishes.

Soaking and draining time: 30 min
Preparation and cooking time: 25 min

Dahi bhat
Rice with yogurt

Served hot or cold, dahi bhat is a popular rice dish of South India. You can dress up this dish with one or more of the following ingredients: diced raw green or red pepper, chopped tomato, fried potato cubes, or steamed peas.

2 cups (350 g) basmati or other good-quality long-grained rice
1 tbs ghee or vegetable oil
1 tsp urad dal
1 tsp black mustard seeds
¾ tsp fennel seeds
2 fresh chillies, seeded and minced
1 tsp grated fresh ginger
3 cups (700 ml) water
2 tsp salt
1 cup (250 ml) yogurt
1 tbs butter

Wash the rice. Then soak it for about 15 minutes and leave it in a colander to drain. Heat the *ghee* or vegetable oil in a medium-sized saucepan and toss in the *urad dal* and mustard seeds. Cover the pot immediately. When the mustard seeds finish popping, put in the fennel seeds, chilies, and ginger. Stir once. Add the rice and stir-fry for about a minute, until the grains turn translucent. Pour in the water and salt and boil for 1 minute. Cover the pan, reduce the heat to the lowest setting, and simmer for 18 to 20 minutes.

Five minutes before the rice is completely cooked, lift the lid, add the yogurt and butter, and stir quickly with a fork. Replace the cover and continue cooking until the grains are fluffy and the rice has absorbed most of the liquid. Allow the rest of the liquid to evaporate by letting the rice cook for 2 or 3 minutes uncovered.

Soaking time: 15 min
Preparation and cooking time: 25 min

Matar pulao
Rice with peas and cheese

Pulaos are exquisitely beautiful. They are the main attraction on the table, and they're often a meal in themselves. Pulaos stand out for their garnishes. Some use a dozen or more. And every pulao recipe uses ghee or butter to saute the rice before the cold water is added.

2 cups (350 g) basmati or other good-quality long-grained rice
7 oz (200 g) pressed paneer
ghee or vegetable oil for deep-frying
1 tsp turmeric
3½ tsp salt
2 tbs ghee or butter
4 cups (950 ml) cold water
6 cardamom pods, bruised
6 cloves
4 oz (100 g) fresh peas, shelled and parboiled
1 tbs butter

Wash the rice in cold water, soak it for 15 minutes, and let it drain. Cut the *paneer* into 1-inch cubes and deep-fry them over medium-high heat until they are lightly browned. Dissolve the turmeric and 2 teaspoons of salt in a cup of warm water or whey and put the *paneer* cubes in to soak. Add the rest of the salt to the water for the rice.

Heat the *ghee* or butter in a saucepan over medium heat and fry the cardamom pods and cloves for a minute. Add the rice and peas, and keep stirring for a few minutes longer. Now pour the salted water into the rice and bring to a rapid boil. Stir once, lower the heat, and simmer for at least 20 minutes without lifting the cover or stirring.

Uncover the pan and allow the water to evaporate for 2 to 3 minutes. Add the drained cheese cubes and a few pats of butter. Mix gently with a fork before serving.

Soaking time: 15 min
Preparation and cooking time: 30 min

Kesar paneer pulao
Saffron rice with cheese balls

Kesar paneer pulao with its fried cheese balls, fried nuts, and raisins, looks like a saffron-colored landscape strewn with flowers. With just a soup and a light bread, it makes a complete meal.

2 cups (350 g) basmati or other good-quality long-grained rice
⅓ cup (50 g) raisins
7 oz (200 g) pressed paneer
½ tsp powdered saffron or 1 tsp saffron strands
2 teaspoon brown sugar
¼ pint (150 ml) warm milk
2 tbs butter
3 cups (700 ml) water
⅓ cup (50 g) blanched almonds or cashew nuts, toasted
2½ teaspoon salt

Wash the rice, soak it for 15 to 20 minutes in cold water, and let it drain. Knead the paneer until it is soft, and roll it into small balls, or press it and cut it into cubes. Deep-fry the paneer balls or cubes until they are browned all over. Drain. Dissolve the saffron and sugar in the warm milk, and put the raisins and deep-fried cheese balls or cubes in the saffron-milk to soak.

Melt a tablespoon of butter in a large saucepan over medium heat and stir-fry the rice for 2 minutes. When the grains become lightly toasted, pour the water and salt into the rice, bring to a boil, then cook covered over very low heat. After 10 minutes, remove the cover and gently stir in the saffron-milk (set the cheese balls aside), nuts, and raisins. Be careful not to break the grains. Cover the pot again and cook 10 minutes more or until the rice is completely cooked. Then remove the cover and allow the rest of the water to evaporate by cooking it another 2 or 3 minutes.

Finally, dot the rice with butter and gently mix with a fork. Garnish with the cheese balls and serve hot.

Soaking time: 15 to 20 min
Preparation and cooking time: 30 to 40 min

Opposite page: *Kesar paneer pulao*

Sabji pulao
Mixed vegetable rice

2 cups (350 g) basmati rice
¾ cup (100 g) fresh peas
1 cup (100 g) green beans
1 cup (100 g) cauliflower buds
1 cup (100 g) diced carrots
2 tbs ghee or butter
1 fresh chili, seeded and minced
½ tsp grated fresh ginger
½ tsp turmeric
4 cups (950 ml) water
2½ tsp salt
3 firm ripe tomatoes, washed and chopped
2 bay leaves
2 lemons or limes, cut into wedges

Begin by wrapping the following spices in a small piece of muslin like a tea-bag:

6 whole cloves
2 cinnamon sticks, crushed
1 tsp cumin seeds
½ tsp ground cardamom seeds
¼ tsp asafoetida

Wash the vegetables and trim them. Wash the rice, soak it for 15 minutes, and let it drain for 15 minutes. Heat the *ghee* or butter in a medium-sized saucepan and fry the chili, grated ginger, and turmeric.

Now add the vegetables (except the tomatoes) and fry for 4 or 5 minutes more. Add the rice and stir for a moment. Then add the salted water, tomatoes, and bay leaves. Stir again and bring to a boil. Suspend the little bag of spices in the rice, cover the pot, and cook over very low heat until the rice has absorbed all the water.

Remove the spice bag and squeeze it over the rice. Turn the rice onto a pre-heated serving dish and garnish with wedges of lemon or lime before serving, either as part of a meal or as a meal in itself.

Soaking and draining time: 30 min
Preparation and cooking time: 35 to 40 min

Seb pulao
Apple rice

This sweet pulao can be served at the end of a meal or as a light meal in itself. It's delicious with whipped cream. You can also use pears or mangos with the apples or in place of them.

1½ cups (275 g) good-quality long-grained white rice
3 medium-sized apples
2 cups (350 g) brown sugar
¼ tsp powdered saffron or
½ tsp saffron strands
1¾ cups (425 ml) water (for the syrup)
3 tbs ghee or butter
1 cinnamon stick, 2 inches (5 cm) long
8 cloves
8 cardamom pods
3 bay leaves
3½ cups (825 ml) water (for the rice)
⅓ cup (50 g) sliced almonds
⅓ cup (50 g) raisins

Wash the rice and drain it. Peel, core, and cut the apples into small chunks. Make a syrup by putting the sugar, a pinch of saffron, and the water in a saucepan and cooking it for 30 minutes over medium heat until it reduces to about one-third of its original volume.

Heat the *ghee* or butter in a saucepan and toss in the cinnamon, cloves, cardamom, and bay leaves. Stir-fry for a moment or two, then add the rice. Stir-fry for 2 or 3 minutes. Add the water and bring to a boil. Toss the rest of the saffron into the water, cover the pan, and cook over low heat for 10 minutes. Then take the saucepan off the heat.

Make a hole in the center of the rice and place the pieces of apple and a little of the syrup in it. Add the raisins and the sliced almonds. Cover the hole with rice and pour the rest of the syrup over the top. Cover the pan again and cook over low heat for 15 more minutes, until the rice is completely cooked. Remove the whole spices, mix gently, and serve hot.

Preparation and cooking time: 40 min

Biriyani
Baked vegetable rice

- 2 cups (350 g) basmati or other good-quality long-grained rice
- 4 cups (950 ml) water
- 3 tsp salt
- ¼ tsp powdered saffron
- 3 tbs ghee or vegetable oil
- 2 tsp garam masala
- 2 tsp ground coriander
- 1 tsp turmeric
- 3 potatoes, peeled and diced
- 1½ cups (200 g) fresh peas, boiled
- 4 tomatoes, blanched and mashed
- 3 tbs minced fresh coriander or parsley leaves
- ¾ cup (175 ml) yogurt
- 2 tsp rose-water
- ¼ cup (35 g) chopped hazelnuts or walnuts

Wash the rice and let it drain. Put the water and 2 teaspoons of the salt in a medium-sized saucepan and bring to a boil. Then add the rice to the water and bring it to a second boil. Cover it and cook it over low heat for about 15 minutes.

While the rice cooks, steep the saffron in a small amount of warm milk. Then heat the *ghee* or vegetable oil in another saucepan and stir-fry the powdered spices. After a few seconds, add the diced potatoes and stir-fry them gently for 5 minutes or until they are lightly browned. Now put in the peas, the tomatoes, half of the fresh coriander leaves, and the remaining salt. Cook with the pan covered until the vegetables are tender. Stir every few minutes. If necessary, add a little water to prevent scorching.

By now the rice should be cooked. Add the yogurt, rose-water, and saffron milk to the rice, mix gently with a fork, and let stand undisturbed for 5 minutes. Grease a cake pan or casserole and cover the bottom with half the rice. Pat the rice down. Spread the vegetables evenly over the rice and cover them with the remaining rice. Pat it down and cover the pan tightly with a piece of aluminum foil. Heat the oven to 275° F (140° C) and bake the rice for 15 to 20 minutes. To serve, cut into portions and remove from the pan with a spatula. Garnish each portion with chopped nuts and coriander leaves. Serve hot.

Preparation and cooking time: 45 min

Pushpanna
Flower rice

With its many garnishes and seasonings, pushpanna *is one of the most opulent of rice dishes, and, as its name implies, it's as colorful as a bouquet of flowers. Some cooks add pieces of chopped dried fruits to heighten the effect.*

8 oz (225 g) pressed paneer
¾ cup (100 g) cashews or blanched almonds
1½ cups (100 g) grated coconut
6 tbs ghee or butter
1 tsp fennel seeds
1 tsp cumin seeds
2 bay leaves
6 cardamom pods, bruised
2 tsp ground coriander
1 tsp turmeric
1 tsp grated nutmeg
1 tsp ground cinnamon
½ tsp cayenne pepper
½ tsp ground black pepper
¼ tsp asafoetida
¼ tsp ground cloves
2 cups (350 g) basmati or other good-quality long-grained white rice
¾ cup (100 g) raisins
3½ cups (825 ml) whey
½ cup (100 g) sugar
1 tbs salt

Cube the *paneer,* or knead it into a dough to be rolled into ½-inch (2.5 cm) balls. Deep-fry the cubes or balls and drain in a colander. Deep-fry the nuts and drain them with the cheese. Toast the grated coconut in 2 tablespoons of the *ghee* and set the coconut aside.

Heat the remaining *ghee* in a large saucepan. When it begins to smoke, toss in the fennel, cumin, bay leaves, and cardamom. After 30 seconds, add all the powdered spices. Stir-fry for a few seconds, then add the rice. Stir until the grains are translucent and lightly browned. Add the fried cheese, raisins, sugar, and salt. Add the whey. (This can be the whey from your *paneer*. If you don't have enough whey, add water). Mix gently. Bring to a boil, then adjust to the lowest heat and cover the pan tightly. Cook for 20 minutes until the rice is tender. Then add the fried nuts and coconut and mix gently before serving.

Preparation and cooking time: 45 min

Dals and Soups

1 Dal tarkari *(Dal and vegetable soup)* 124
2 Tamatar mung dal *(Toasted mung dal soup with tomatoes)* 125
3 Gujarati urad dal *(Urad dal with spiced yogurt)* 126
4 Tamatar toor dal *(Tomato and toor dal soup)* 127
5 Jagannath Puri channe ki dal *(Sweet dal)* 129
6 Swadisht dal *(Mixed dal)* 130
7 Sambar *(Vegetable and dal stew)* 131
8 Mitha ghani dal *(Sprouted mung beans in yogurt sauce)* 132
9 Khitchri *(Boiled rice, dal, and vegetables)* 133
10 Geeli khitchri *(Boiled rice, dal, and spinach)* 136
11 Channa masala *(Spiced chick-peas)* 137
12 Channa raita *(Fried chick-peas in spiced yogurt)* 138
13 Channa aur simla mirch *(Fried chick-peas and peppers)* 139
14 Mili-juli sabji ka soup *(Creamy vegetable soup)* 140
15 Tamatar ka soup *(Tomato soup)* 141

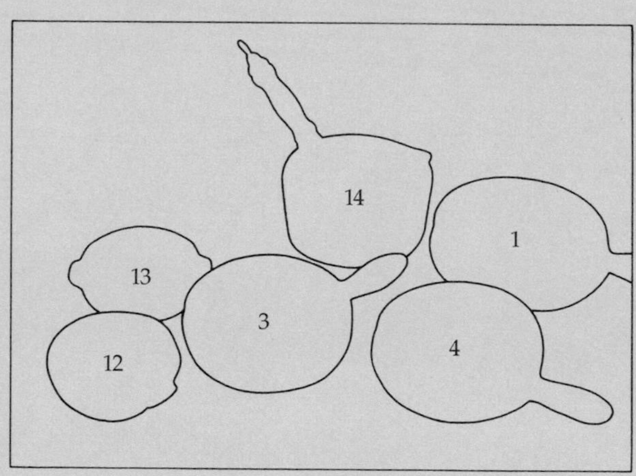

LENTILS or peas that have been husked and split are called *dal,* and that's also the name for the soup-like dish they make. In India, *dal* is served with the main meal and is often spooned over plain rice or eaten with bread.

Besides being rich in iron and the B vitamins, *dal* is a main source of protein in the Vedic diet. The amount of protein in some *dals* is equal to or greater than that in meat, and *dal* reacts synergistically with other protein-rich foods, such as grains, nuts, and milk products, to increase the usable protein in the meal by as much as forty percent. For example, the usable protein of rice (60%) and that of *dal* (65%) increase to 85 percent when the two are eaten together.

More than sixty varieties of *dal* grow in India. The four types used in this book are common varieties available at Asian grocers and most health food shops. Their characteristics are listed below.

• *Mung dal:* Small, pale yellow, and rectangular. This *dal* comes from mung beans, which are often used for making bean sprouts. *Mung dal* is easy to cook and has a mild taste. It is so digestible that it's recommended for children, elderly people, and convalescents.

• *Urad dal:* Small, grayish-white, and rectangular. This *dal* has twice as much protein as meat. It's often used in savories or ground into a powder and allowed to ferment to make foods light and spongy.

• *Channa dal:* Larger than *mung dal,* yellowish, and round. *Channa* is one of the smaller members of the chickpea family and has a rich sweet taste. If it's unavailable, you can substitute yellow split peas and get a good-tasting if not quite authentic dal.

• *Toor dal:* Larger than *channa dal,* pale yellow, and round. This *dal* comes from what is known in the West as pigeon peas. The split grains are sometimes coated with a film of oil that should be washed off before cooking.

Chickpeas (or garbanzo beans), called *kabuli channa* in India, are a wonderful source of protein. They are extremely hard and require soaking before being used. Cooked chickpeas are usually eaten by themselves in the morning with a little grated ginger, or accompanied by other dishes such as *upma* or *khichri.*

In Vedic cooking, a meal without *dal* in one form or another is rare. There are *dal* dishes to suit any meal, from breakfast to late dinner. You can make *dal* into soups, thick sauces, stews, fried savories, moist chutneys, crisp pancakes, sprouted salads, and sweets.

You should wash your *dal* before using it. And with all *dals,* except those packaged especially for supermarkets, you have to pick out the tiny stones. The best way to do this is to put the *dal* at the end of a large cookie sheet or round plate and slowly move all the grains from one side to the other, a few at a time, carefully picking out any stones or other foreign matter. To wash the *dal,* take only as much as you will use right away, put it into a metal strainer, and lower the strainer into a large bowl two-thirds full of water. Rub the beans between your hands for about 30 seconds. Then lift the strainer, pour off the water, and fill the bowl again. Repeat this rubbing and rinsing several times, or until the rinse water is reasonably clear. Then drain or soak the *dal,* as the recipe requires.

Dal soup, made thick or thin, depending on the recipe, usually requires long cooking so that the split grains break up and merge, giving the *dal* a smooth texture. Some cooks blend the *dal* in an electric blender for a few minutes when it is finished to make it even smoother.

When *dal* cooks, it forms a thick froth that blocks the passage of steam. Leave the cover slightly ajar and spoon off most of the froth as it forms, so that the soup doesn't rise and spill over. Adding a tablespoon of butter to the *dal* will help keep down the froth.

The chaunce (fried seasonings and spices) added to the *dal* in the last few minutes of the cooking is what gives *dal* its punch. Heat a small amount of *ghee* or vegetable oil in a ladle or small pan. Then add the spices. When the spices are browned, pour them into the cooked *dal*. Watch out! Be ready to slap the cover on the pot immediately, because the contact of the hot *ghee* with the *dal* creates a mild explosion—•one of the delights of Vedic cooking.

Dal tarkari

Dal and vegetable soup

1 cup (200 g) mung dal or green split-peas
8 cups (1.9 liters) water
3 tsp salt
2 bay leaves
1 cinnamon stick, 3-inches (7.5 cm) long, broken in half
1 tsp turmeric
1 tbs butter
10 oz (275 g) assorted vegetables, washed and cubed
1 tbs ghee
1½ tsp cumin seeds
2 dried chillies, crushed
1 tsp grated fresh ginger
¼ tsp asafoetida
1 tbs chopped fresh coriander leaves
2 lemons, washed and cut into 8 wedges each

Clean and wash the *dal*. Drain. Combine the water, salt, bay leaves, and pieces of cinnamon stick in a heavy saucepan or pot to boil. Put the *dal* into the boiling water.

When the water comes to a second boil, partially cover the pot, lower to a medium heat, and cook for about 20 minutes, or until the *dal* grains are quite tender. Remove any froth that collects at the top. Then put in the turmeric and butter. Drop in the cut vegetables, replace the lid, and continue cooking on the same heat until the vegetables are tender and the dal is completely broken up. Let the *dal* simmer while you prepare the seasonings.

Heat the 2 tablespoons of *ghee* in a small frying pan and toss in the cumin seeds and the crushed chili. Stir once. When the cumin seeds darken, put in the grated ginger and the asafoetida and fry a few more seconds. Swirl and tilt the pan, and then pour the seasonings into the *dal* in one swoop. Cover the pot immediately and allow the seasonings to blend into the dal for 4 or 5 minutes. Serve this *dal* for lunch steaming hot with rice, vegetables, and a bread, garnished with fresh minced herbs and a wedge of lemon.

Dal tarkari should have a thin consistency; if it is too thick, add some hot water.

Preparation and cooking time: 1 hr

Tamatar mung dal
Toasted mung dal soup with tomatoes

1 cup (200 g) mung dal
8 cups (1.9 liters) water
3 bay leaves
1 tbs butter
2½ tsp salt
2 tbs ghee
1 tsp mustard seeds
1 tsp cumin seeds
2 dried chilies, crushed
2 tsp grated fresh ginger
¼ tsp asafoetida
1 tsp turmeric
5 medium-sized tomatoes, washed and chopped
2 tbs lemon juice
1 tbs chopped fresh coriander leaves

Pick through the *dal* and put it (unwashed) into a heavy saucepan. Place the pan over medium-low heat and dry-roast the *dal* for 4 to 5 minutes, stirring constantly, until most of the *dal* grains are slightly browned. Now pour the *dal* into a metal strainer. Wash the *dal* under running water and return it back to the saucepan. Add the water, bay leaves, butter and salt. Now place the pan over high heat and bring to a boil. Cover and cook over medium-high heat for 30 minutes.

When the *dal* begins to break up, heat the *ghee* in a small saucepan and toss in the mustard seeds. Cover the pan. When they finish sputtering, add in quick succession, the cumin seeds, chilies, ginger, asafoetida, and turmeric. Stir-fry for about 20 seconds, then drop in the chopped tomatoes and turn them with a spoon for a minute or two.

Scrape the tomatoes and spices into the soup, cover, and simmer until the *dal* is fully cooked and smooth. Finally, add the lemon juice and coriander leaves and stir well. Serve hot with any rice dish or Indian bread.

Preparation and cooking time: 1 hr

Gujarati urad dal

Urad dal with spiced yogurt

Urad dal *is so rich in protein that the* Āyur-veda *recommends eating it not more than four times a week, otherwise the body becomes overloaded with protein. The addition of seasoned yogurt gives this soup a creamy consistency. It goes well with a simple steamed rice dish and an Indian bread.*

1½ cups (375 ml) plain yogurt
1 tbs brown sugar
7 cups (1.6 liters) water
1 cup (200 g) urad dal
½ tsp turmeric
2 bay leaves
2½ tsp salt
1 tbs ghee or vegetable oil
1 tsp black mustard seeds
2 dried chillies, crushed
1 tsp fennel seeds
1 tsp grated fresh ginger

Mix the yogurt and the brown sugar in 1 cup (250 ml) of water. Set aside. Clean, wash, and drain the *dal.* In a heavy saucepan bring the remaining water to a boil. To this water, add the *urad dal,* bring to a boil again and cook uncovered for 10 minutes. Remove any froth that accumulates on the surface. Add the turmeric, bay leaves, and salt, stir once, cover the pot, and cook for 20 minutes over medium-low heat until the *dal* grains can be mashed between two fingers. Now, remove the bay leaves, and mix the *dal* in a blender until it is smooth. Then let simmer.

Put the *ghee* or vegetable oil in a small saucepan over medium heat and fry the black mustard seeds. Cover the pan for a moment to prevent the mustard seeds from jumping out. When the mustard seeds have finished popping, toss in the crushed chilies, the fennel seeds, and the grated ginger. Stir-fry for a moment. Finally, put this *masala* into the yogurt and pour the yogurt into the *dal.* Stir to blend well. Continue cooking for 5 minutes before serving.

Preparation and cooking time: 1 hr

Tamatar toor dal

Tomato and toor dal soup

In the Indian province of Gujarat, toor dal *is so widely used that the word* dal *means only* toor dal. *All other* dals *are known by their specific names. In Barcelona* toor dal *is also becoming well known to the hundreds of people who come to our restaurant for lunch. This dish is a favorite there, and many people ask the devotees how to cook it.*

1 cup (200 g) toor dal
8 cups (1.9 liters) water
3 tsp salt
½ tsp turmeric
1 tbs ghee or vegetable oil
1 tsp cumin seeds
1 tsp grated fresh ginger
1 tsp ground coriander
½ tsp asafoetida
3 medium-sized tomatoes, washed and chopped
1 tbs chopped fresh coriander leaves
1 lemon, sliced

Pick through the *dal* and wash it under warm running water until the grains appear free from their oily coating. Then drain them.

Bring the water with the salt and turmeric added to a boil. Pour the *dal* into the water, cover, and cook over medium heat for 30 minutes, stirring every now and then. When the *dal* is tender, heat the *ghee* or oil in a small saucepan and fry the cumin seeds. Let them sizzle for a few seconds. Put in the grated ginger, ground coriander and asafoetida, then stir in the tomatoes. Stir-fry for 2 or 3 minutes. Finally, pour the fried tomatoes and seasonings into the *dal* and simmer, stirring occasionally, until the grains are soft and fully cooked.

Garnish each serving with fresh chopped coriander or parsley leaves and a slice of lemon.

Preparation and cooking time: 1 hr

Jagannātha Purī channe ki dal
Sweet dal

Anyone who has ever had the good fortune to see the form of Kṛṣṇa traditionally worshiped in the Indian city of Jagannātha Purī, will never forget it. This form of Kṛṣṇa, called Jagannātha, "the Lord of the universe," is very merciful and attractive. His eyes are large and brilliant, and His broad smile extends from ear to ear.

Jagannātha Purī channe ki dal *is a favorite dish of Lord Jagannātha, and in many of our temples the devotees regularly offer it to Him. After tasting this soup for the first time, a guest once remarked that he now understood why Lord Jagannātha is always smiling.*

1 cup (200 g) channa dal
8 cups (1.9 liters) water
3 tsp salt
2 bay leaves
5 medium-sized tomatoes
1 tbs butter
2 tbs ghee or vegetable oil
½ tsp cumin seeds
1 tsp grated fresh ginger
½ tsp powdered asafoetida
3 tbs grated fresh or 4 tbs dry coconut
2 tbs brown sugar
2 tsp molasses

Soak the *dal* overnight and leave in a strainer to drain. Bring the water with the salt to a boil in a heavy saucepan or pot, then add the *dal* and bay leaves. Cook partially covered over high heat for 30 to 40 minutes. (Remove any froth that collects on the surface). Then lift the cover, stir the *dal* several times, and lower to a simmer.

Wash the tomatoes, cut each one into 8 wedges, and add to the *dal* with the butter. Replace the cover and let the *dal* simmer while you prepare the seasonings.

Heat the *ghee* or oil in a small saucepan and fry the cumin seeds. Let them fry for a few seconds, then add the grated ginger, asafoetida, and grated coconut. Fry this mixture for 1 or 2 minutes, stirring constantly. Now pour the ghee and spices into the cooked *dal* along with the sugar and the molasses. Stir well and simmer for 5 more minutes before serving.

Preparation and cooking time: 1 hr

Opposite page: *Jagannātha Purī channe ki dal*

Swadisht dal

Mixed dal

⅓ cup (75 g) each: toor dal, mung dal, and urad dal
5 tbs ghee or vegetable oil
1 tbs grated fresh ginger
½ tsp turmeric
8 cups (1.9 liters) water
1 tsp black mustard seeds
1 tsp cumin seeds
2 green chilies, seeded and minced
4 curry leaves or 2 bay leaves
½ tsp asafoetida
1 small eggplant, cubed
3 medium-sized tomatoes, chopped
1 tsp sugar
2½ tsp salt
½ tsp garam masala
2 heaping tbs chopped fresh coriander leaves

Wash the *dals* and soak them for one hour; then let them drain. Heat 2 tablespoons of the *ghee* or vegetable oil and fry the ginger. Add the turmeric and the dals. Stir-fry for a minute, add 1¼ pints (725 ml) water, and cook over medium heat (skimming off the foam as it accumulates) until the *dal* becomes soft. Remove the saucepan. Mix the *dal* in a blender or mash it into a paste. Set aside.

Heat the remaining 3 tablespoons of *ghee* or vegetable oil in a saucepan. Fry the mustard seeds, cumin seeds, chilies, curry leaves, and asafoetida. Add the cubed eggplant. Stir-fry for 10 minutes until they are butter-soft. Now add the tomatoes, sugar, salt, *garam masala, dal paste,* and the remaining water. Stir well to mix the ingredients, cover and cook until the vegetables are tender. Garnish with the coriander leaves and serve hot with plain rice.

Preparation and cooking time: 45 min

Sambar

Vegetable and dal stew

Sambar is thicker than ordinary dal *and is especially easy to digest. It is traditionally served with* masala *or* atta dosa, *or with white rice and one of the breads described in the next chapter.*

6 cups (1.4 liters) water
3 tsp salt
1¼ cups (250 g) mung dal, toor dal, green split-peas, or whole lentils
1½ lb (675 g) assorted vegetables such as eggplant, carrots, tomatoes, green beans, or squash
2 oz (50 g) tamarind
3 tbs ghee or vegetable oil
1 tsp black mustard seeds
1½ tsp ground cumin
2 tsp ground coriander
½ tsp cayenne pepper or 2 fresh chillies, minced
1 tsp turmeric
4 tbs grated coconut

Start by putting the water, with the salt added, over heat to boil. Sort, wash, and drain the *dal.* Add the *dal* to the boiling water. Cook uncovered for 10 minutes. Remove any froth and *dal* skins that collect on the surface, then cover and cook over medium heat for 15 to 25 minutes, stirring occasionally. The *dal* should become softer but not mushy.

While the *dal* is cooking, wash and cut the vegetables into small cubes. Break up the lump of tamarind, boil it in a small amount of water, and extract the juice.

Heat the *ghee* or vegetable oil in a saucepan and fry the mustard seeds. After they finish popping, add the powdered spices, fry for a few seconds, then add the vegetables. (If you use eggplant, cook it first until it is butter-soft). Stir-fry for 10 to 15 minutes, until all the vegetables are browned. Add the grated coconut and fry for 2 more minutes.

By this time the *dal* should be ready. Empty the vegetables and the tamarind juice into the *dal* and mix well. Lower the heat and cook uncovered until the dal is fully cooked and thick and the vegetables are soft.

Preparation and cooking time: 45 min

Mithi ghani dal

Sprouted mung beans in yogurt sauce

1½ cups (300 g) whole mung beans
1 cup (250 ml) yogurt or buttermilk
2 tbs chickpea flour
1 tsp cumin seeds
1 tbs grated fresh ginger
¼ tsp asafoetida
5 curry leaves (if available)
1 tsp turmeric
2 tsp salt
3 fresh chillies, seeded and minced
1½ tsp sugar
4 tbs chopped fresh coriander leaves
2½ cups (600 ml) water
3 tbs ghee or vegetable oil

Wash the *mung* beans and soak them overnight. The next morning, tie them in a moist cloth and hang them for at least 24 hours before cooking, so they can begin to sprout. Check from time to time to make sure the cloth does not dry out.

Mix the chickpea flour with the yogurt or buttermilk and set aside. Heat the *ghee* or vegetable oil and fry the cumin, ginger, chilies, and asafoetida. When the cumin seeds darken, add the curry leaves, turmeric, salt, and sprouted *mung* beans. Pour the water into the pan and cook over medium heat for 30 to 40 minutes, adding a little more water if necessary. When the beans are soft, add the yogurt or buttermilk; then add the sugar and cook for 5 more minutes. Garnish with the chopped coriander leaves. Serve with plain white rice or an Indian bread.

Preparation and cooking time: 45 min

Khichri

Boiled rice, dal, and vegetables

This inexpensive dish is so satisfying that Śrīla Prabhupāda once said, "A bowl of khichri *and a small portion of yogurt is a poor man's feast fit for a king."*

This recipe is for "dry" khichri, *which has the consistency of rice that is slightly overcooked, soft, and a little moist.*

1 cup (200 g) mung dal, split peas, or whole mung beans
1½ cups (250 g) medium or long-grained rice
½ cauliflower, washed and separated into small flowerets
3 tbs ghee or vegetable oil
2 tsp cumin seeds
4 medium-sized tomatoes, washed and quartered
2 fresh chilies, seeded and minced
2 tsp grated fresh ginger
1 tsp ground cumin
½ tsp asafoetida
7 cups (1.6 liters) water
2 tsp salt
2 tsp turmeric
4 medium-sized potatoes, washed, peeled, and cubed
3 tablespoon lemon juice
2 tablespoon butter
½ teaspoon ground black pepper

Pick through the *dal* and wash it and the rice together. Let drain.

Meanwhile, wash, trim, and cut the vegetables. Heat the *ghee* or vegetable oil and fry the cumin seeds, chilies and ginger. After they sizzle for a minute, toss in the ground cumin and the asafoetida. After a few seconds, put in the diced potatoes and the flowerets of cauliflower. Turn the vegetables with a spoon for 4 to 5 minutes until they become flecked with brown spots. Now add the drained *dal* and rice and stir-fry for one minute. Pour in the water. Add the salt, turmeric, and tomatoes, and bring to a full boil over high heat. Reduce to low heat and cook with the pot partially covered for 30 to 40 minutes (if you use *mung* beans, cook a little more; split peas a little less) until the *dal* is soft and fully cooked. Stir once or twice in the beginning to prevent the rice from sticking to the bottom of the pot.

Finally, squeeze the lemon juice over the *khichri,* put the butter on top, and simmer over low heat until the grains have absorbed all the liquid. Season with the pepper. Mix all the ingredients gently but quickly with a fork.

For an extra special *khichri,* serve it with a little *kadhi* sauce. If you use brown rice, cook the *khichri* for an extra 20 minutes.

Preparation and cooking time: 45 min

Opposite page: *Geeli khichri (p. 136)*
Khichri

Geeli khichri

Boiled rice, dal, and spinach

In Calcutta the devotees hold a Hare Kṛṣṇa festival at a different city park every weekend. The local people, informed of the upcoming festival, come with generous contributions of rice, dal, and vegetables, which the devotees transform into a sumptuous "wet" khichri. *The* khichri *is first offered to Kṛṣṇa, then distributed to at least 5, 000 people each weekend. Here is a recipe for that* geeli, *or wet* khichri.

1½ cups (250 g) medium or long-grained rice
1¼ cups (250 g) mung dal, split-peas, or whole mung beans
¼ cup (50 g) butter or ghee
3 bay leaves
1 tbs chopped ginger
2 cloves
2 tsp salt
1 tsp turmeric
¼ tsp ground nutmeg
8 oz (225 g) fresh spinach, washed, stemmed, and finely chopped
3 tomatoes, chopped

Wash the *dal* and rice, soak them for 1 hour, and let them drain. Heat the butter or *ghee* in a heavy saucepan, add the bay leaves, chopped ginger, and cloves, then add the drained rice and *dal*. Fry for about 8 to 10 minutes, stirring well, until the butter has been absorbed. Stir in enough water to cover the grains by 2 inches (5 cm). Add the salt, turmeric and nutmeg, stir, and boil for 1 minute. Cover tightly and start to cook over medium-low heat.

Lower the heat gradually as the grains absorb the water. Cook slowly for about 30 minutes, checking from time to time to insure that the mixture is always covered with a little water. (If necessary, add a few tablespoons). Then gently stir in the chopped spinach and tomatoes and cover again. Continue cooking for another 15 minutes, or until the grains are well cooked but the mixture is still quite moist. Mix well before serving.

Soaking time: 1 hr
Preparation and cooking time: 1 hr

Channa masala
Spiced chickpeas

For a simple, nutritious breakfast, eat a small portion of spiced chickpeas, with *khichri* or *sambar* or by themselves.

1½ cup (250 g) chickpeas, picked through and washed
1 tsp grated fresh ginger
¼ tsp asafoetida
1½ tsp salt
2 tsp lemon juice
½ tsp ground black pepper

Soak the chickpeas overnight in water double their volume. Drain them and put them into a medium-sized saucepan, and add enough water to cover them by about 3 inches (7.5 cm). Add ½ teaspoon of salt, and bring to a boil. Remove any froth that may collect on the surface. Cover and simmer for 45 minutes to 1 hour, or until a chickpea is tender enough to be crushed between two fingers. Now drain the chickpeas and transfer them to a mixing bowl.

Add the lemon juice, the remaining **teaspoon** of salt, and the spices. Mix well before offering.

Soaking time: overnight
Preparation and cooking time: 1 hr

Channa raita
Fried chickpeas in spiced yogurt

Channa raita *is a tasty breakfast item. The yogurt added at the end of the cooking gives* channa raita *a rich, saucy texture that goes well with* puris *and* upma *or* khichri.

1 cup (175 g) chickpeas
1½ tsp salt
4 tsp ghee
1 tsp garam masala or ground coriander
¼ tsp asafoetida
⅔ cup (150 ml) plain yogurt
¼ tsp ground black pepper

Soak the chickpeas overnight in water double their volume. Drain them and put them into a medium-sized saucepan. Add enough water to cover them by about 3 inches (7.5 cm). Add ½ teaspoon of salt. Boil for 10 minutes and remove any froth that may accumulate. Cover the pot and lower the heat to medium. Cook until the chickpeas are tender. Check from time to time that there is enough water to prevent burning. Drain.

Heat the *ghee* or vegetable oil in a saucepan over medium heat. Add the *garam masala* and asafoetida and stir once. Then immediately add the drained chickpeas. Turn them constantly with a spoon while they fry for 8 to 10 minutes. When they become flecked with brown spots, remove the saucepan from the heat and stir in the yogurt. Season with salt and pepper. Serve hot.

Soaking time: overnight
Preparation and cooking time: 45 min to 1 hr

Channa aur simla mirch
Fried chickpeas and peppers

This recipe is traditionally served with wedges of firm tomato and hot bhaturas. *If you like, you can serve it with any of the Vedic breads described in the next chapter, or as a breakfast with yogurt and ginger tea.*

1½ cups (250 g) chickpeas
1½ tsp salt
2 tbs ghee or vegetable oil
2 tsp cumin seeds
1 or 2 fresh chilies, minced
1 tsp grated fresh ginger
½ tsp turmeric
½ tsp asafoetida
1 green bell pepper, cut into ½ inch (1.5 cm) pieces
1 medium-sized tomato, washed and chopped (optional)
2 medium-sized tomatoes, washed and cut into 8 wedges each

Soak the chickpeas overnight in water double their volume. Drain them and put them into a pot. Add enough water to cover them by about 3 inches (7.5 cm) and add ½ teaspoon of salt. Boil for 10 minutes. Remove any froth that has collected on the top, cover, and gently simmer over medium-low heat for 40 minutes to 1 hour, until the chickpeas are tender. Then drain off the water. (Save ½ cup [125 ml] of this water if you plan to make a sauce).

Over medium heat, heat the *ghee* or vegetable oil in a frying pan and fry the cumin seeds. Then add the minced chili and ginger. Add the turmeric and asafoetida and then follow immediately with the cut pepper. Turn the pieces of pepper with a spoon. When they appear soft and browned, add the drained chickpeas and stir for 3 minutes. Then add the remaining salt.

If you would like a sauce, add the water you saved, or 1 chopped tomato, and cook 5 minutes more.

Soaking time: overnight
Preparation and cooking time: 1 hr

Mili-juli sabji ka soup
Creamy vegetable soup

This soup is a favorite with the customers of our London restaurant, Govinda's. Svarūpa-siddhi dāsa, the head cook, says he often shows people how to make it.

3 tbs ghee
2 bay leaves
1 tsp ground coriander
¼ tsp ground asafoetida
1¼ tsp turmeric
1½ lb (675 g) assorted vegetables, washed and diced
6 cups (1.4 liters) water
3 tsp salt
¼ tsp pepper
2 cups (475 ml) milk
2 tbs butter
3 tbs white flour

Heat the *ghee* in a heavy saucepan. Fry the bay leaves, coriander, asafoetida, and turmeric for a few seconds, then immediately add the diced vegetables. Stir-fry the vegetables for 4 to 5 minutes, allowing them to brown in spots. Now add the water, salt, and pepper. Cover and simmer over medium-low heat (stirring occasionally) until the vegetables are tender and soft. Leave the vegetables intact if you prefer, or mash them to a puree or blend them in an electric blender. Remember to remove the bay leaves if you blend the soup.

While the vegetables are cooking, heat the butter over medium heat in a small saucepan. Add the flour and stir-fry carefully for 1 or 2 minutes until it begins to brown. Add the hot milk. Whisk the mixture constantly for about 2 minutes, until the sauce is fairly thick. Mix it into the soup and heat just until boiling. Then serve.

Preparation and cooking time: 45 to 50 min

Tamatar ka soup
Tomato soup

4½ lbs (2 kg) firm red tomatoes
6 tbs ghee or vegetable oil
1 tsp ground coriander
¼ teaspoon asafoetida
4 tbs chopped fresh coriander leaves
1½ tbs brown sugar
1½ tsp salt
¼ tsp ground black pepper
¼ tsp cayenne pepper
2 tbs butter
2 tbs white flour
1¾ cups (425 ml) milk
1 tbs lemon juice

Wash the tomatoes and cut each one into 8 wedges. Put them in an electric blender and blend them for a minute; then press the sauce through a sieve to remove bits of skin. (If you don't have a blender, blanch the tomatoes and press them through a sieve). Set aside.

Heat the *ghee* or vegetable oil in a heavy saucepan and fry the ground coriander and asafoetida for a few seconds. Add the tomatoes. Adjust the heat to medium-low and cook the tomatoes for 20 to 25 minutes. Then add the chopped coriander, sugar, salt, pepper, and cayenne.

Heat the butter in another saucepan and stir-fry the flour over low heat to brown it lightly. Now slowly add the milk and continue to cook (while stirring all the time to prevent lumps from forming) until the sauce thickens. Finally, mix this into the tomatoes, add the lemon juice, and serve hot.

For a garnish, you can pan-fry a tablespoon of vermicelli in a little butter and spread it over the surface of the soup.

Preparation and cooking time: 30 to 40 min

Breads and Pancakes

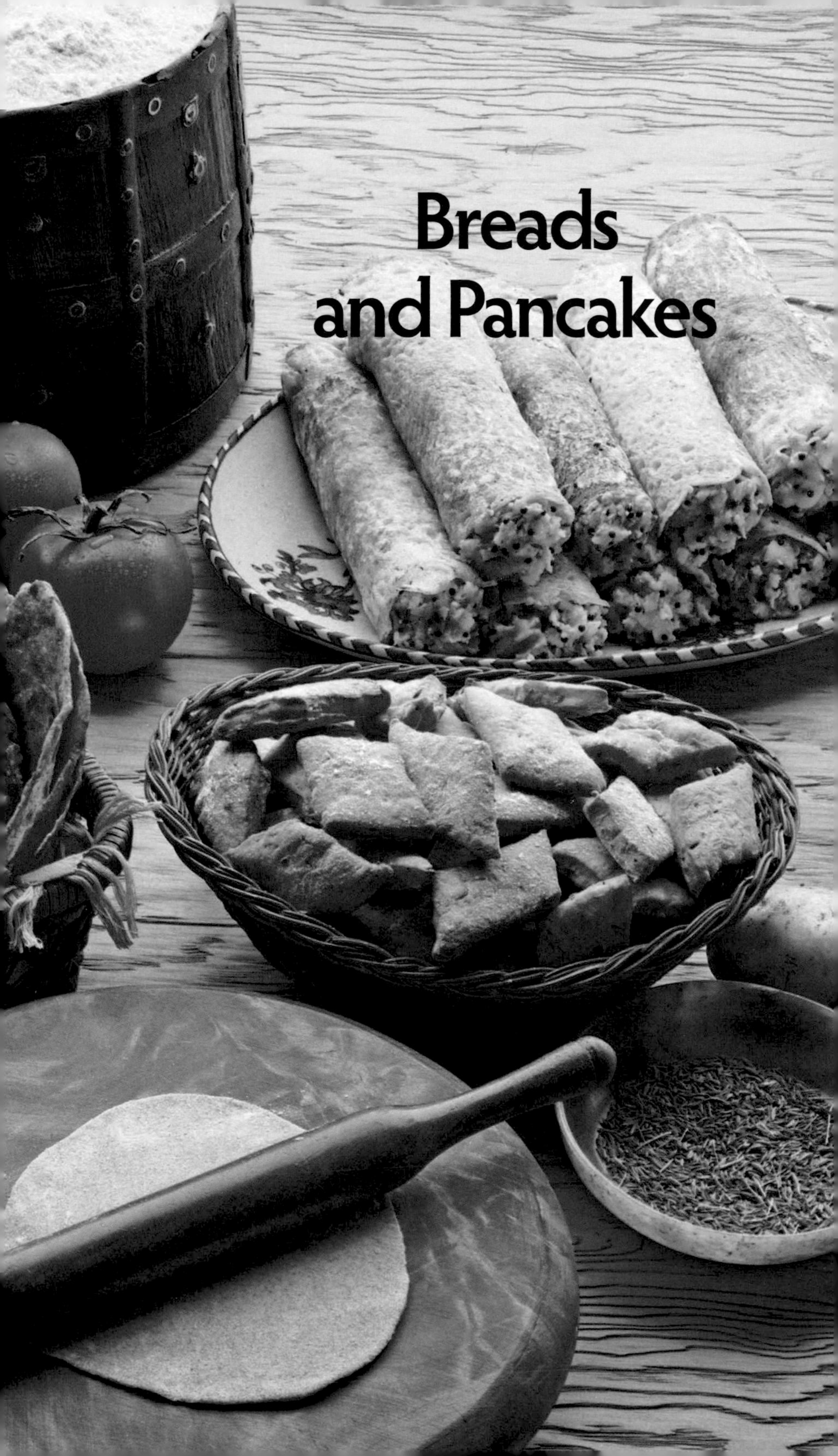

1 Chapati *(Whole-wheat flat bread)* 147
2 Puri *(Deep-fried puffed bread)* 151
3 Kela puri *(Banana)* 126
4 Bhatura *(Thick, leavened puris)* 153
5 Paratha *(Layered whole-wheat bread)* 154
6 Alu paratha *(Flat bread filled with spiced potatoes)* 155
7 Besan roti *(Chick-pea flour bread)* 156
8 Matthi *(Indian crackers)* 157
9 Masala dosa *(Pancakes filled with spiced potatoes)* 158
10 Atta dosa *(Whole-wheat pancakes)* 160
11 Pudla *(Chick-peas pancakes)* 161

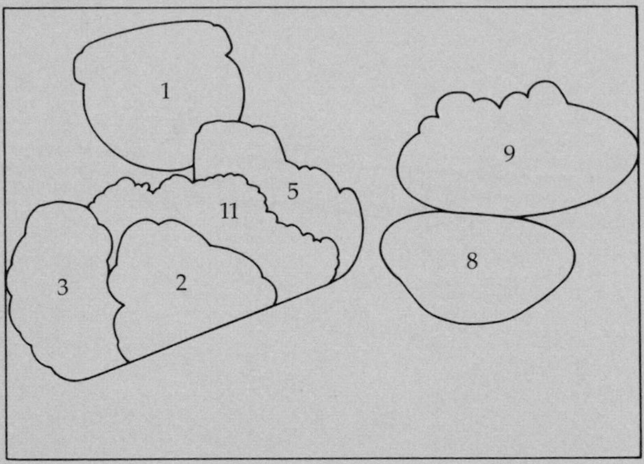

THE aphorism "Bread is the staff of life" has a much fuller meaning in India than in the West, where most of us eat denatured bread with few life-giving qualities. In India natural, wholesome homemade breads are a part of almost every meal. Varied in shape, texture, and taste, Indian breads are easily and quickly prepared.

The Vedic way of serving bread adds a special touch to a meal: as soon as your guest finishes one hot bread, you immediately serve him another.

You may wonder how you can offer the bread to Kṛṣṇa and still serve it hot to your guests. The trick is to cook the bread last. Just before the offering, cook enough for Kṛṣṇa's plate. Then, while the offering is on the altar, cook the rest and keep it hot. (For large gatherings, you may find it more practical to cook all the bread before the offering and warm it in the oven just before you serve it).

In Western dining, we often use bread to push other foods onto the fork. But in Indian dining the bread itself is the fork. The Indian way is to tear off a small piece of bread, wrap it around a bit of food too soft to pick up with your fingers, and pop both your food and your "fork" into your mouth.

At each Hare Kṛṣṇa center, every day we have a simple Vedic lunch of rice, *dal*, vegetables, and *chapatis*. Like most Vedic breads, *chapatis* are made with a kind of stone-ground whole-wheat flour called *chapati* flour or *atta*. This flour, available in Indian stores, is quite different from the whole-wheat flour in supermarkets and health food stores. *Chapati* flour consists of whole grains of wheat finely milled to a buff-colored powder. Doughs made with *atta* turn out velvety smooth, knead readily, and respond easily to shaping. If *chapati* flour is unavailable, whole-wheat pastry flour is the next best. If coarse whole-wheat flour is all you can get, sift it to reduce its coarse texture or mix it with unbleached or all-purpose flour. Two parts sifted whole-wheat flour to one part all-purpose flour generally gives good results.

In most of the bread recipes, the amount of water given is approximate. It will vary with the quality of the flour and the moistness of the air. Start by adding a little less water than specified, and if that isn't enough, add more, a little at a time, until the dough has the desired consistency. Then knead the dough.

The most important step in preparing any dough is the kneading. If the dough has been evenly and thoroughly kneaded, the rolling and cooking are easy. Here is how to do it. Lightly flour the dough and your hand, then push the heel of your hand into the dough, away from you. Fold the dough over, give it a slight turn, and push down again. Keep pushing, folding, and turning until the motion becomes rhythmic. Knead the dough in this way until it is smooth and elastic. If the dough still sticks to your hands or the bowl after you've added all the ingredients, keep kneading and adding flour a little at a time until the ball of dough comes away clean.

The breads in this chapter are either cooked on the *tava* (a heavy, slightly concave cast-iron frying pan) or deep-fried in a *karhai* or wok. Usually you set the *tava* on the flame before you cook the first bread. A pre-heated *tava* or pan cooks the bread faster and prevents it from becoming dry and brittle. The *karhai* or wok saves *ghee,* and its wide concave sides give plenty of room for deep frying. If you don't have a *tava,* you can substitute a cast-iron frying pan; if you don't have a *karhai* or wok, any wide, heavy saucepan will do.

Rolling these breads calls for a little practice, but don't be discouraged if it seems difficult at first. After a few times, you'll become expert. Besides, even your mistakes will taste good.

At the end of this chapter you'll find recipes for three types of savory pancakes, each made with a different kind of flour.

Chapati
Whole-wheat flatbread

Chapatis, *the daily bread of millions of Indians, are cooked first on a dry hotplate, then held directly over a flame, where they swell with steam to the point of bursting.*

2½ cups (250 g) atta or sifted whole-wheat flour
⅔ cup (150 ml) lukewarm water
½ tsp salt
2 or 3 tbs melted butter

Combine the flour and the salt in a large salad bowl. Slowly add water, gathering the flour together as you do so, until a soft, moist dough is formed. Transfer the dough to a work surface and knead it for 6 – 8 minutes until it is smooth and firm. Sprinkle the ball of dough with water, cover it with a damp cloth, and set it aside for half an hour to two hours.

When the dough is ready, place a tava or a heavy cast-iron griddle over medium heat. With moistened hands, knead the dough again, then shape into 15 equal-sized patties. Dip them into flour and roll them out thin and even on a floured board. Make them as round as possible and about 5½ inches (14 cm) across. Keep some plain whole-wheat flour on the side to dust the *chapatis* as you roll them.

Knock the excess flour off a *chapati* with a few slaps between the hands and place it on the pre-heated griddle. (You can cook several at a time if the size of your griddle allows). When small white blisters appear on the surface of the *chapati* and the edges begin to turn up, turn it over with a pair of flat tongs and cook the other side until the surface bulges with air pockets. Lift the *chapati* and toast both sides over a direct flame for a few seconds until it puffs up like a ball. A finished *chapati* should be cooked completely (no wet spots) and should be freckled with brown spots on both sides. Press the air out and brush one surface with melted butter.

You can also cook a *chapati* on electric heat. Let it stay on the griddle. Turn it over as many times as it takes for both sides to cook, then gently press the top of the *chapati* all over with a soft cloth, and the *chapati* will swell. Serve the *chapatis* soon after cooking or wrap them in a cloth to keep them warm and soft.

Preparation time: 15 min
Standing time: 30 min to 2 hrs
Rolling and cooking time: 2 to 3 min for each *chapati*

Opposite page: *Preparation of chapati*
Overleaf: *Preparation of puri (p. 151)*

Puri
Deep-fried puffed bread

Making puris*—watching little deep-fried rounds of dough inflate like balloons—is one of the delights of Vedic cooking. Eating them is even more delightful: they have a taste and a texture that go perfectly with any meal.*

2½ cups (250 g) whole-wheat flour
1 cup (100 g) white flour
½ tsp salt
1 tbs butter or ghee
¾ cup (175 ml) warm water
ghee or vegetable oil for deep-frying

Sift the two flours and the salt into a mixing bowl and rub in the tablespoon of butter (or *ghee*) with your fingertips. Slowly add the water, and mix until all the flour sticks together and you can knead it. Put a little *ghee* on your hands and knead the dough for 5 to 8 minutes until it is smooth and firm. (For a change, you can make *masala puris* by adding 2 teaspoons of cumin seeds, ¾ teaspoon of turmeric, and ¼ teaspoon of cayenne pepper to the dough).

In a *karhai,* wok, or saucepan, put the *ghee* or oil over medium high heat. Meanwhile, smear a few drops of *ghee* on the rolling surface (don't use flour—it burns and discolors the *ghee),* shape the dough into 16 patties, and roll them all out thin and even.

When the *ghee* begins to smoke, lower the heat to medium. Lay a *puri* on the surface of the *ghee,* being careful not to burn your fingers. The *puri* will sink for a second, then rise to the surface and sputter. Immediately submerge it with soft swift pushes, using the back of a slotted spoon, until it inflates like a balloon. Fry the other side for a few seconds; then remove the *puri* from the *ghee* and stand it on edge in a colander to drain. (When your skill increases, try frying several *puris* at a time). Cook all the *puris* the same way.

Serve hot *puris* with any meal or as a snack spread with applesauce, honey, jam, or fresh cheese.

Preparation time: 15 min
Rolling and cooking time: 2 min for each *puri*

Kela puri
Banana puris

Kela puris *will make you grateful that Vedic cooking has come to the West. Make sure the dough is kneaded until firm, and that the* puris *are deep-fried until golden and mottled brown.*

2½ cups (250 g) whole-wheat flour
½ cup (50 g) chickpea flour
½ tsp cayenne pepper
1 tsp turmeric
1 tsp cumin seeds
1 tsp salt
1 tbs melted ghee or butter
2 small ripe bananas
2 tsp brown sugar
ghee or vegetable oil for deep-frying

Sift the two flours into a large mixing bowl and add the spices and salt. Dribble the melted *ghee* or butter over the top. Rub it into the flour until the flour resembles coarse breadcrumbs.

In another bowl, mash the bananas into a smooth paste. Stir the sugar into the mashed bananas, then pour the mixture into the other ingredients, mixing thoroughly so that all the flour sticks together. If more moisture is needed to bind the flour, add more mashed banana or a tablespoon or two of warm water. If the dough is too sticky, add more flour. Knead the dough for several minutes until it is smooth and fairly firm. Then set it aside.

Let the dough stand for 15 to 30 minutes. Then roll and deep-fry the *kela puris* as in the recipe for *puris*.

Preparation time: 15 min
Standing time: 15 to 30 min
Rolling and cooking time: 3 min for each *kela puri*

Bhatura

Thick, leavened puris

Commercial yeast is seldom used in Vedic breads. More often, a batter is left in a warm place to ferment. In hot climates, batter will ferment in hours; in the colder climates we sometimes use baking powder to speed up the process.

In India bhaturas *are often eaten for breakfast with* channa raita *(spiced chickpeas) and yogurt.*

⅔ cup (150 ml) plain yogurt
2 tsp brown sugar
½ tsp baking powder
⅔ cup (150 g) white flour
3 cups (300 g) atta or sifted whole-wheat flour
2 tsp salt
1 tbs ghee or butter
½ cup (125 ml) warm water
ghee or vegetable oil for deep-frying

Start the night before by mixing together the yogurt, sugar, baking powder, and white flour in a large bowl. Cover the bowl with a cloth, and set it aside in a warm place overnight to allow natural fermentation to take place. The mixture is ready for the next step when bubbles appear on the surface.

In another bowl, mix together the *atta* or sifted whole-wheat flour with the salt, and rub the ghee or butter into it with your fingertips. Into this bowl, add the fermenting mixture and the warm water. Work it with your hands until it holds together and forms a dough. Knead the dough for 5 to 10 minutes or until it is silky smooth. Add a little flour if it is too wet. Now gather it into a compact ball, cover it with a damp cloth, and set it aside in a warm place.

After 2 hours, knead the dough again. Form it into 15 balls and roll them into 5-inch (13 cm) discs. Heat the *ghee* and deep-fry the *bhaturas* exactly as you would *puris*.

Preparation time: 20 min
Standing time: overnight plus 2 hrs
Rolling and cooking time: 4 min for each *bhatura*

Paratha

Layered whole-wheat bread

Parathas *are rich and flaky because they've been spread with* ghee *or butter and folded several times. Serve them with a wet vegetable dish, yogurt, and mint or coriander chutney.*

2 cups (200 g) atta or sifted whole-wheat flour
1 cup (100 g) white flour
2 tbs melted ghee or butter
⅔ cup (150 ml) warm water
1 tsp salt

Put the two kinds of flour in a large mixing bowl and mix them together. Rub the melted *ghee* or butter into the mixture and prepare the dough as directed for *chapati*. Set it aside, covered with a damp cloth. After 30 minutes, set a large cast-iron griddle or *tava* over medium-low heat. While the *tava* heats, knead the dough again and form it into 10 equal-sized balls and roll them into discs, (not too thin), dusting your work surface with flour when necessary, to prevent sticking. Brush the surface of each disc with melted butter and fold it in half. Butter the surface again and fold each *paratha* in half a second time, making triangles. Roll them out rather thin into larger triangles.

Place a *paratha* on the dry, pre-heated griddle or *tava*. Move the *paratha* around as you cook it so that all ends cook evenly. *Parathas* take more time to cook than *chapatis*. Adjust the heat so they don't burn. When both sides are golden brown, turn the *paratha* over to the first side and rub ½ teaspoon of *ghee* (or butter) over its surface with the back of a spoon. The *paratha* should then puff up. Turn it over and rub *ghee* over the other side. The *paratha* is finished when both sides are golden brown and flecked with dark spots. Cook all the *parathas* by this same method.

If you're not serving the *parathas* right away, wrap them in a cloth to keep them warm.

Preparation time: 15 min
Standing time: 30 min
Rolling and cooking time: 8 min for each *paratha*

Alu paratha

Flat bread filled with spiced potatoes

2 cups (200 g) atta or sifted whole-wheat flour
1 cup (100 g) white flour
4 tbs butter
½ cup (125 ml) warm water
1 tsp salt
3 medium-sized potatoes
1 tbs ghee
½ tsp cumin seeds
1 tsp grated fresh ginger
½ tsp cayenne pepper
½ tsp turmeric
1½ tbs lemon juice
1 tsp salt
2 tbs chopped coriander leaves

Make the dough as directed in the recipe for *paratha* and set aside while you prepare the filling.

Boil the potatoes until soft, rinse under cold water, peel, and mash coarse. Heat a tablespoon of *ghee* in a saucepan, put in the cumin seeds, and stir-fry. A few seconds later, add the grated ginger, cayenne pepper, and turmeric. Stir-fry a few seconds more. Add the mashed potatoes and fry for 4 to 5 minutes, stirring all the time. Pour the lemon juice over the mixture, sprinkle in the salt and coriander leaves. Mix thoroughly. Spread the mixture on a plate to cool.

When the filling has cooled, form the dough into 10 balls and roll one out into a 6-inch (15 cm) disc. Brush some ghee over the surface of the disc. Place a tablespoon of filling in the center. Lift the edges of the dough over the filling and twist them together. Pull off the excess dough and seal the opening by pinching it firmly. Now dust with flour, flatten into a patty, and roll out as thin as possible, being careful that the filling does not break through.

Grease a heavy-bottomed frying pan or griddle with ghee. Fry the *paratha* (or several, if the size of your pan allows) slowly, turning it over as many times as it takes to cook both sides. When both sides are golden brown with reddish spots, it is done. Repeat the procedure to make 10 *parathas.*

Alu parathas are delicious served hot with a wet vegetable dish and a raita or plain yogurt.

Preparation time: 30 min
Standing time: 30 min
Rolling and cooking time: 8 min for each *paratha*

Besan roti

Chickpea-flour bread

One kilometer from Varṣāṇā, the birthplace of Lord Kṛṣṇa's eternal consort, Śrīmatī Rādhārāṇī, there's a small village named Annapura, known for its prasādam, *which is said to be cooked with more devotion than that of any other place in the universe. The residents of Annapura are famous for their hospitality. For the past five thousand years, it is said, every visitor to this village has received a warm welcome, and a meal, usually with as many* besan rotis *as he could eat.*

2 cups (200 g) sifted whole-wheat flour
2 cups (200 g) chickpea flour
1½ tsp salt
½ tsp ground black pepper
½ tsp cumin seeds
1 or 2 fresh chillies, minced
3 tbs chopped fresh coriander or spinach leaves
1 tbs ghee or butter
⅔ cup (150 ml) warm water

Combine the flours, salt, spices, and coriander leaves in a large bowl. Rub the *ghee* or butter into the mixture. Gradually add warm water while mixing and kneading, until you have a smooth and elastic dough. Cover the dough with a moist cloth and set aside.

After 30 minutes or more, put a heavy griddle or *tava* over medium-low heat. Break the dough into 12 parts. Take each part, form it into a ball, and roll it out. Fold and roll it out again like a *paratha*. When the pan is hot, place a *besan roti* on it and cook each side for 2 or 3 minutes, using a little *ghee* or butter if the roti sticks to the pan. Then spread ½ teaspoon of *ghee* or melted butter over one side and rub it into the roti with the back of the spoon. Do the same with the other side. The *besan* roti is finished when both sides are golden brown and freckled with reddish spots. Cook all 12 the same way.

Preparation time: 15 min
Standing time: 30 min
Rolling and cooking time: 5 min for each *roti*

Matthi
Indian crackers

These crackers are easy to make and can be eaten as a snack, with soups, or as part of a meal. If rock salt is unavailable, you can use ordinary salt instead.

3 cups (300 g) sifted whole-wheat or white flour
2 tbs caraway or sesame seeds
1½ tsp rock salt
½ tsp baking powder
2 tbs ghee or butter ghee or vegetable oil for deep-frying
¾ cup (175 ml) water

Combine the flour, caraway seeds, salt, and baking powder in a large mixing bowl. Rub the *ghee* or butter into the flour. Add enough water to form a fairly firm dough. Knead well for at least 5 minutes, until the dough is smooth and elastic. Then set it aside for a few minutes.

Fill the *karhai* or wok to two-thirds with *ghee* or vegetable oil and put it over medium heat. While the *ghee* is heating, roll out the dough into a large square, ½ inch (1 cm) thick. With a sharp knife, cut the dough into diamonds or rectangles 2 inches (5 cm) long. Gently drop half of them into the hot *ghee*. The heat should be adjusted so that the crackers become golden brown on both sides in 4 or 5 minutes. Remove with a slotted spoon and put in a colander to drain. Then cook the other half the same way.

Preparation and cooking time: 30 min

Masala dosa
Pancakes filled with spiced potatoes

This thin, crisp pancake with a spicy potato filling is a popular snack all over South India. Masala dosa *should be eaten fresh and hot, so serve them as soon as you cook them. Coconut chutney and chopped coriander leaves are the traditional garnishes.*

1 cup (175 g) short-grained white rice, washed
½ cup (100 g) urad dal, sorted and washed
½ tsp brown sugar
2½ tsp salt
10 medium-sized potatoes
ghee or vegetable oil for greasing the griddle
2 fresh chilies chopped
4 tbs grated coconut
3 tsp grated fresh ginger
4 tbs ghee
2 tsp cumin seeds
2 tsp black mustard seeds
1½ tsp turmeric
2 tbs chopped coriander leaves
2 tbs butter

Soak the rice and the *dal* overnight in separate bowls. Wash and drain them separately, then blend them separately in an electric mixer with just enough water to make smooth batters. Now combine both batters in a large bowl along with 1 chopped chili, the brown sugar, and ½ teaspoon of the salt. Beat thoroughly. Cover the bowl and set aside in a warm place for an hour or two, or, if possible, overnight.

When you're ready to cook, grease the griddle with about ½ teaspoon of *ghee* or vegetable oil and put it over medium heat. Beat the batter again—it should be of pouring consistency. Flick a few drops of water onto the pan. If they bounce and sputter, the pan is ready. Pour on 4 tablespoons of batter and use the back of a spoon to spread it out thin with a circular motion, starting from the center. This amount of batter should make a thin *dosa,* about 8 inches (20 cm) in diameter. (The art of making *dosas* lies in the ability to spread the batter thin before the heat of the skillet hardens the mixture). Cook for 2 or 3 minutes until it becomes golden brown. Turn once. Cooking the second side takes only about half as long as the first. The second side never browns as evenly as the first.

Continue making *dosas* until the batter is finished, greasing the pan only when the *dosas* stick. Pile them on a plate so that they will stay warm and moist while you prepare the filling, as follows.

Boil the potatoes until soft, and peel and mash them coarse with a fork or potato masher. Grind together the coconut, the remaining chopped chili, the ginger, and a few drops of water to make a *masala* paste. In a medium-sized saucepan, heat the *ghee* or vegetable oil, and stir-fry the cumin and mustard seeds in it. When the mustard seeds start sputtering, add the *masala* paste. A minute later, toss in the turmeric, then immediately add the potatoes, the chopped coriander, and the remaining salt. Stir-fry for 5 minutes before setting them aside.

Divide the filling into as many portions as you have *dosas*. Put one portion in the center of each *dosa* and fold in half. Now grease the frying pan with butter, and toast both sides of each filled dosa. *Masala dosa* with *sambar* and fresh tomato salad is a traditional South Indian meal.

Preparation time: 30 min
Standing time: 1 to 2 hrs or overnight
Cooking time: 5 min for each *dosa*

Atta dosa

Whole-wheat pancakes

2½ cups (250 g) sifted whole wheat flour
2 tbs chopped fresh coriander leaves
1 fresh chili, minced
1 tsp salt
2 cups (475 ml) lukewarm water

Mix all the dry ingredients together in a large bowl. Slowly add the water and whisk it into the flour until you have a smooth pancake batter. Cover the bowl with a cloth and let stand for at least half an hour.

Beat the batter again and cook the *dosas* as in the previous recipe. If you use about 4 tablespoons of batter to make each *dosa,* you should get about 15 *dosas*. Serve *atta dosas* with coconut chutney or plain yogurt, or both.

Preparation time: 10 min
Standing time: 30 mins
Cooking time: 5 min for each *dosa*

Pudla

Chickpea-flour pancakes

This is the basic recipe for pudla. *You can make many tasty variations by adding cooked or quick-cooking vegetables such as mung bean sprouts, grated carrots, chopped parsley, or small cubes of potato.*

2 cups (200 g) chickpea flour
½ cup (50 g) white flour
1 tsp ground cumin
1 or 2 fresh green chilies, seeded and minced
¼ tsp asafoetida
¾ tsp turmeric
1½ teaspoon salt
¼ tsp pepper
1 tsp ground coriander
2 tbs fresh coriander or parsley leaves, minced
1¼ cups (300 ml) cold water
1 tsp grated fresh ginger
2 medium-sized tomatoes, chopped
1 green bell pepper, diced
ghee or butter for frying
3 tbs lemon juice

In a large bowl, mix together the chickpea flour, white flour, and the next eight ingredients. Slowly add the cold water, stirring as you do, until you have a thickish pancake batter. If the batter seems too thick, remember that the juice from the tomatoes will thin it. Now stir in the grated ginger and pieces of tomato and pepper. Set aside.

Melt a tablespoon of ghee or butter in a 10 to 12 inch (20 to 26 cm) frying pan over medium heat. Pour in enough batter to make two 4 to 5 inch (10 to 13 cm) pancakes at a time. It is more important that the pancakes be uniformly thick, than perfectly round. Cook slowly on both sides so that they become golden brown and crisp (about 4 – 5 minutes). Finish the batter in this way, using about 1 teaspoon of ghee or butter for each *pudla*. Sprinkle the lemon juice over the top of the *pudlas*. Serve hot.

Preparation time: 15 min
Cooking time: 5 min for each *pudla*

Vegetables

1 Alu phul gobi paneer sabji *(Fried cauliflower, potatoes, and fresh cheese)* 167
2 Alu phul gobi ki baji *(Curried vegetables)* 168
3 Alu gauranga *(Potatoes au gratin)* 169
4 Bandgobhi alu sabji *(Fried cabbage and potatoes)* 171
5 Tamatar bharta *(Scrambled cheese with tomatoes)* 172
6 Tamatar paneer malai *(Flat bread filled with spiced potatoes)* 173
7 Phansi kadhi *(Green beans in chickpea flour sauce)* 174
8 Matar paneer *(Peas and cheese in tomato sauce)* 175
9 Bengali tarkari kari *(Bengali curried vegetables)* 176
10 Matar alu tarkari *(Vegetable and cheese stew)* 178
11 Sukta *(Bitter-melon stew)* 179
12 Maha brinjal *(Puréed eggplant, spinach, and tomatoes)* 181
13 Palak baingan aur channa *(Vegetables and chickpeas)* 182
14 Sak *(Vegetable greens cooked in their own juices)* 183
15 Paneer sak *(Steamed spinach with fresh cheese)* 184
16 Khati mithi sabji *(Sweet and sour vegetables)* 185
17 Masala bhindi sabji *(Seasoned okra slices with coconut)* 187
18 Upma *(Vegetable semolina)* 188
19 Bhari hui sabji *(Stuffed vegetables)* 190
20 Alu tikkia tamatar sahit *(Deep-fried stuffed tomatoes)* 192
21 Bhindi Massaledarh *(Stuffed okra)* 193
22 Alu kofta *(Deep-fried vegetable balls in tomato sauce)* 194
23 Palak kofta *(Deep-fried spinach and cheese balls)* 196
24 Bandgobhi kofta *(Stuffed cabbage leaves)* 198
25 Nargisi kofta *("Royal" kofta)* 200

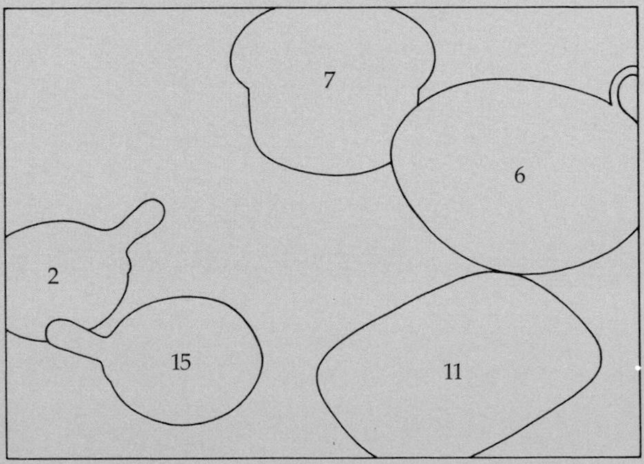

THE Vedic art of cooking vegetables is unsurpassed in all the world. Vedic cuisine offers an infinite variety of vegetarian vegetable dishes. Śrīla Prabhupāda would sometimes tell the devotees that Śrīmatī Rādhārāṇī (Lord Kṛṣṇa's eternal consort) has been cooking for Kṛṣṇa eternally and She has never offered Him the same preparation twice—each dish always has an original taste. And in *Caitanya-caritāmṛta,* the Bengali scripture describing the pastimes of Lord Caitanya, there are vivid descriptions of feasts offered to the Lord by His devotees, that contain hundreds of delectable vegetable dishes.

Cooking vegetables Indian style means cooking them to bring out their flavors while retaining their nutritional value. The recipes in this chapter show you how to transform the most ordinary vegetables into wonderfully flavored dishes. The secret lies in knowing how to cook the vegetables with the proper spices. You can also combine vegetables with grains, yogurt, cheese, nuts, or fresh herbs.

Your neighborhood grocery should have almost all of the vegetables in these recipes. You can also shop around and see what else is available from local farmers and ethnic grocery stores. When selecting vegetables and other foodstuffs try to be conscious of their origin because, as the *Vedas* predict, this Age in which we are living is characterized by gradual degradation of the environment, including our foods. Already we can see that despite today's highly advanced medical technology, the most prevalent disease in the industrialized world is premature aging.

Many scientists attribute this to the contamination of our air, water, and food. Agribusiness is much more concerned about profit than people's health, and what we usually find in the supermarket is over-cultivated, hybridized, glossy-skinned produce with more eye-appeal than nutritional value. As far as possible use naturally grown produce that is compact and full of color. It's better to buy or grow vegetables that may be blemished but are free of chemicals. The *Āyur-veda* states that an important aspect of achieving physical health, and harmony with our surroundings, is to eat food grown locally and in season.

There are two principal ways to cook vegetables: wet and dry. To cook wet vegetables, first brown the spices in a little *ghee* or vegetable oil and then saute the vegetables in the spices. Then add some water and a thickening agent such as shredded coconut, yogurt, or pureed tomatoes. Keep the heat low and the pan covered to trap the steam. For dry vegetables, first saute the vegetables and then cook them without water, or with just enough water to prevent scorching. Then towards the end of the cooking take off the lid and cook off most of the moisture. Both wet and dry dishes may be eaten with rice or Indian breads.

There are also some other methods of cooking vegetables that are mentioned in other chapters of this book such as making vegetable pancakes, or cooking vegetables together with rice and *dal,* or deep-frying vegetables dipped in batter. For these methods, and for braising, baking, steaming, stuffing, and deep-frying, at one stage or another, you brown spices in hot *ghee* or oil. When the spices are browned, you add the vegetables. And provided your ghee is hot enough, the moist vegetables hitting the hot *ghee* and seasonings will make the "*chuum*" sound familiar to all Indian cooks.

You'll never find canned or frozen vegetables in Kṛṣṇa's kitchen. Why use canned or frozen food when fresh produce is so readily available? The taste of fresh vegetables more than makes up for the time it takes to prepare them. Vegetables should be cooked just until tender and always eaten hot.

Alu phul gobhi paneer sabji
Fried cauliflower, potatoes, and fresh cheese

This is a simple, quick-cooking dish. The cauliflower and potatoes are deep-fried, then simmered in a liquid masala *until done. Serve this vegetable dish with an Indian bread and a smooth dal or vegetable soup.*

2 tbs ghee or vegetable oil
½ tsp black mustard seeds
2 fresh chilies, seeded and minced
1 tbs grated fresh ginger
2 bay leaves
1 tsp turmeric
1 tsp ground coriander
1 tsp ground cinnamon
2½ cups (600 ml) water
4 potatoes, peeled and cubed
12 oz (350 g) pressed paneer, cubed
1 medium-sized cauliflower, washed, trimmed, and cut into flowerets
2 tsp salt
½ tsp garam masala
2 tbs chopped fresh coriander or parsley leaves

Heat the *ghee* or oil in a medium-sized saucepan over medium heat. Toss in the mustard seeds and cover the pot so they don't jump all over the stove. When they finish popping, add the chilies, ginger, and bay leaves. Stir for 30 seconds. Now stir in the powdered spices—except for the *garam masala*—and immediately add the water. Bring to a rapid boil, then lower the heat and simmer gently.

While this liquid *masala* is simmering, deep-fry separately the potato cubes and the cheese cubes until they are golden brown, then drain them. Deep-fry the cauliflower flowerets until they are lightly browned and partially cooked. Now put the cauliflower in the *liquid masala,* cover, and cook over low heat. After 5 minutes, lift the cover, drop in the fried potatoes and cheese cubes, stir once, and cook for 2 or 3 minutes more, until all the ingredients are heated thoroughly.

Season with the salt and *garam masala* and sprinkle in the fresh coriander or parsley leaves. Mix and serve hot.

Preparation and cooking time: 30 min

Alu phul gobhi ki bhaji
Cauliflower and potatoes in yogurt sauce

This technique of frying vegetables first in a masala, *then steaming them, can be applied to other types of vegetables as well. People sometimes refer to this method as "curried" vegetables.*

1 medium-sized cauliflower
5 tbs ghee or vegetable oil
2 tsp cumin seeds
1 or 2 dried chilies, crushed
2 tsp ground coriander
1 tsp turmeric
½ tsp asafoetida
4 medium-sized potatoes, peeled and cubed
4 tbs water
1½ tsp salt
1 cup (250 ml) plain yogurt
¾ tsp garam masala
2 firm ripe tomatoes, washed and sliced
1 lemon or lime

Trim the cauliflower and cut it into flowerets 1½ inches (4 cm) long by 1 inch (2.5 cm) thick. Rinse them in a colander and let drain.

Heat the *ghee* or oil in a heavy saucepan over medium heat. Drop in the cumin seeds and crushed chilies and fry them for 30 to 45 seconds, until the cumin seeds turn golden brown. Add the powdered spices, fry a few seconds longer, then immediately add the cubed potatoes. Turn the potatoes for 2 or 3 minutes, letting them brown in spots. Now stir in the cauliflower and stir-fry for another 2 or 3 minutes. Then add the water and salt and put the lid on the pan to trap the steam. Cook over medium heat, shaking the pan occasionally, for about 15 minutes, until the vegetables are tender but still firm.

Finally, stir in the yogurt and simmer for a few minutes until the sauce is thick. Sprinkle with *garam masala* and stir gently to mix. Garnish each serving with slices of tomato and a twist of lemon or lime.

Preparation and cooking time: 30 min

Alu gauranga
Potatoes au gratin

The devotees of Kṛṣṇa have named this dish after Śrī Caitanya Mahāprabhu, the incarnation of Kṛṣṇa who came to earth to teach the chanting of the Hare Kṛṣṇa mantra. He was also known as Gauranga (the golden one) because of His fair complexion.

Add a vegetable dish and some chapatis, *and you'll have a most satisfying meal.*

1 lb (450 g) paneer
10 medium-sized potatoes
½ tsp asafoetida
3 tsp salt
1 tsp ground black pepper
3 tbs chopped fresh coriander or thyme leaves
3 tbs ground coriander
3 cups (725 ml) sour cream mixed with 1 tsp turmeric
¼ cup (50 g) butter
2 tbs powdered milk

Rinse the *paneer* well under cold running water. Then gather the cheesecloth tight around the paneer and squeeze out most of the water. Wash and peel the potatoes and cut them into thin slices.

Cover the bottom of a greased casserole or cake pan with one third of the potato slices. Sprinkle this layer with one third of each spice, in this order: asafoetida, salt, pepper, fresh coriander, ground coriander. Cover with a layer of one third of the crumbled *paneer* and a layer of one third of the cream. Dot with one third of the butter.

Cover this with a second layer of sliced potatoes and other ingredients in the same manner as the first layer. Make the third layer with the rest of the sliced potatoes, and repeat the procedure using the rest of the ingredients. Finally, sprinkle the powdered milk over the top in a thin layer. Cover the casserole with a sheet of aluminum foil wrapped tightly around the edges and put it in the oven for at least 45 minutes at 400°F (200°C). Remove the aluminum foil 10 minutes before the end of cooking to allow the top to brown.

Preparation and cooking time: 1 hr

Bandgobhi alu sabji
Fried cabbage and potatoes

It's curious how some of the world's most famous cuisines are always in search of excellence. From classical French cuisine came cuisine nouvelle, *and now* cuisine moderne *blends the classic and the nouvelle. And in Italy, the most discerning chefs hail la* nuova cucina italiana, *the new Italian cooking.*

Vedic cooking, in contrast, never changes. This simple dish of cooked vegetables and sweet spices, coming from the head priest of the ancient Minaksi temple in Madurai, India, is as tasty and healthful today as it has been for thousands of years.

1 lb (450 g) cabbage
2 cloves
2 cardamoms
1 cinnamon stick, 3 inches (7.5 cm) long
4 tbs ghee or vegetable oil
4 medium-sized potatoes, peeled and cubed
1 tbs grated fresh ginger
½ tsp cayenne pepper
1 tsp turmeric
4 medium-sized ripe tomatoes, each cut into 8 wedges
1½ tsp salt
½ tsp sugar
⅔ cup (150 ml) water

Wash the cabbage, shred it, and let it drain. Grind the cloves, cardamom, and cinnamon stick into a fine powder and set aside.

Heat 3 tablespoons of the *ghee* or vegetable oil in a saucepan over moderate heat. Put the cubed potatoes in the pan and stir-fry them, scraping the bottom of the pan frequently, until they are lightly browned. Remove them from the pan and set them aside.

Put the remaining tablespoon of *ghee* or vegetable oil in the same saucepan and stir-fry the grated ginger, cayenne pepper and turmeric. Fry for a few seconds more. Add the shredded cabbage and fry for 3 or 4 more minutes, stirring regularly to mix it with the spices and prevent scorching. Add the tomatoes, fried potatoes, salt, sugar, and water. Cover the pan and simmer over low heat until all the vegetables are tender. Before serving, sprinkle the previously prepared ground sweet spices over the top and mix gently.

Preparation and cooking time: 30 min

Opposite page: *Bandgobhi alu sabji*

Tamatar bharta

Stewed tomatoes with flat noodles

15 medium-sized tomatoes
8 large papadams or 12 small
1 cinnamon stick, 2 inches (5 cm) long
1½ tsp cumin seeds
5 curry leaves or 3 bay leaves
1 fresh chili, seeded and minced
½ tsp asafoetida
1 tbs grated fresh ginger
2 tsp salt
1 tsp brown sugar
2 tsp chopped coriander or parsley leaves
⅔ cup (150 ml) sour cream or yogurt (optional)

Start by blanching the tomatoes. Then either chop them fine, blend them in a mixer, or force them through a sieve. Set aside. Cut the *papadams* into 1-inch (2 cm) strips and set them aside.

In a medium-sized saucepan, heat the *ghee* or vegetable oil over medium heat. When the *ghee* begins to smoke, drop in the cinnamon stick, cumin seeds, curry leaves (or bay leaves), chili, and a few seconds later, the asafoetida. Now put the tomatoes in the saucepan with the ginger, salt, and sugar. Bring to a boil and stir well. Cover the saucepan halfway, and simmer over medium-low heat for about 15 minutes, stirring frequently.

While the tomatoes simmer, bring some salted water to boil in another medium-sized saucepan, and drop in the strips of *papadam*. Boil them for 8 – 10 minutes until they are quite soft. Finally, drain the *papadam* strips and then fold them and the coriander into the stewed tomatoes a few minutes before removing the saucepan from the heat. (If you use cream or yogurt, fold it into the preparation and allow to heat for a few minutes more).

Tamatar bharta goes well with any rice dish or Indian bread.

Preparation and cooking time: 40 min

Tamatar paneer malai

Scrambled cheese with fried tomatoes

Serve tamatar paneer malai *with* puris *as part of a meal or as a light meal in itself. For a variation, you can reduce the* paneer *by half and add 2 cups (200 g) of steamed peas or golden-fried cauliflower flowerets at the same time as the paneer. A* karhai *or wok is ideal for cooking this recipe.*

1 lb. (450 g) paneer
6 medium-sized tomatoes
3 tbs ghee or vegetable oil
2 tsp cumin seeds
1 tsp turmeric
2 tsp salt
1/2 tsp pepper
2/3 cup (150 ml) sour cream
2 tbs chopped coriander or parsley leaves

Keep the *paneer* in the cheesecloth and rinse it under cold water for a moment, then squeeze out some of the water.

While the *paneer* is still moist, break it into roughly 1-inch cubes (2.5 cm) and set aside. Now wash the tomatoes and cut each of them into 8 wedges. Heat the ghee or oil in a *karhai,* wok, or medium-sized saucepan. Add the cumin seeds, and as soon as they darken (about 30 seconds) add the tomato wedges. Turn the tomato wedges gently until they are lightly browned. Put in the chunks of *paneer*. Season with the turmeric, salt, and pepper, and stir-fry gently for 2 or 3 minutes, taking care not to break the pieces of *paneer* and tomato.

Finally, fold in the cream and toss all the ingredients. Serve hot, garnished with chopped coriander or parsley leaves.

Preparation and cooking time: 40 min

Phansi kadhi

Green beans in chickpea flour sauce

Although this recipe is traditionally prepared with green beans, most other vegetables can be cooked the same way. This recipe has been used for fifteen years in the kitchens of New Vrindaban, the Hare Kṛṣṇa community in West Virginia, which is as well known for its sumptuous prasādam *as for its devotional atmosphere.*

2 lbs (900 g) fresh green beans
4¼ cups (1 liters) water
¾ cup (75 g) sifted chickpea flour
1 cup (250 ml) plain yogurt
1 tbs ghee or vegetable oil
1 tsp black mustard seeds
½ tsp grated fresh ginger
¼ tsp cayenne pepper
½ tsp asafoetida
1 tsp turmeric
1 tsp sugar
2 tsp lemon juice
2½ tsp salt
1 lemon, washed and quartered
2 tomatoes, cut into 8 wedges each

Wash and trim the beans, then snap them in half. Cover the bottom of a medium-sized saucepan with 1 inch (2.5 cm) of water, insert a metal steam-rack, then add the beans. Bring the water to a boil and cover the pan to trap the steam. Cook for about 10 minutes, until the beans darken and become tender. Drain off the stock and save it.

Boil the water and add the chickpea flour while stirring well, using a whisk if available. Then add the yogurt and stock and bring to a second boil, stirring always. Boil rapidly for about 15 minutes.

Heat the *ghee* or oil in a small saucepan and fry the mustard seeds. When they sputter, add the grated ginger, cayenne pepper, and asafoetida. Turn with a spoon for a few seconds, then pour the *ghee* and seasonings into the *kadhi* sauce. Add to the sauce the turmeric, sugar, lemon juice, and salt. Mix well. Reduce the heat and simmer for 5 minutes, stirring more frequently as the mixture thickens. Then fold in the beans and heat to serving temperature, stirring constantly. Garnish with wedges of lemon and tomato.

Preparation and cooking time: 30 to 40 min

Matar paneer
Peas and cheese in tomato sauce

This simple combination of vegetables and cheese needs only a fancy rice or a hot Indian bread to make a complete meal.

You can adjust the thickness of the sauce to your taste by varying the amount of the water. Thin, it goes well with rice; thick, with chapatis.

8 oz (225 g) paneer
ghee or vegetable oil for deep-frying
4 tsp salt
2½ tsp turmeric
2 tbs ghee
½ tsp cumin seeds
1 or 2 fresh chilies, seeded and minced
1 tsp grated fresh ginger
¼ tsp asafoetida
1 lb (450 g) fresh peas, shelled
⅔ cup (150 ml) water
6 tomatoes, chopped
1½ tbs lemon juice
1 tsp garam masala

Knead the paneer well until it is smooth and soft. Then, form it into grape-sized balls and deep-fry them in *ghee* or vegetable oil until they are crisp and golden brown. Remove them from the ghee with a slotted spoon and drop them into a solution of 3 teaspoons of salt, 2 teaspoons of turmeric, and 2 cups of warm water or whey. Let them soak while you go on to the next step.

In a medium-sized saucepan, heat the 2 tablespoons of *ghee* over medium heat. Then add the cumin seeds, followed by the minced chilies and grated ginger. When the cumin seeds are browned (in about 30 – 45 seconds), toss in the asafoetida, the remaining turmeric, and a few seconds later the peas. Now add the water, cover the pan, and cook the peas until they are tender. Add the tomatoes and the cheese balls. Cook over the same medium heat for 5 more minutes.

Just before serving, add a generous squeeze of lemon, and season with the remaining teaspoon of salt and the *garam masala*.

Preparation and cooking time: 25 min

Bengali tarkari
Bengali mixed vegetable stew

5 medium-sized potatoes, peeled and diced
1 large eggplant, diced
12 oz (350 g) squash, diced
1 lb (450 g) peas or cut green beans
3 tbs ghee or vegetable oil
1½ tsp black mustard seeds
2 dried chilies, crushed
3 bay leaves
1 tsp fenugreek seeds
1 tsp anise seeds
1 tsp ground cumin
2 1/2 cups (600 ml) water
2 tsp brown sugar
2 tsp salt
2 lemons, quartered
6 sprigs of parsley

Heat the *ghee* or oil in a large saucepan over medium heat. Toss in the mustard seeds, chilies, bay leaves, and fenugreek seeds. Cover the pan to prevent the mustard seeds from jumping out. When the mustard seeds stop sputtering and the fenugreek seeds darken, add the anise seeds and ground cumin. Then immediately put in the diced potatoes. Turn the potatoes for about 8 minutes, letting them get golden brown on all sides. Then add the squash and eggplant. Keep cooking and stirring for 5 more minutes.

Next put in the peas or green beans along with the water and cover the pan. Cook over medium-low heat, stirring gently every 5 minutes or so. After 15 minutes, add the sugar and salt, stir to mix, and cook slowly on the same low heat until the vegetables are tender and the sauce is thick.

Serve this *tarkari* with hot *puris* or *parathas*. Garnish each portion with a wedge of lemon and a sprig of parsley.

Preparation and cooking time: 30 to 40 min

Opposite page: *Bengali tarkari*

Matar alu tarkari

Vegetable and cheese stew

In France, many Kṛṣṇa devotees are excellent cooks, but Kiśorī is the best. She often cooked for Śrīla Prabhupāda in India. Śrīla Prabhupāda especially liked matar alu tarkari. *In fact, he told Kiśorī that he could eat it every day.*

2 tbs ghee or vegetable oil
6 cloves
2 cinnamon sticks, 3 inches (7.5 cm) long
½ tsp ground cardamom seeds
3 bay leaves
6 potatoes, peeled and cubed
1 lb (450 g) fresh peas, shelled
1 tsp turmeric
1¾ cups (425 ml) water
6 medium-sized tomatoes, washed and quartered
1 tsp grated fresh ginger
¼ tsp grated fresh nutmeg
½ tsp brown sugar
2 tsp salt
⅔ cup (150 ml) sour cream
1 tbs chopped fresh coriander or parsley leaves
¾ cup (100 g) almonds, lightly toasted
8 oz (225 g) paneer, cubed and deep-fried

Put the *ghee* or oil in a large saucepan over medium heat. When it begins to smoke, toss in the cloves, cinnamon sticks, ground cardamom, and bay leaves. Stir-fry for about 30 seconds; then put in the potatoes. Fry them for 5 minutes, frequently scraping the bottom of the pan with a spatula, until they are lightly browned. Add the peas and turmeric. Stir once, pour in the water, and cook for 10 minutes with the pot covered. Then add the tomatoes, along with the grated ginger and nutmeg, the sugar, and the salt. Stir to mix, and cook covered for 5 more minutes.

Now fold in the cream, the coriander or parsley, the almonds, and the fried *paneer* cubes. Remove the whole spices. Heat for a few minutes before serving.

Preparation and cooking time: 40 min

Sukta

Bitter-melon stew

Usually made with several types of vegetables, sukta *derives its distinctive flavor from one vegetable in particular:* karela, *also known as bitter melon or bitter squash.* Karela *is usually available at oriental groceries. Śrīla Prabhupāda appreciated its taste and health-giving qualities so much that he would sometimes carry a supply of dried* karela *with him when he traveled.*

2 or 3 karelas, green and firm
1 lb (450 g) each: cauliflower flowerets, washed and drained; potatoes, peeled and cubed; squash or eggplant, cubed; fresh peas, or green beans cut into 2-inch (5 cm) pieces
4 tbs ghee
1 tsp fenugreek seeds
6 curry leaves (if not available, use 4 bay leaves)
¾ cup (425 ml) water
1 tsp cumin seeds
2 tsp grated ginger
1 or 2 fresh chilies, seeded and minced
½ tsp turmeric
1 tsp panch masala
2 tsp coriander
½ tsp asafoetida
1 cup (250 ml) plain yogurt
2½ tsp salt

Remove the seeds from the *karelas* and cut them into 1-inch (2.5 cm) cubes. Heat 2 tablespoons of *ghee* over medium-high heat in a large saucepan (about 5 quarts / 5 liter). Fry the fenugreek seeds for 30 seconds, then add the cut vegetables. Add the curry leaves (or bay leaves) and stir-fry the vegetables for 5 minutes, turning them gently with a wooden spoon. Now pour in half of the water, cover the pan, and allow to cook over medium heat for 10 minutes.

Meanwhile, use a mortar and pestle or a small blender to grind together the cumin seeds, grated ginger, minced chilies, turmeric, and a few drops of water, to make a smooth *masala* paste. Heat the remaining 2 tablespoons of *ghee* or oil in a small saucepan and stir-fry the *masala* paste for a minute or two. Then add the *panch masala*, ground coriander, and asafoetida. Stir for a few seconds. Pour the remaining water into the seasonings and bring to a boil for 1 minute. Empty the liquid *masala* into the cooking vegetables and continue cooking over medium heat for 15 – 20 minutes, stirring every now and then, until the vegetables are barely tender.

Lift the lid and fold in the yogurt, and salt. (If you like, you can add *sada pakoras* or *bhajas* at this point, but not later, as they need a few minutes of simmering to absorb some of the sauce and blend with the other ingredients). Stir and toss gently to mix the spices and sauce evenly with the vegetables. Simmer for a few minutes uncovered, then serve as a main dish with rice or an Indian bread.

Preparation and cooking time: 45 min

Mahā brinjal

Puréed eggplant, spinach, and tomatoes

Mahā *means "great" and* brinjal *means "eggplant, " the most popular of all vegetables in India. This dish is made by cooking the vegetables until they form a thick sauce.* Mahā brinjal *goes well with a light rice and hot* chapatis.

2 lbs (900 g) eggplant, peeled and diced
1 lb (450 g) fresh spinach, washed, stemmed, and chopped
2 lbs (900 g) tomatoes, blanched, peeled, and chopped
5 tbs ghee or vegetable oil
1 or 2 dried chilies, crushed
1 tsp ground coriander
½ tsp ground cumin
½ tsp turmeric
½ tsp asafoetida
⅔ cup (150 ml) water
1 tsp brown sugar
2½ tsp salt
½ tsp garam masala

Heat the *ghee* or oil in a large saucepan and fry the chili and the ground coriander for a few seconds. Follow with all the other powdered spices, fry a few seconds longer, then immediately drop in the eggplant cubes. Stir-fry gently over medium-high heat until the eggplant becomes soft and begins to release its seeds.

Now stir in the chopped tomatoes, spinach, and water. Mix well. Partially cover the saucepan and simmer (stirring occasionally) for about 20 minutes, or until the eggplant is very soft. Turn up the heat to medium and cook for 10 more minutes, stirring frequently, until the spinach, eggplant, and tomatoes have merged into a thick velvety sauce. Finally, season with the sugar, salt, and *garam masala*. Mix well.

Preparation and cooking time: 40 min

Palak baingan aur channa

Spinach, eggplant, tomatoes, and chickpeas

2/3 cup (100 g) chickpeas, soaked overnight
4 tbs ghee or vegetable oil
2 tsp cumin seeds
1 tsp grated fresh ginger
2 tsp ground coriander
1 tsp turmeric
2 fresh chilies, seeded and minced
1 lb (450 g) eggplant, peeled and cubed
6 tomatoes, chopped
1 lb (450 g) fresh spinach, washed, stemmed, and chopped
4 tbs water
2 tsp salt
1 tbs butter

Boil the soaked chickpeas in water until tender. Then set them aside to drain. Place a medium-sized saucepan over medium heat and heat the *ghee* or vegetable oil. When it is hot, toss in the cumin seeds, minced chilies, grated ginger, ground coriander, and turmeric, in that order and in quick succession. Stir-fry for about 30 seconds, then drop in the eggplant cubes and turn them with a spoon until they are browned and butter-soft.

Now add the tomatoes and chopped spinach. Stir to blend the spices into the vegetables. Pour in the water and add the salt. Lower the heat to medium low and simmer with the pot covered. After 10 minutes, remove the cover and fold in the chickpeas. Then dot with butter and simmer gently, stirring every few minutes, until most of the excess liquid has been cooked off. Serve hot with *nimbu chawal* or *alu paratha.*

Soaking time: overnight
Preparation and cooking time: 45 min

Sak

Vegetable greens cooked in their own juices

Sak *was the favorite dish of Śrī Caitanya Mahāprabhu, the incarnation of Kṛṣṇa who appeared in West Bengal five hundred years ago to propagate the chanting of the Hare Kṛṣṇa mantra.* Sak *can be made with spinach or other leafy greens such as radish or broccoli leaves.*

2 lbs (900 g) fresh green vegetable leaves
2 tbs ghee
½ tsp fennel seeds
½ tsp grated fresh ginger
2 fresh chilies, seeded and minced
½ tsp turmeric
¼ tsp asafoetida (optional)
2 potatoes, peeled and diced (optional)
1 tsp salt
2 tbs lemon juice

Wash the vegetable greens in several changes of water, and discard the tough stems. Let the greens drain, then chop them into small pieces. In a *karhai* or medium-sized saucepan, heat the *ghee* or vegetable oil and fry the fennel seeds, grated ginger, and minced chilies together for 30 to 40 seconds. Add the powdered spices and fry them very briefly. Then immediately drop in the diced potatoes and stir-fry for 8 to 10 minutes, scraping the bottom of the pan as you stir. Let them brown to a nice golden color on all sides.

Next, put in the chopped vegetable leaves, cover, and cook slowly for about 15 minutes or until the greens are cooked and the potatoes are soft. (Leafy greens that are juicy and cook quickly may not need additional water, but leaves that stay dry and need to cook longer will need a small amount of water). Add the salt and lemon juice, stir, then remove from the heat.

Sak goes well with white rice or hot *chapatis* and any of the *dal* soups described in the previous section.

Preparation and cooking time: 30 min

Paneer sak

Steamed spinach with fresh cheese

High in the Tirumala hills lies Tirupati temple, the home of the richest Deity in the world, Lord Veṅkateśvara, and described by Śrīla Prabhupāda in Kṛṣṇa *book as "the most important place of pilgrimage in southern India." Catering to the needs of tens of thousands of pilgrims who visit every day, the temple executives have developed a management system which Śrīla Prabhupāda said was superexcellent and which he urged ISKCON leaders to study.*

The Hare Kṛṣṇa movement has a unique relationship with this temple. Out of respect for Śrīla Prabhupāda's concern that the local preaching be increased, the temple executives gave the devotees land, funds to build a temple, and an open-air restaurant to manage, so that the pilgrims can have the opportunity to associate with devotees and purchase their books. This is the recipe for paneer sak *served at the ISKCON canteen situated at the halfway point on the eight kilometer footpath to the temple.*

1 lb (450 g) fresh spinach, washed and stemmed
1 tbs ghee or vegetable oil
2 tsp ground coriander
½ tsp turmeric
¼ tsp cayenne pepper
½ tsp garam masala
2 pinches asafoetida
3 tbs water
⅔ cup (150 ml) sour cream (optional)
8 oz (225 g) paneer, cubed
1 tsp salt
½ tsp sugar

Chop the washed and drained spinach leaves into small pieces. Heat the *ghee* in a saucepan over medium heat and fry the powdered spices for a moment. Put the chopped spinach into the saucepan with the 3 tablespoons of water. Cover, and cook gently until the spinach is tender. This should take about 10 minutes. Now fold in the cream and the cubes of *paneer*. Add the salt and sugar, stir well, and continue cooking over the same low heat for 5 more minutes.

Serve *paneer sak* as a main dish with rice or hot *chapatis* or both.

Preparation and cooking time: 30 min

Khati mithi sabji

Sweet and sour vegetables

Viṣṇu Gada is a devotee well known for his devotional cooking. While he was chief cook of the New York temple, he cooked a sumptuous feast for over three hundred people every Sunday for eight years. This dish was often the highlight of those feasts.

6 oz (175 g) tamarind
2 tbs ghee
1 tsp cumin seeds
2 tbs grated fresh ginger
2 green chilies, sliced
½ tsp ground black pepper
¼ tsp asafoetida
1¼ cups (275 ml) whey
⅔ cup (100 g) brown sugar
1 pineapple, trimmed and cubed
3 carrots, sliced
2 tsp mango powder
2 tsp paprika
2 tsp ground coriander
10 oz (275 g) pressed paneer, cubed
3 zucchinis, cubed
4 tomatoes, quartered
3 stalks celery, diced
3 tsp salt
4 potatoes, washed, peeled, cubed, and deep-fried, or 3 green plantains, sliced

Start by making tamarind juice (see page 84). Then make the *masala*. Heat the *ghee* in a large saucepan and fry the cumin seeds, then the grated ginger and green chilies. Next toss in the ground pepper and the asafoetida and fry for a few seconds more. Then pour the whey into the *masala* and simmer for a moment. Add the tamarind juice, brown sugar, pineapple chunks, sliced carrots, mango powder, paprika, and ground coriander. Allow to boil and thicken, stirring occasionally to prevent scorching. Meanwhile, deep-fry the paneer cubes until light brown and set them aside.

Add the zucchini and celery to the *masala,* cover the pan, and cook until barely tender. Then add the fried paneer cubes, tomatoes, and salt. Stir well. If you are using sliced green plantains, add them at this point. If you are using fried potatoes, add them after the *paneer* cubes have soaked up some of the sauce and become juicy. Cover the pan, and cook until all the ingredients are tender.

Preparation and cooking time: 30 min

Masala bhindi sabji

Seasoned okra slices with coconut

Known as "lady fingers" in India, okra is widely used in creole cooking and is a popular soul food in America. If you can't find okra in supermarkets, look for it at Asian grocers. Choose pods that are small, firm, tender, and bright green.

1½ lbs (675 g) fresh okra
3 tsp ground coriander
1 tsp turmeric
2 pinches cayenne pepper
1½ tsp salt
5 tbs ghee or vegetable oil
2 tsp cumin seeds
1 tsp black mustard seeds
¼ tsp asafoetida
1 cup (75 g) grated coconut
1½ tsp sugar
2 tbs lemon juice

Rinse the okra pods and pat them dry. Cut off the two ends and slice the pods into rounds 1/4 inch (5 mm) thick. You can cut 2 or 3 pods at the same time. Put the slices in a mixing bowl and sprinkle over them the ground coriander, turmeric, cayenne pepper, and salt. Toss the slices to coat them evenly with the spices.

Heat the *ghee* or vegetable oil in a frying pan, *karhai,* or wok and drop in the cumin seeds and black mustard seeds. Cover the pan for a moment to prevent the mustard seeds from popping out. Then toss in the asafoetida. Fry for a few seconds, and then add as many of the seasoned okra slices as will fit in one layer. You will probably have to fry them in 2 or 3 batches. You should have an idea of how many batches it will take before you start cooking, so that you can divide the ingredients accordingly.

Stir-fry each batch for 3 – 4 minutes until the pods appear to wilt and brown. For each batch, add a portion of the grated coconut and a portion of the sugar. Keep frying and stirring until the pods turn a reddish-brown and are very tender. Sprinkle the lemon juice over them and serve them hot.

Preparation and cooking time: 25 min

Opposite page: *Masala bhindi sabji*
Kathi mithi sabji (p. 185)

Upma
Vegetable semolina

At many Hare Kṛṣṇa centers around the world, after the morning spiritual program, the devotees start their day of devotional work with a substantial breakfast of upma, *chickpeas, and ginger tea.*

Making upma *involves three simultaneous operations: cooking the vegetables, boiling the water, and toasting the semolina. When everything is ready, all the ingredients are combined.*

4 medium-sized tomatoes
1 lb (450 g) other assorted vegetables
3 tbs ghee
2 tsp cumin seeds
1 tsp black mustard seeds
½ tsp fenugreek seeds
2 tsp grated fresh ginger
1 dried chili, crushed
6 curry leaves (if not available, use 3 bay leaves)
½ tsp turmeric
¼ tsp asafoetida
6 cups (1.4 liters) water
⅓ cup (50 g) raisins (optional)
3 tsp salt
3 cups (450 g) semolina
1 cup (200 g) butter or ghee
½ tsp pepper
2 tbs lemon juice
2 tbs butter

Begin by cutting the vegetables. The tomatoes can be quartered, green beans and peppers cut into pieces, carrots sliced, potatoes cubed, and cauliflower cut into flowerets. Heat the tablespoon of *ghee* in a saucepan over medium heat and fry the cumin seeds, black mustard seeds, and fenugreek seeds, curry leaves, ginger, and chili. After 30 to 45 seconds, toss in the turmeric and asafoetida, then add the cut vegetables. (If you want to give your *upma* a special taste and texture, lightly deep-fry the cubed potatoes, sliced carrots, and cauliflower flowerets and add them to the *upma* at the end). Stir the vegetables until they brown, then add a little water to prevent scorching. Lower the heat, cover, and gently simmer until the vegetables are tender. While the vegetables simmer, put the water and salt in a small pot to boil.

Melt the butter or *ghee* in a 5-pint (3-liter) saucepan, add the semolina, and stir-fry gently over medium-low heat, stirring every time the bottom layer of semolina appears lightly browned. It should take 10 to 15 minutes for all the semolina to turn faintly brown.

When the grains are ready and the water is boiling, put the cooked vegetables into the grains, toss in the raisins (if desired), then pour the boiling water into this mixture. Be careful! The mixture will erupt and sputter. Lower the heat. Stir several times to break up any lumps, then cover the pot to trap the steam. Let it simmer on the lowest heat. After 5 minutes, lift the cover to see if the grains have absorbed all the water. If not, stir briskly several times and cook a few more minutes uncovered. Finally, add the pepper, lemon juice, and butter. Mix again.

Preparation and cooking time: 35 min

Bhari hui sabji
Stuffed vegetables

6 medium-large tomatoes,
or 6 medium-small green bell peppers,
or 6 medium-small eggplants

Wash and dry the tomatoes, then cut a "lid" off the top of each. Scoop out the pulp and force it through a strainer. Discard the seeds and save the pulp, to be used in the filling. Sprinkle some salt inside the tomato shells and turn them upside down to drain.

Do the same with the peppers, but discard their pulp. Cut the eggplants in half lengthwise and scoop out the pulp, leaving a thick shell. Chop the eggplant pulp into tiny pieces and fry it in a small quantity of *ghee* or oil until it is tender. Mash it and use it in any of the fillings.

Prepare one of the fillings described below and stuff it into the hollowed vegetables. There are three recipes for fillings. Each is sufficient to stuff 6 vegetables.

FILLINGS

Rice and cheese filling:

3 tbs ghee
4 oz (100 g) pressed paneer crumbled
1 cup (175 g) cooked long grained white rice
½ cup (75 g) lightly toasted cashew nuts, crushed
½ tsp asafoetida
1 tsp salt
⅔ cup (150 ml) sour cream

Heat the *ghee* in a small saucepan over medium heat. Crumble the *paneer,* add it to the pan, and stir-fry it for a minute or two. Then add the cooked rice and all the other ingredients. Remove the pan from the heat, fold in the cream, and mix the ingredients well.

Coconut filling:

¾ cup (100 g) fresh grated coconut or ¾ cup (75 g) dry coconut
⅔ cup (150 ml) sour cream
1 tbs grated fresh ginger
1 tsp ground coriander

1 cup (100 g) chickpea flour, lightly toasted
2 oz (50 g) paneer
¼ tsp cayenne pepper
¼ tsp powdered cloves
1 tsp salt

Put all the ingredients in a large bowl and knead well to make a smooth filling.

Vegetable filling:
4 medium-sized potatoes
1 small eggplant
ghee or vegetable oil for deep-frying
2 tsp ground coriander
¼ tsp cayenne pepper
½ tsp garam masala
1 tsp salt
3 tbs chopped coriander leaves
⅔ cup (150 ml) plain yogurt

Boil the potatoes in their skins, then peel and mash them coarse with a fork. Peel and cube the eggplant and deep-fry the cubes until golden brown. Then let them drain. Now mix together the vegetables, spices, herbs, and yogurt to make a thick filling.

When you stuff the tomatoes or peppers, don't forget to replace their lids. You can make a paste from a tablespoon of flour and a dash of water to help the lids stick to the top.

Arrange the stuffed tomatoes or peppers (or both together) in a greased, ovenproof dish. Add 4 tablespoons of water, cover, and bake in the oven at 300°F (150°C) for 15 to 20 minutes. Eggplants take about 1 hour to cook, so cook them separately.

Instead of baking stuffed vegetables, you can steam them in a saucepan. If you have a metal steam-rack, you can steam them over boiling water for 15 to 20 minutes. If you don't have a steam-rack, heat a tablespoon of vegetable oil or *ghee* and fry the bottom of the stuffed vegetables for 2 or 3 minutes. Then add several tablespoons of water, cover the pan tightly, and cook for 15 to 20 minutes. For either method, make sure there is enough water at all times.

Sprinkle the lemon juice and some fresh minced herbs over each serving. Serve hot with a soup and an Indian bread.

Preparation and cooking time: 45 min to 1 hr

Alu tikkia tamatar sahit

Deep-fried stuffed tomatoes

2 lbs (900 g) potatoes, washed and peeled
2¼ cups (225 g) chickpea flour
3 tsp kalinji seeds (optional)
2½ tsp salt
¾ tsp cayenne pepper
2 tbs butter
1½ tsp garam masala
10 medium-small tomatoes
1 tsp sugar

Boil the potatoes until tender; then let them drain. Set them aside in a mixing bowl. Prepare the batter by mixing the chickpea flour, *kalinji* seeds, 1 teaspoon of salt, ½ teaspoon of cayenne pepper, and enough water to make a smooth batter; then set aside. Make one of the fillings from the previous recipe for stuffed vegetables and set aside. Add the butter, ¾ teaspoon of salt, ¼ teaspoon of cayenne pepper, and 1 teaspoon of *garam masala* to the boiled potatoes and mash into a smooth paste.

Wash the tomatoes. Cut a thin lid from the top of each and scoop out the pulp. Sprinkle a mixture of ¾ teaspoon salt, ½ teaspoon of *garam masala,* and 1 teaspoon of sugar into the tomato cases; then stuff them with the filling.

Divide the potato mixture into 10 equal parts. Flatten one part into a round shape by placing it on the greased palm of your left hand and pressing with the fingertips of your right hand. Place a stuffed tomato upside down on the center of the flattened mixture and work the edge of the mixture upwards until the tomato is completely covered. Smooth it over between your hands. Prepare all the tomatoes in this way.

Beat the batter and pour some over each potato-covered stuffed tomato. Deep-fry them all in smoking hot *ghee,* turning often, until they are golden brown. Drain them. Serve hot.

Preparation and cooking time: 50 min to 1 hr

Bhindi Massaledarh
Stuffed okra

7 oz (200 g) paneer
1 tsp cumin seeds
½ tsp grated fresh ginger
3 fresh green chilies
3 tbs chopped coriander leaves
1 tsp turmeric
1 tsp salt
1 lb (450 g) fresh okra
3 tbs ghee or vegetable oil
¼ tsp asafoetida

Wrap a piece of cheesecloth around the *paneer* and gently squeeze out most of the water. Remove the cheesecloth, put the *paneer* into a bowl, and set it aside. Grind the cumin, ginger, chilies, and coriander leaves into a fine paste in a mortar and pestle or electric grinder. Mix the paste, along with the turmeric and salt, into the *paneer*. Knead it into a smooth dough. Cover it with a moist cloth and set it aside.

Wash the okra pods and pat them dry with paper towels. Trim off their heads and lower tips. Slit each pod lengthwise, being careful not to cut all the way to the ends or through to the opposite side. Gently pry back one side of the cut okra with your thumb, then the other side, carefully loosening the pod from the seeds in the center. Stuff each pod with just enough *paneer* mixture to fill it. Take care not to force the edges too wide, otherwise it will break in half.

Heat the *ghee* in a wide saucepan. When it begins to smoke, toss in the asafoetida. Add the stuffed okra pods, carefully placing them with the stuffing facing upward. Reduce the heat to very low and cook covered for 10 minutes. Remove the lid and turn the pods stuffing-side down. Cook uncovered for 10 minutes more until they become golden brown.

Lift the pods out gently and serve them on a warm platter.

Preparation and cooking time: 45 min

Alu kofta

Deep-fried vegetable balls in tomato sauce

Alu koftas *are the most popular type of* kofta. *They are easy to prepare and go well with any meal. After covering them with the tomato sauce, serve them promptly, otherwise they may absorb too much liquid and fall apart.*

15 medium-sized tomatoes
2 tbs ghee or vegetable oil
2 tsp grated fresh ginger
2 dried chilies, crushed
1 tsp ground cumin
1½ tsp turmeric
3 tsp salt
5 medium-sized potatoes, washed
½ medium-sized cauliflower, washed, trimmed, and separated into flowerets
1 cup (100 g) chickpea flour
3 tbs chopped fresh coriander or parsley leaves
1 tsp garam masala
¼ tsp asafoetida
½ tsp ground black pepper
ghee or vegetable oil for deep-frying
1 cup (250 ml) plain yogurt (optional)

Start by making the tomato sauce. Drop the tomatoes into a pot of rapidly boiling water for 15 – 20 seconds. Drain them, and rinse them under cold water. Then peel and mash them. Heat the tablespoon of *ghee* or vegetable oil in a saucepan over medium heat and fry 1 teaspoon of the grated ginger, then the dried chilies. Follow with the ground cumin and ½ teaspoon of the turmeric. Stir-fry for a few seconds. Put the tomatoes into the pan, add half the salt, cover, and lower the heat. Cook slowly for 20 minutes, stirring every 5 minutes or so.

While the sauce simmers, peel the potatoes and break up the cauliflower into large flowerets. Wash both vegetables thoroughly, then grate them through the large holes of a metal grater. Combine the grated vegetables, the chickpea flour, 2 tablespoons of the chopped coriander leaves, and all the remaining spices in a mixing bowl. Mix thoroughly. The grated potatoes should give enough moisture to bind the ingredients together. Knead the mixture for 2 minutes, then form it into 20 to 30 small balls. Heat the ghee or vegetable oil until almost smoking, and drop in the vegetable balls. Deep-fry them for 4 to 5 minutes until they are uniformly golden brown and crisp. Then drain them.

If you use yogurt, stir it into the tomato sauce and allow the sauce to heat for 2 minutes. Put the *kofta* balls in a serving bowl and cover them with the hot sauce. Garnish with the remaining chopped fresh coriander or parsley leaves. Serve with a rice or an Indian bread.

Preparation and cooking time: 45 min

Palak kofta
Deep-fried spinach-and-cheese balls

Broadcasting from our community in Florence, Italy, "Radio Krishna Centrale" reaches more than fifteen million people. The most popular program, "Radio Cucino" (cooking lessons), is hosted by Kṛṣṇa Caitanya dāsa, who sometimes recites the prayers for his listeners' offerings during the show. Listeners often telephone the station to express their thanks for this recipe.

1 lb (450 g) fresh spinach
1 tbs ghee or vegetable oil
1 tsp grated fresh ginger
2 dried chilies, crushed
½ tsp turmeric
½ tsp garam masala
½ tsp ground coriander
¼ tsp asafoetida
7 oz (200 g) paneer, drained and chopped
2 tsp salt
2¾ cups (275 g) chickpea flour
ghee or vegetable oil for deep-frying

Wash the spinach thoroughly, remove the larger stalks, then wilt the leaves by plunging them into boiling water for a few minutes. Let them drain well, and then press out any remaining water. Chop the leaves into small pieces on a cutting board.

Use a medium-sized saucepan to heat the *ghee* or vegetable oil and fry the ginger and the chilies, followed by the ground spices. Add the chopped *paneer* and stir-fry for 1 minute. Then add the spinach. Toss in the salt and mix the ingredients well with a spoon. Transfer the mixture onto a smooth working surface, add the chickpea flour as a binder, and knead well.

Now roll the mixture into 1-inch (2.5-cm) balls and deep-fry them in ghee or vegetable oil until lightly browned. Then drain. *Palak koftas* are tasty served with a tomato sauce or eaten as is.

Preparation and cooking time: 45 min

Opposite page: *Bandgobhi kofta (p. 198)*
Nargisi kofta (p. 200)
Palak kofta

Bandgobhi kofta

Stuffed cabbage leaves

2 tbs ghee
1 cinnamon stick, 2 inches (5 cm) long
5 cloves
1 tsp ground cumin
¼ tsp asafoetida
2 lbs (900 g) tomatoes, blanched, peeled, and mashed
4 tbs raisins
1 tbs lemon juice
1 tsp turmeric
3½ tsp salt
1 cup (100 g) chickpea flour
1 pinch ground pepper
1 small green cabbage
2 tbs ghee
⅓ cup (50 g) almonds or cashew nuts, crushed
1 tsp grated fresh ginger
1 or 2 dried chilies, crushed
12 oz (350 g) paneer, drained and chopped
3 tbs finely chopped fresh coriander leaves or 1 tsp ground coriander
½ tsp paprika

In a small saucepan, heat the *ghee* and stir-fry the cinnamon, cloves, ground cumin, and asafoetida for 30 to 45 seconds. Put in the pureed tomatoes and cook gently for 30 minutes to obtain a smooth sauce. Then fold in the raisins and add the lemon juice, turmeric, and 2 teaspoons of the salt. Discard the whole spices, and remove the saucepan from the heat. Put the chickpea flour in a bowl with a pinch of salt and a pinch of pepper. Mix with just enough water to make a thick batter. Cover the bowl with a cloth and set aside.

Cut off the stem of the cabbage and remove any damaged outer leaves. Wash the head of cabbage and place it in boiling water with 1 teaspoon of salt. After 8 or 10 minutes, carefully remove the cabbage and rinse it under cold water. Cut the cabbage at the base and peel off 6 – 8 leaves without breaking them. (You can use the rest of the cabbage for another recipe). Use a small paring knife to pare down the thick section that runs down the middle of each leaf (without cutting through the leaf). This will make the leaves more pliable. Pat them dry and set them aside.

Heat the ghee in a small saucepan and brown the crushed nuts, grated ginger, and chilies. Drop in the chopped paneer with the chopped coriander leaves, paprika, and the remaining salt. Cook over medium heat, stirring constantly until all the ingredients are well mixed. Next, spread out the cabbage leaves and place a tablespoon of this filling in the center of each one. Fold over the edges of the leaf and roll it into a tight roll.

Dip the rolls in the thick batter and deep-fry them for 4 to 5 minutes in hot *ghee* or vegetable oil until golden brown. Put the stuffed cabbage rolls on a serving plate and cover them with the preheated tomato sauce.

Instead of frying the rolls, you can also bake them. For this method you leave out the batter. Place the rolls in an oven in a casserole side-by-side, seam-side down. Cover them with the tomato sauce and bake at 300°F (150°C) for 15 to 20 minutes.

Preparation and cooking time: 1 hour 15 min

Nargisi kofta
"Royal" kofta

Vedic recipes range from very simple to very complex. Nargisi kofta *is a little on the complex side, but well worth the time it takes to make it. It is a favorite in Rajasthan, the "playground of kings". Serve* nargisi kofta *with a chutney as a snack or with a wet vegetable as a side dish to a main meal.*

1 cup (200 g) white rice
8 medium-sized potatoes
3¾ tsp salt
6 oz (175 g) paneer
2¼ cups (225 g) chickpea flour
1 tsp kalinji or black cumin seeds (optional)
½ tsp turmeric
¼ tsp powdered saffron
2 tsp warm milk
12 oz (350 g) whole spinach leaves, with stems removed
¼ tsp ground black pepper
1 tsp garam masala
½ tsp turmeric
¼ tsp asafoetida
ghee for deep-frying

Steam the rice in twice its volume of water (to which one teaspoon of salt has been added) for about 18 minutes, or until all the water is absorbed. Drain and set aside. Boil the potatoes until they are tender, then peel them. Mix ½ teaspoon of salt into the *paneer* and knead it into a soft dough. Cover the paneer with a moist cloth and set aside. Combine the chickpea flour, 1 teaspoon salt, *kalinji* seeds, and turmeric in a bowl. Mix with enough water to make a smooth batter. Let stand. Steep the saffron in the warm milk; then mix it well with the cooked rice. Wilt the spinach by plunging it into boiling water for a minute; then let it drain. Mix the spinach with the black pepper and ¼ teaspoon of salt and set it aside. Add the *garam masala,* turmeric, 1 teaspoon of salt, and ¼ teaspoon of asafoetida to the potatoes. Mash into a smooth paste.

Divide the rice, the *paneer,* the spinach, and the potato mixture into six parts each. Take one part of the rice in your hands and roll it into a compact ball. Flatten one part of the *paneer* dough into a round shape in the palm of your left hand and put the ball of rice in the center of it. Bring up the edges to completely cover the ball; then roll it between your palms to make it smooth. Cover the ball with a layer or two of unraveled spinach leaves and a layer of the potato mixture. Make the ball compact and smooth by tossing it gently from one hand to the other.

When several balls are ready, beat the batter and pour some over each one. Then put them in smoking hot *ghee*. Turn them frequently to keep them from burning. Fry until they are browned all over. Remove and serve hot.

Preparation and cooking time: 50 min to 1 hour

Savories

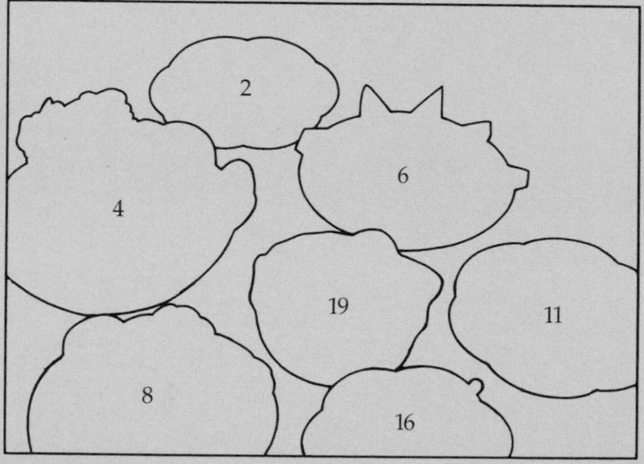
2
4
6
19
11
8
16

SAVORIES can be a meal in themselves, a side dish, or a snack. Most go well with a matching chutney. Some savories, such as *pakoras* or *sevian* noodles, can be made at a moment's notice. Others, like *samosas* and *kachoris,* take longer because you have to stuff and roll them. But the time is well spent. *Samosas,* in fact, are so delectable that Śrīla Prabhupāda predicted they will become a favorite snack in the West, as they now are in India.

This chapter will introduce you to some classic cooking techniques: stuffing *kachoris* and twisting them closed, folding *samosas* and pleating their tops, forming *vadas* in one hand, and making chickpea flour noodles. There are no shortcuts or modern gadgets to do it for you, but with a little practice it becomes easy. And you can cook most savories in advance and reheat them a few minutes before serving.

An essential ingredient for making certain savories is *ghee,* used for pan-frying and deep-frying. Although you can choose between *ghee* and vegetable oil, the delicate flavor of *ghee* will give your savories a master's touch.

Chickpea flour, called *besan* in Hindi, is another ingredient often used in savories. It has a distinctive rich flavor, and is available at most health food shops and in Asian groceries.

Papadam

Dal-flour wafers

Papadams *are thin, crisp, sun-dried wafers of dal-flour. They are available in Indian grocery stores. All you have to do is cook them, which is quick and easy.*

The three main varieties are: red chili (hot and spicy), black pepper (spicy but not hot), and plain. They come in several sizes. The large ones can be broken in half before cooking if necessary. Papadams *should be served crisp; so don't fry them far in advance, otherwise they will become limp.* Papadams *can be served with any sort of Indian meal.*

ghee or vegetable oil for deep-frying
8 to 12 papadams

Heat the *ghee* or vegetable oil in a *karhai* or shallow frying pan until it is almost smoking. Place a *papadam* in the *ghee*. In just a few seconds, it will expand and curl at the edges. Submerge it for a moment with the back of a slotted spoon to flatten it, then turn it over. The *papadam* should be golden yellow. Watch it all the time and be careful not to let it brown or burn.

After a few seconds, remove it from the *ghee* and place it on edge in a colander to drain.

Papadams can also be cooked directly over a low flame. Hold the *papadam* with a pair of tongs just over the flame until the part nearest the flame begins to blister and turn a lighter color. This should take no more than a few seconds. Then, turn the *papadam* so that another part cooks. Repeat the turning and cooking until the entire *papadam* is cooked.

Cooking time: about 10 seconds for each *papadam*

Paneer masala

Fried and soaked cheese cubes

There are many ways to cook paneer. *For this one, you soak the fried cheese cubes in a spicy broth until they absorb the flavor of the spices and become soft and juicy. Having soaked from twenty minutes to two days, the cubes can be used to enhance vegetable dishes, or served as a snack or side dish.*

10 oz (275 g) paneer
ghee or vegetable oil for deep-frying
1 tbs ghee or vegetable oil
½ tsp cumin seeds
2 cinnamon sticks, 2 inches (5 cm) long
4 cloves
½ tsp ground coriander
½ tsp turmeric
½ tsp asafoetida
¼ tsp ground black pepper
1 tsp salt

Make *paneer* as described on page 94 and reserve 2½ cups (600 ml) of the whey. Gather the *paneer* in a cheesecloth and rinse it under cold water for a few seconds. Now, flatten the cheese in the cheesecloth to a thickness of about 1 inch (2.5 cm) and weight it down evenly so the result will be a flat slab of firm cheese. Do this on top of the sink so the liquid has a place to drain. Leave it for 30 minutes.

Remove the cheesecloth and cut the cheese into 1-inch (2.5 cm) cubes, or into rectangles or diamonds 2 inches (5 cm) long. Deep-fry them in *ghee* or vegetable oil. It should take about 4 or 5 minutes to brown the cubes lightly. Drain.

Start a *masala* by heating a tablespoon of *ghee* or vegetable oil in a small saucepan. Stir-fry the cumin seeds, cinnamon sticks, and cloves. After about 30 seconds, follow with the powdered spices and stir-fry for a few seconds more. Now pour the whey into the *masala*, add the salt, and bring to a boil, then remove from the heat. Put the fried cheese cubes into this liquid *masala* and allow them to soak for at least 20 minutes. Just before serving, reheat the *paneer masala;* then drain off the liquid.

Preparation and cooking time: 25 min
Soaking time: 20 min

Tali hui paneer
Pan-fried seasoned cheese

For frying pieces of paneer, *a heavy skillet works very well. Turn them over with a spatula to avoid breaking the crust that forms.*

Paneer *can also be made into pakoras. Dip the pieces of paneer into spiced chickpea-flour batter and deep-fry them as described in the next recipe.*

10 oz (275 g) paneer
3 tsp turmeric
3 tsp salt
1 tbs ghee or vegetable oil
1 tbs finely chopped fresh coriander or parsley leaves
1 lemon or lime

Make *paneer* and press with a weight for 10 minutes, so that the cheese is firm but quite moist. Cut the cheese into pieces about 4 inches (10 cm) long, 2 inches (5 cm) wide, and ½ to 1 inch (1 to 2.5 cm) thick.

Make a coating for the cheese by mixing the turmeric and salt in a small dish. Press the pieces of moist *paneer* lightly into the mixture one by one to coat both sides. The coating should be thin and even. If the coating is thick, you'll not have enough mixture to go around. Heat a tablespoon of oil or *ghee* in a skillet (or frying pan) and put in as many pieces of *paneer* as the frying pan will easily hold. Cook them slowly, about 4 or 5 minutes on each side, until they are lightly browned and have a thin crust.

Serve *tali hui paneer* garnished with chopped coriander leaves and a slice of lemon or lime.

Preparation and cooking time: 20 min

Pakora
Vegetable fritters

Practically any type of vegetable can be made into pakoras. *Whatever vegetable you use, cut the pieces about the same size, so that they cook at the same speed. Eggplants, zucchini, potatoes, squash, and carrots can be sliced or cut into small chunks, cauliflower and broccoli into flowerets, and bell peppers into rings or strips. Brussels sprouts, asparagus, and folded spinach leaves can be put in whole. A welcome addition to any meal or feast, pakoras are an easy-to-make snack that goes well with a chutney.*

2¼ cups (225 g) chickpea flour
1 tbs kalinji seeds
½ tsp ground cinnamon
¼ tsp cayenne pepper
2 tsp ground coriander
2 tsp ground cumin
1½ tsp turmeric
¼ tsp asafoetida
2 tsp salt
½ tsp baking powder
1 cup (250 ml) cold water
1½ lbs (675 g) trimmed vegetables
ghee or vegetable oil for deep-frying

Sift the chickpea flour into a large mixing bowl and add the spices, salt, and baking powder. Slowly add the cold water and whisk until you have a smooth batter, thick enough to coat the vegetables.

Cut all the vegetables before heating the *ghee*. You may need to parboil large cauliflower flowerets. Use other vegetables raw.

Put the *ghee* or vegetable oil over medium-high heat. The *ghee* is hot enough when a drop of batter put into it rises immediately to the surface and sizzles. Now put a handful of cut vegetables into the batter and coat them well. Put in one type of vegetable at a time—you're going to fry each type separately. Take the coated vegetables out of the batter one by one and put them quickly into the hot *ghee* until the surface of the *ghee* is covered. Fry for several minutes until the *pakoras* are golden brown and crisp, then remove them and let them drain. Fry all the *pakoras* in this way, never putting in more than one layer at a time.

Preparation and cooking time: 20 min

Sada pakora
Spiced chickpea-flour fritters

Sada pakoras *go well with white or brown rice and kadhi sauce. If you make them smaller, about the size of a grape, they can be added to wet vegetables such as* sukta *or* mater alu takari. *Mix them into the vegetable dish at least ten minutes before serving so they have time to soak up some of the sauce. They can also be eaten with a chutney as a snack.*

8 oz (225 g) chickpea flour
1 tbs kalinji seeds
½ tsp ground cinnamon
¼ tsp cayenne pepper
1 tsp ground coriander
1 tsp ground cumin
1 tsp turmeric
¼ tsp asafoetida
1 tsp salt
½ tsp baking powder (optional)
⅓ pint (200 ml) cold water
ghee or vegetable oil for deep-frying

Prepare the batter as in the previous recipe for *pakora,* but make it thicker, almost pastelike. Get air into the batter by beating it vigorously. Scoop up some batter with a tablespoon or small ice-cream scoop, and put 2 to 3 lumps of it into the hot *ghee* or vegetable oil. The lumps will immediately swell and sizzle on the surface of the *ghee* or oil. Quickly add more lumps of the batter until the surface of the *ghee* is covered with sizzling *pakoras.*

Adjust the heat so that it takes the *pakoras* 4 to 5 minutes to become crisp and uniformly golden brown (turn them once or twice with a slotted spoon). Remove and drain.

Bhajas are a variation of *sada pakoras.* You can prepare and cook them in exactly the same way, except for the spicing. Instead of the ground cinnamon, coriander, and cumin, use ½ teaspoon of cumin seeds, 2 tablespoons of chopped fresh coriander leaves, and one fresh chili, chopped fine.

Preparation and cooking time: 20 min

Dokla

Steamed dal and yogurt

2 cups (350 g) channa dal, cleaned
⅔ cup (150 ml) yogurt
1 cup (250 ml) water
3 or 4 fresh chilies
2 tbs grated fresh ginger
½ tsp turmeric
1½ tsp salt
1 tbs lemon juice
3 tbs melted ghee
1½ tsp baking powder
2 tbs ghee
1 tbs black mustard seeds
2 tbs sesame seeds
1 pinch asafoetida
5 tbs grated fresh coconut
4 tbs chopped fresh coriander leaves

Wash the *dal* and soak it for at least 4 hours. Drain it. Put it in a blender or food processor with the yogurt and water. Blend until smooth and let it stand at least 6 hours in a warm place, covered.

Find a pot into which you can fit an 8-inch (20-cm) round cake-pan. You will need some sort of ring to keep the cake-pan off the bottom. Its center should have an opening wide enough to allow steam to reach the bottom of the pan. Put about 2 inches (5 cm) of water in the pot and bring to a boil.

Grind the fresh chilies into a paste with a little water and add to the batter. Then add the ginger, turmeric, salt, lemon juice, melted *ghee*, and baking powder. Mix well. Grease the cake-pan with a little butter or ghee and pour in the batter. Cover the pot tightly and steam the *dokla* for 20 to 25 minutes or until springy to the touch.

To prepare a topping, heat the 2 tablespoons of *ghee* in a small pan and fry the mustard seeds, the sesame seeds, and a pinch of asafoetida. When the mustard seeds finish popping, spread these seasonings over the top of the *dokla* and then sprinkle over it the grated coconut and coriander leaves.

When cool, cut into 3-inch (7.5-cm) rectangles or diamonds and carefully remove them from the pan. Serve with coconut chutney.

Soaking time: *Dal,* at least 4 hours
Resting time: Batter, at least 6 hrs
Preparation and cooking time: 25 min

Samosa

Vegetable turnovers

Once you've tasted a good samosa, *you'll understand why* samosas *are the most popular of all Indian savories. For variations, mix fresh paneer into the filling and try different blends of spices.*

4 cups (400 g) white flour
½ tsp salt
½ cup (100 g) melted butter or ghee
⅔ cup (150 ml) cold water
2 or 3 medium-sized potatoes
½ cauliflower, separated into flowerets
1½ cups (200 g) fresh peas
4 tablespoon ghee or vegetable oil
1 tsp cumin seeds
½ tsp fenugreek seeds
½ tsp grated fresh ginger
1 tsp turmeric
½ tsp ground coriander
¼ tsp asafoetida
¼ tsp ground cloves
½ tsp ground cinnamon
2 tsp salt
¼ teaspoon pepper
ghee or vegetable oil for deep-frying

Put the white flour and salt in a bowl and dribble the melted butter or *ghee* over the top. Rub the butter or *ghee* into the flour with your fingertips until the mixture resembles coarse breadcrumbs. Slowly mix in the water and gather the flour together to make a dough. Knead vigorously for 5 minutes, until it is smooth and soft but doesn't stick to your fingers. Gather the dough into a ball, sprinkle with a few drops of water, and cover with a damp cloth while you prepare the filling.

Peel the potatoes and dice them. Either grate the cauliflower flowerets through the largest holes of a metal grater or cut them into tiny flowerets. Boil the peas until they are tender; then drain and set them aside.

Place a large frying pan over medium heat, and fry the cumin and fenugreek seeds in 2 tablespoons of *ghee* or oil. When they begin to darken, toss in the grated ginger and the powdered spices and fry for a few seconds more. Now put in the potato cubes; stir-fry for 3 or 4 minutes, then add the cauliflower. Stir-fry for

---

Opposite page: *Preparation of samosa*

another 3 or 4 minutes. Add 2 tablespoons of water, cover, and cook for about 15 minutes, until the vegetables are tender (watch closely to prevent burning). Stir the peas into the mixture, season with the salt and pepper, then spread the contents of the pan on a clean surface to cool while you roll out the dough.

Dust the rolling surface with flour. Form the dough into 10 balls. Roll out each ball to make a 6-inch (15-cm) circle. Cut each circle in half. Take each half circle and moisten the edge of its straight side from the center to one end. Bring the two ends of the straight side together to make a cone. Firmly press the dry side over the wet side to seal the cone tight. Stuff the cone to two-thirds with filling. Then close the opening by pinching and folding the two edges together to form a pleated top.

Heat the *ghee* or oil in a deep-frying vessel over medium heat. Fry a few *samosas* at a time (as many as will cover the surface of the *ghee* in one layer). Fry them for 10 to 15 minutes, turning them often until both sides are golden brown. Remove and drain.

Preparation and cooking time: 1 hr 15 min

Alu patra
Fried spicy potato swirls

4 medium-sized potatoes
2 tbs grated coconut
2 tsp sesame seeds
2 tsp brown sugar
2 tsp grated fresh ginger
2 fresh green chilies, minced
1 tbs fresh coriander leaves, minced
2 tsp garam masala
1½ tsp salt
2 tbs lemon juice
2 cups (200 g) white flour
½ tsp turmeric
¼ tsp cayenne pepper
2 tsp melted ghee
½ cup (100 ml) water
ghee or vegetable oil for deep-frying

Prepare the filling first, so that it will be cool by the time the dough is ready. Boil the potatoes until they are soft. Then peel them. Use a fork to mash them in a bowl with the grated coconut and the next 8 ingredients including 1 teaspoon of the salt. Now spread the mixture on a surface to cool while you prepare the dough.

Combine the flour, turmeric, cayenne pepper, and the remaining salt in a mixing bowl. Rub the melted *ghee* into the flour, then add the water slowly while mixing with your hand until a dough forms. Transfer the dough to a rolling surface and knead well so that it becomes soft and elastic. If the dough is too wet, add more flour.

Flour the rolling surface liberally, then roll out the entire dough into a rectangle with a thickness of about 1/8 inch (3 mm). Spread the cool potato mixture evenly on the surface. While dusting with flour to prevent the dough from sticking to your fingers, roll it up to make a tight, compact roll. Use a sharp serrated knife to cut the roll into slices of ½ inch (1 cm). Pat and form the slices so they retain their shape. Place them on a platter.

Heat the *ghee* or vegetable oil in a *karhai* or shallow pot. The oil or *ghee* is hot enough when a pinch of dough dropped into it rises immediately to the surface and sizzles. Put several slices into the *ghee* and fry them for 3 to 5 minutes, turning them over once, until they are golden brown. Serve hot as a side dish in a feast or a meal, or as a snack with a chutney.

Preparation and cooking time: 40 min

Alu ki tikki

Fried potato patties

Slow cooking forms a crust on both sides of these potato cutlets, which gives them a special texture and flavor. Without the peas and the chickpea flour, alu ki tikki *is often served on* Ekādaśī *days (see page 55), when devotees fast from grains.*

5 medium-sized potatoes
1½ cups (200 g) fresh peas
1 cup (100 g) carrots, diced
1 cup (100 g) cauliflower, minced
1 tsp garam masala
½ tsp cumin seeds
¼ tsp asafoetida
2 dried chilies, crushed
2 tbs chopped fresh coriander or parsley leaves
1 tsp salt
1 tbs lemon or lime juice
3 tbs chickpea flour, dry-roasted
2 tbs butter or ghee

Boil the potatoes. Steam the other vegetables until they are soft. Drain the potatoes and other vegetables. Peel the potatoes, then break them into chunks and combine them in a large mixing bowl with the other drained vegetables, the spices, the lemon juice, and finally the chickpea flour. Use a fork or masher to mash all the ingredients thoroughly.

Form the mixture into 8 patties about 1 inch (2.5 cm) thick. Then heat a heavy-bottomed frying pan over low heat and put in a little butter or *ghee*. Put in several patties at a time, leaving enough room between them to insert the spatula. Cook each side for 12 to 15 minutes. When one side becomes golden brown, work your spatula under the patty, without breaking the crust, and turn it over. If the patties are cooking too quickly, lower the heat.

Alu ki tikkis go well with tomato chutney and a *raita*.

Preparation and cooking time: 40 min to 1 hr

Urad dal kachori

Deep-fried savories filled with spiced dal

Śrīla Prabhupāda was fond of kachoris *from his earliest childhood, so much so, in fact, that his mother gave him the nickname* Kachori-mukha *(one who fills his mouth with* kachoris*).*

4 cups (400 g) white flour
3/8 cup (75 g) butter or ghee
1¼ tsp salt
1 cup (250 ml) water
¾ cup (150 g) urad dal, washed and soaked overnight
1 tbs ghee
½ tsp cumin seeds
½ tsp ground anise seeds
½ tsp ground cumin
½ tsp grated fresh ginger
1 tsp turmeric
¼ tsp asafoetida
1 tsp chopped fresh coriander leaves
2 tbs lemon juice
1½ tsp salt

Put the flour and salt into a large mixing bowl. Blend the butter or *ghee* into the mixture with your fingertips. Slowly add the cold water and form a soft (not wet) dough. Knead the dough vigorously for 5 minutes, then cover with a moist cloth and set aside.

Drain the *dal* and blend it in an electric blender (or a grinder) with just enough water to make a smooth paste. Heat the tablespoon of *ghee* in a small frying pan and fry the cumin seeds until brown (about 30 seconds). Then add the powdered spices and the pureed *dal*. Stir-fry for several minutes until partially cooked. Mix in the chopped coriander leaves, lemon juice, and salt. Set aside to cool.

Form the dough into 12 balls. Divide the *dal* mixture into 12 parts. With your thumb, poke a hole in each one. Fill it with one part of the *dal* mixture. Seal the hole, flatten the ball into a patty between your hands, and roll it out like a very thick *puri*. Put the *ghee* over medium heat. After some time, test the *ghee* by dropping a piece of dough in it. If the dough immediately rises to the surface and sizzles, the *ghee* is ready. Put in the *kachoris* and deep-fry them for about 10 minutes, until they are flaky and golden brown.

Soaking time: overnight
Preparation and cooking time: 50 min to 1 hr

Matar dal bara
Split-pea croquettes

This is one of the recipes that have earned Gopībhāva dāsī the reputation of being the finest cook among the Hare Kṛṣṇa devotees in South Africa. When visiting devotees taste her cooking, they know that even though they have traveled far, they are still close to home.

2½ cups (600 ml) plain yogurt
1¾ cups (350 g) green or yellow split-peas
2 tbs chopped coriander or parsley leaves
2 tbs grated fresh ginger
2 tsp ground coriander
2 tsp cumin seeds
2 tsp ground cinnamon
1 fresh green chili, seeded and minced
1 tsp turmeric
½ tsp cayenne pepper
¼ tsp asafoetida
5 tsp salt
4½ cups (1 liter) warm water
ghee or vegetable oil for deep-frying

Soak the split-peas overnight in water twice their volume. Then drain them.

Blend the split-peas in an electric blender, adding just enough fresh water to make a very thick paste. Scrape the paste into a bowl. Add half of each spice to the paste, along with 1 teaspoon of the salt. Mix well and set it aside. Reserve a teaspoon of the remaining salt and dissolve the rest into the warm water. Set the water aside.

Heat the *ghee* in a *karhai* or saucepan over medium heat. Moisten your hands and form the paste into small patties. Fry them in the *ghee,* turning once or twice, until they are nicely browned on all sides. Remove, and let them drain over the ghee for a moment. Then drop them into the salted water to soak for at least 15 minutes.

Combine the yogurt with the remaining spices and salt in a bowl. Mix well. After the *baras* have soaked, remove them from the salted water and place them in a serving bowl. Cover them with the spiced yogurt and serve.

Soaking time: overnight, plus 15 min in salted water
Preparation and cooking time: 25 min

Urad dal bara
Dal croquettes in yogurt

1¾ cups (350 g) urad dal, soaked overnight
2 fresh chilies, minced
¼ tsp asafoetida
1 tsp baking soda
4 tsp salt
4¼ cups (1 liter) warm water
ghee or vegetable oil for deep-frying
2½ cups (600 ml) plain yogurt
1 tsp cumin seeds, toasted and ground

Drain the *dal* and blend it in an electric blender (or a grinder) with the minced chilies, asafoetida, baking soda, 1 teaspoon of the salt, and just enough water to make a smooth paste. Beat the mixture vigorously until it is so light that a drop will float on water. Set aside. Reserve ½ teaspoon of the salt and dissolve the rest into the warm water.

Heat the *ghee* or vegetable oil in a deep-frying vessel until it is hot but not smoking. Drop lumps of the batter, one after another, into the *ghee.* (A small ice-cream scoop is ideal for this purpose). In seconds the *baras* will become round and float, sizzling. Fry them on all sides. They should become nicely browned in 5 or 6 minutes. Then drain them and put them in the salt water to soak. Add the remaining ½ teaspoon of salt to the yogurt, mix well, and set the yogurt aside.

After 20 to 30 minutes, when the *baras* begin to become light-colored, gently remove them and squeeze the excess water out of each one. Place them in a serving dish, cover with the yogurt, and garnish with the ground cumin. Serve *urad dal baras* as part of a main meal or as a special treat.

Soaking time: overnight, plus 20 to 30 min in salted water
Preparation and cooking time: 30 min

Kathmir vada

Chickpea-flour–and–coriander-leaf tidbits

2 oz (50 g) fresh coriander or 3 oz (75 g) spinach leaves
2 cups (200 g) sifted chick-pea flour
1 cup (275 ml) plain yogurt
1 or 2 fresh chilies, seeded and chopped
2½ tsp salt
1¾ cups (425 ml) water
ghee or vegetable oil for deep-frying

Wash the coriander or spinach leaves thoroughly and remove the largest stems. Chop the leaves into small pieces and combine in a mixing bowl with the chickpea flour, yogurt, chilies, and salt. Slowly add water, stirring as you do, until the batter has a milk-like consistency.

Pour the batter into a medium-sized pot and place over low heat. Cook gently for 15 – 20 minutes. As the batter thickens, stir frequently with a wide wooden spoon to avoid scorching. The batter is ready when a dab of it solidifies on a cool surface. Now pour the batter into a shallow cake-pan (1 to 2 inch/ 2.5 to 5 cm high) and let it cool for at least 15 minutes. When it becomes firm, cut it into diamonds and deep-fry the pieces in *ghee* or vegetable oil until golden brown.

Remove, drain, and serve hot or at room temperature with date and tamarind or mint *chutney*.

Preparation and cooking time: 45 min

Opposite page: *Kathmir vada*
Gajar vada (p. 222)
Dahi vada (p. 223)

Gajar vada
Spiced carrot croquettes

This savory will impress anyone. Be sure the mixture is thick enough not to fall apart when deep-fried. Add more chickpea flour if necessary, until it holds together.

4 or 5 medium-sized carrots, washed and scrape
1 cup (100 g) chickpea flour
2 tbs walnuts or hazelnuts, coarsely chopped
1 tbs grated fresh coconut
1 tbs chopped fresh coriander or parsley leaves
2 fresh chilies, seeded and chopped
1 tsp garam masala
½ tsp turmeric
½ tsp salt
¼ tsp baking powder
ghee or vegetable oil for deep-frying

Grate the carrots on the fine holes of a metal grater until you have about 2 cups (250 g) of grated carrots. Put the grated carrots and all the other ingredients in a large bowl. Mix with just enough water to make a paste thick enough to hold together when deep-fried.

Heat the *ghee* or vegetable oil in a *karhai,* wok, or saucepan over medium heat. Pick up a lump of batter with a tablespoon. Use your finger to push the lump into the hot *ghee* or oil. (You can also use a small ice cream scoop to flick the batter into the *ghee*). Do this until you have 8 to 10 *vadas* cooking at the same time. Adjust the heat and turn the *vadas* often so that they become nicely browned on all sides in 4 or 5 minutes. Remove with a slotted spoon. Drain in a strainer or colander.

Serve *gajar vadas* hot or at room temperature with a wet vegetable, a *raita,* or plain yogurt.

Preparation and cooking time: 25 min

Dahi vada

Dal croquettes in yogurt sauce

Dahi vada *is a variation of* urad dal bara. *In India, a moistened banana leaf is used to hold the* vada *before it is slid into the* ghee. *In the absence of a banana leaf, however, you can use your hand. Just make sure that the batter is thick enough to hold its shape.*

1 cup (200 g) urad dal, sorted and washed
1 tsp cumin seeds
2 fresh chilies, seeded and chopped
1 tbs grated fresh ginger
½ tsp asafoetida
1½ tsp salt
ghee or vegetable oil for deep-frying
1¾ cups (425 ml) plain yogurt
1 tbs grated coconut
2 tbs chopped fresh coriander leaves
2 pinches cayenne pepper

Soak the *dal* in warm water for several hours. Drain it and grind it in an electric blender (or a grinder) with just enough water to make a thick, smooth paste. Scrape this paste into a bowl and mix in the cumin seeds, chilies, ginger, asafoetida, and ½ teaspoon of salt.

Heat the *ghee* or oil in a *karhai,* wok, or saucepan over medium heat. Moisten your left hand and put 2 oz (50 g) of the mixture on it. Flatten it slightly with the thumb of your left hand to form a flat "bread." Poke it in the center with the little finger of your right hand to make a depression. Now carefully slide it into the *ghee*. Because the *dal* is not very firm, this operation may require some practice (if it seems difficult, don't worry: you can also use a spoon to put lumps of the batter in the hot *ghee*). Fry the *vadas* for 6 to 8 minutes on each side until they become reddish brown. Remove and drain in a colander.

Mix the grated coconut, fresh coriander, cayenne pepper, and the remaining salt into the yogurt and cover the *vadas* with this sauce one hour before serving. Garnish each *vada* by filling the dent in the center with a dab of date-and-tamarind chutney.

Soaking time: several hours for the dal
Preparation and cooking time: 40 min

Sevian

Chickpea-flour noodles

Sevian *is one of India's favorite snacks. It is sold virtually everywhere, in different shapes and different mixtures.* Sevian *may be eaten plain or as a garnish on a vegetable dish or salad. It is also delicious mixed with raisins and toasted nuts. The only problem is stopping after one handful.*

2 cups (200 g) sifted chickpea flour
½ tsp cayenne pepper
1 tsp turmeric
1½ tsp salt
½ cup (125 ml) cold water
ghee or vegetable oil for deep-frying

Mix together the chickpea flour, spices, salt, and cold water to make a smooth, thick paste. Heat the *ghee* or oil over medium heat. Beat the paste a few seconds. Then use a spatula to force a spoonful of paste through a large-holed colander into the *ghee*. Now run the spatula over the bottom of the colander to scrape any remaining batter back into the bowl. Force another spoonful of paste through the holes into the ghee. Repeat until the surface of the *ghee* is covered with noodles. If the paste is too thin and falls in elongated drops instead of noodles, thicken it with more chickpea flour. Turn and fry the noodles until only slightly browned—they will continue to darken after being removed from the *ghee*. Drain.

You can also use a cloth icing bag with a small hole to make spirals or loops. If these noodles are too large, you can break them into pieces after they drain.

Preparation and cooking time: 25 min

Khandvi

Spiced chickpea-flour–and–yogurt swirls

1 or 2 fresh chilies, minced
1 tsp grated fresh ginger
3 cups (700 ml) plain yogurt
1 cup (100 g) chickpea flour
2 tsp salt
¾ tsp turmeric
3 tbs ghee
1½ tsp black mustard seeds
½ tsp asafoetida
4 tbs grated coconut
3 tbs chopped fresh coriander leaves

Make a paste of the fresh chilies and grated ginger. Combine the yogurt, chickpea flour, chili paste, turmeric, and salt in a saucepan and bring to a boil. Lower the heat to medium and cook for 10 to 15 minutes, stirring constantly, until the mixture thickens and pulls away from the sides of the pan. Take care that no lumps form while cooking.

Clear a space on a smooth, clean surface. Take a few tablespoons of the thickened mixture and use a spatula to spread it on the work surface as thin and as even as you can without wasting much time. Repeat this procedure until you've spread all the mixture into a large square or rectangle.

In only a few minutes, the mixture should solidify. Cut it into strips about 1 inch (2.5 cm) wide. Roll each strip into a swirl, in the manner of a jelly roll or an ice cream roll and set aside on a platter. When all the strips have been rolled up, heat the *ghee* in a saucepan and fry the mustard seeds until they finish popping. Add the asafoetida, wait a few seconds, and add the grated coconut. Stir-fry the coconut for a few seconds; then pour the fried seasonings over the swirls. Sprinkle the chopped coriander leaves over them and serve them hot or at room temperature.

Preparation and cooking time: 25 min

Chidwa

Mixed fried and seasoned tidbits

One day in India, Kiśorī dāsī wanted to please Śrīla Prabhupāda by cooking something special for him, so she went to the best chidwa wallas (professional chidwa makers) *in New Delhi to learn their secrets. When she made her own* chidwa *the next day and put it on Śrīla Prabhupāda's lunch* thali, *Śrīla Prabhupāda liked it so much that he called for Kiśorī and asked how she had made it. Kiśorī was delighted to tell him.*

1 cup (50 g) deep-fried puffed rice
1 cup (200 g) dried green peas, soaked overnight in water double their volume
⅓ cup (50 g) grated potatoes
½ cup (50 g) tiny cauliflower flowerets
¾ cup (50 g) diced skinned eggplant
⅓ cup (75 g) cashew nuts, slivered almonds, or pistachio nuts
⅓ cup (50 g) raisins
1 fresh chili, chopped
½ tsp ground black pepper
½ tsp brown sugar
¼ tsp asafoetida
1¼ tsp salt

If the puffed rice is not already deep-fried, deep-fry it for a few seconds in smoking hot *ghee* and let it drain. Drain the soaked green peas thoroughly and deep-fry them for 45 seconds to 1 minute, until they swell and become crisp. Deep-fry the grated potatoes, the tiny cauliflower flowerets, the diced skinned eggplant, and the nuts. Set them aside in a colander to drain. Once all the items have drained, combine them in a mixing bowl. Add the raisins, the spices, and the sugar and mix well. *Chidwa* can be eaten as a snack or as a side dish.

Preparation and cooking time: 30 min

Malai kofta

Deep-fried cheese balls in cream sauce

1 lb (450 g) paneer
3 tbs white flour
1 fresh chili, minced
1 tbs chopped fresh coriander leaves
2½ teaspoon salt
ghee or vegetable oil for deep-frying
6 medium-sized tomatoes
2 tbs grated coconut
2 fresh chilies, seeded and minced
1 teaspoon ground coriander
1 teaspoon grated ginger
1 teaspoon cumin seeds
¼ teaspoon asafoetida
2 tbs ghee or vegetable oil
1⅔ cups (400 ml) sour cream
1 tbs chopped fresh coriander or parsley leaves
1 lemon or lime

Knead the *paneer* vigorously until it is smooth and soft. Add the flour, chili, fresh coriander leaves, and 1 teaspoon of salt. Knead it again to blend the ingredients evenly. Break off pieces and roll them into walnut-sized balls. Heat the *ghee* or oil until almost smoking hot. Deep-fry the cheese balls for several minutes until they are golden brown and crisp. Drain and set aside.

Blanch the tomatoes, peel them, and mash them to a purée. Then make a *masala* paste by grinding (or blending) together the coconut and all the spices except the remaining salt and coriander leaves. Heat the 2 tablespoons of *ghee* or oil in a medium-sized saucepan and fry this paste for about 1 minute. Now add the tomato purée, cream, coriander leaves, and remaining salt. Simmer for 10 minutes, stirring often.

Put the *kofta* balls into the sauce 10 minutes before serving. Garnish each portion with a wedge of lemon or lime.

Preparation and cooking time: 20 to 40 min

Chutneys and Raitas

1 Tamatar chatni *(Tomato chutney)* 232
2 Seb ki chatni *(Apple chutney)* 233
3 Anannas ki chatni *(Pineapple chutney)* 234
4 Narial chatni *(Coconut chutney)* 235
5 Dhanya chatni *(Fresh coriander chutney)* 236
6 Pudina chatni *(Fresh mint chutney)* 237
7 Khajur imli ki chatni *(Date and tamarind chutney)* 238
8 Aam chatni *(Mango chutney)* 239
9 Alu narial raita *(Potato and coconut salad)* 240
10 Kakri raita *(Cucumber and yogurt salad)* 242
11 Palak ka raita *(Spinach and yogurt salad)* 243
12 Bundi raita *(Chickpea flour pearls in seasoned yogurt)* 244
13 Kela raita *(Sliced bananas in yogurt sauce)* 245

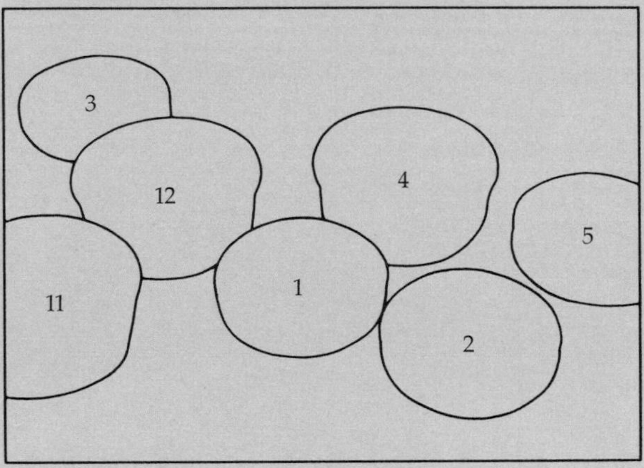

CHUTNEYS and *raitas* bring out the flavor of the main courses. Spicy chutneys enhance mild dishes, cool *raitas* enhance spicy dishes, and the vivid colors of both enhance the appearance of a meal. With a little experience, you'll be able to choose the right chutney or *raita* to match the main dish.

In this chapter you'll find two kinds of chutneys: cooked and fresh. Cooked chutneys are made sometimes from vegetables but most often from fruits. They take a long time to cook so that the ingredients merge and thicken. Fresh chutneys are not cooked. You make them by grinding fresh ingredients into a smooth paste.

Whether cooked or fresh, all chutneys are sweet and spicy. They also perk up the appetite and stimulate digestion. A good chutney, Śrīla Prabhupāda said, is so hot you can hardly eat it but so sweet you can't resist. You need only a teaspoon or two to accent a meal. Serve it in a little bowl or directly on the plate or *thali,* next to the rice. The uninitiated should be warned not to take a whole mouthful at once.

Some chutneys make a good dip for savories. Tomato chutney, for example, goes well with vegetable *pakoras, kachoris,* and fried potato patties.

Raitas consist of either cooked or raw vegetables, or fresh fruits, combined with spiced yogurt. Served in small bowls they are light, refreshing, and easily prepared.

Tamatar chutni
Tomato chutney

Although tomato chutney may look like ketchup, it tastes a lot better. Besides, ketchup can't be offered to Lord Kṛṣṇa, or eaten by devotees, because it contains vinegar and onions, which according to the Vedas *increase the quality of ignorance.*

8 ripe tomatoes
4 tbs water
2 tbs ghee
2 tsp black mustard seeds
2 or 3 fresh chilies, minced
5 cloves
2 bay leaves
1 cinnamon stick, 2 inches (5 cm) long
1 tsp cumin seeds
2 tsp ground coriander
1 tbs grated fresh ginger
1 pinch asafoetida
1 tsp salt
4 tbs brown sugar

Blanch the tomatoes, purée them with 4 tablespoons of water, and set them aside. In a medium-sized saucepan, heat the ghee over medium heat and toss in the mustard seeds. Cover the pan. When the mustard seeds stop sputtering, stir-fry the next six spices and the ginger for 1 minute. Put the tomatoes in the saucepan with the asafoetida and salt. Mix with a wooden spoon, and cook uncovered over low heat for 20 – 30 minutes. Stir occasionally at first, then more often as the chutney thickens, until there is hardly any liquid in the pot.

Now stir in the sugar and raise the heat. With a quicker motion stir the chutney for 5 minutes more, or until it has thickened to the consistency of thick tomato sauce. Discard the cloves, bay leaves, and cinnamon stick. Transfer the chutney into a bowl and serve at room temperature with a meal or as a dip for savories.

Preparation and cooking time: 40 to 50 min

Seb ki chutni
Apple chutney

Practically any type of apple will make a good apple chutney. Select firm, ripe ones and avoid those that are oversized and mealy.

The recipe may also be used for making chutneys from other fruits, such as peaches, plums, apricots, mangos, guavas, gooseberries, and blackberries. Omit the asafoetida if you like, and use the dried chilies according to taste.

6 medium-sized apples
4 tbs ghee or vegetable oil
2 tsp grated fresh ginger
2 cinnamon sticks, 2 inches (5 cm) long
1 tsp anise seeds
2 or 3 dried chilies, crushed
5 cloves
1 tsp turmeric
1 pinch asafoetida (optional)
4 tbs water
4 tbs brown sugar

Wash, peel, and core the apples. Then cut them into small chunks. Heat the *ghee* or vegetable oil in a saucepan. When it begins to smoke, drop in the ginger, cinnamon sticks, anise seeds, chilies, and cloves. Stir-fry until the anise seeds darken (about 30 seconds). Immediately add the turmeric and asafoetida, then the chunks of apple. Stir-fry to brown the apples for 5 or 6 minutes. Then add the water.

Cover and cook over high heat for about 15 minutes, stirring often, until the apples are quite soft. Mash the apples in the pot. Add the sugar, increase the heat, and stir continuously until the chutney thickens. Remove the cinnamon sticks and cloves. Serve at room temperature with hot *puris,* or with a sweet at the end of the meal.

Preparation and cooking time: 30 min

Anannas ki chutni
Pineapple chutney

Pineapples are popular in India. The field-ripened ones are best. A pineapple is ripe when some of the inner leaves pull out easily, the eyes protrude, and the fruit has a sweet smell.

1 medium-large pineapple
1 tbs ghee
1 tsp cumin seeds
2 fresh chilies, seeded and minced
½ tsp turmeric
½ tsp ground cinnamon
4 tbs water
1 cup (175 g) brown sugar

Hold the pineapple upright and pare off the skin with a sharp knife, then dig out the eyes. Cut the pineapple lengthwise into quarters, ad remove the core from each quarter. Then cut each quarter lengthwise into three strips, and cut each strip into chunks. Set the pineapple aside in a bowl.

Heat the *ghee* in a saucepan and fry the cumin seeds and chilies until they darken. Toss in the turmeric and ground cinnamon; then immediately follow with the pineapple chunks. After stir-frying for 4 to 5 minutes, add the water. Cover the pan. Cook over low heat for 15 minutes, stirring every now and then. Remove the cover and continue to cook until most of the liquid is cooked off. Finally, stir in the sugar and cook over the same low heat until the chutney thickens again (about 10 minutes).

Pineapple chutney can be served with puris towards the end of a meal, or with another dessert such as *shrikhand* or *kulfi*.

Preparation and cooking time: 30 min

Narial chutni
Coconut chutney

Take care to buy coconuts that are fresh. There should be no cracks in the shells, and they should be heavy with milk. The coconut milk should smell pleasant and taste sweet. If it smells oily and tastes sour, the coconut will be sour. Coconut chutney goes well with dosas, *and can be used as a dip for savories such as* doklas, pakoras, *and* gajar vadas.

1½ cups (200 g) fresh coconut or 1½ cups (100 g) desiccated coconut
1 tbs granulated sugar
1 tbs grated fresh ginger
1 tbs finely chopped fresh coriander leaves
2 or 3 fresh chilies, seeded and minced
3 tbs lemon juice
½ tsp salt

Break the coconut and save the coconut milk. Detach the pulp from the shell and pare off the brown skin. Cut the pulp into small pieces and blend them in an electric blender with all the other ingredients. Add enough coconut milk or water to make the mixture smooth. If you don't have a blender, grate the coconut and use a mortar and pestle or a grinding stone to make a smooth mixture. As an alternative to coconut milk or water, you can use 1¼ cups (300 ml) yogurt, which gives a creamier texture.

Preparation time: 20 min

Dhanya chutni

Fresh coriander chutney

Fresh coriander can be recognized, by its smell and by its leaves, which are feathery on the top of the plant and fan-like on the bottom. When making coriander chutney, use only the upper, leafy portions of the plant; the lower stalks become stringy when pulverized.

Coriander chutney should be eaten on the same day it is made. The yogurt makes it a relatively mild chutney. A small amount—two or three tablespoons—is sufficient with a meal.

2 oz (50 g) fresh coriander leaves (weight without stems)
4 tbs grated coconut
1 tbs fresh ginger, grated
1 or 2 fresh chilies, chopped
3 tbs lemon or lime juice
1 cup (250 g) plain yogurt
1 tsp sugar
1 tsp salt
½ tsp cumin seeds, roasted and ground

Thoroughly wash the coriander leaves and chop them fine. Put all the ingredients into an electric blender. Mix until they form a smooth paste.

Cover and refrigerate until ready to serve.

Preparation time: 15 min

Pudina chutni

Fresh mint chutney

This chutney goes well in small quantities with any meal.

2 oz (50 g) fresh mint leaves
1 tbs grated fresh ginger
2 fresh chilies, minced
4 tbs lemon juice
1 tsp salt
2 tsp sugar

Wash the mint thoroughly and shake it dry. Use only the leaves and the thinnest stalks; discard the thick stems. Blend all the ingredients together in an electric blender, with just enough water to make a smooth paste.

Serve, preferably chilled.

For a tasty chutney using both mint and coriander leaves, mix the same ingredients in an electric blender, and add only 1 oz (25 g) of mint leaves. Add 1 oz (25 g) of coriander leaves, 3 oz (75 g) of roasted or deep-fried peanuts, and 2 oz (50 g) of tamarind pulp. Blend well. This recipe may take about 10 minutes longer than *pudina chutni*.

Preparation time: 15 min

Khajur imli ki chutni
Date and tamarind chutney

This chutney is simultaneously sweet, sour, and hot. It goes well with most fried savories.

2 oz (50 g) tamarind
1¼ cups (275 ml) water
¾ cup (150 g) dates, pitted and chopped
2 tsp sugar
½ tsp salt
½ tsp ground cumin
1 pinch cayenne pepper

Break the lump of tamarind into small pieces and boil them in the water for 10 minutes. Then pour the tamarind and water through a strainer. With a wooden spoon push as much of the pulp as possible through the strainer into the water, scraping the bottom of the strainer every few seconds. Continue until all the pulp has been extracted from the seeds and fiber.

To this juice, add all the other ingredients. Cook over medium heat, uncovered, until most of the liquid cooks off and the chutney takes on the consistency of marmalade. This chutney goes very well with savories such as *kathmir vadas, dahi vadas,* and *urad dal kachoris.*

Preparation and cooking time: 35 min

Aam chutni
Mango chutney

You may be surprised to discover that the flavor of a green, unripe mango may rival the flavor of a colorful ripe mango. Often the flesh beneath the skin of a green mango will be orange colored. Adding the sugar to this recipe will give the chutney a sweet and sour taste.

1 large green mango
1 fresh chili
½ tsp grated fresh ginger
1 tsp salt
1 tsp sugar (optional)
2 tbs fresh mint leaves

Peel the mango, cut the flesh off in strips, and scrape the rest off the seed. Chop the flesh. Then grind it with all the other ingredients in an electric blender (or in a mortar and pestle) to form a thick pulp. Serve portions of the chutney in small dishes as an accompaniment to a meal.

Preparation time: 15 min

Alu narial raita
Potato and coconut salad

This raita, consisting of boiled potatoes, grated coconut, and seasoned yogurt, goes well with any meal.

Potatoes are full of vitamins B, C, and G, plus minerals and protein. Don't use potatoes whose skins are greenish (they're apt to be bitter) or sprouted potatoes (they tend to be watery).

6 medium-sized potatoes
1¾ cups (425 ml) plain yogurt
2 tsp salt
1½ cups (100 g) grated coconut
1 tbs ghee
1 tsp black mustard seeds
1 tbs grated fresh ginger
1 fresh chili, minced
2 firm ripe tomatoes washed and cut into 8 wedges each
several sprigs of parsley

Boil the potatoes until they are soft. Peel them, cut them into cubes, and put them in a bowl. Refrigerate.

Mix together the yogurt, salt, and grated coconut. Heat the *ghee* in a small pan; then toss in the mustard seeds. Cover the pan immediately so that the seeds don't jump all over the stove. When they finish popping, add the ginger and the chili. Stir for a few seconds. Empty this *masala* into the bowl of yogurt, drop the potatoes in, mix, and toss gently to give the potatoes an even coating of the yogurt and the spices.

Serve chilled, garnished with a sprig of parsley and wedges of tomato.

Preparation and cooking time: 30 min

Opposite page: *Alu narial raita*

Kakri raita
Cucumber and yogurt salad

Hari Caraṇa dāsa, the head cook of Gopal's Restaurant in Auckland, New Zealand, says that cucumbers are at their best when they're about 10 inches (25 cm) long, firm, bright green, and shiny. If the skin is tough, you can peel or score it; if the seeds are large, it will be worth the extra time to scrape them out.

½ tsp cumin seeds
2 medium-sized cucumbers
1¼ cups (300 ml) plain yogurt
¼ tsp garam masala
¼ tsp salt
¼ tsp ground black pepper
2 pinches asafoetida (optional)

Dry-roast the cumin seeds and grind them into a powder. Wash the cucumbers and grate them through the large holes of a metal grater. Squeeze out the excess liquid and combine the grated cucumber with all the other ingredients in a mixing bowl. Toss. Serve chilled.

Preparation time: 15 min

Palak ka raita
Spinach and yogurt salad

Any kind of spinach or spinach-like leafy green can be used for palak ka raita. *New Zealand spinach (which, by the way, is not a true spinach) can be easily grown at home all through the summer and fall.*

1 lb (450 g) fresh spinach, washed and stemmed
2 cups (475 ml) plain yogurt
1 tsp cumin seeds; dry-roasted and ground
½ tsp garam masala
¼ tsp ground black pepper
1 tsp salt

Make sure the spinach is washed in several changes of water. Then plunge the leaves in boiling water for a minute or two to wilt them. Drain, press out the excess water, and chop the leaves coarse.

Put the yogurt in a large bowl with the spinach and other ingredients. Mix with a fork. *Palak ka raita* is tasty served with puris or as a refreshing side dish to an elaborate meal.

Preparation and cooking time: 20 min

Bundi raita

Chickpea-flour pearls in seasoned yogurt

1 cup (100 g) chickpea flour
3 tsp salt
¼ cup (50 ml) cold water
½ cup (275 ml) warm water
2½ cups (600 ml) plain yogurt
½ tsp ground cumin
2 pinches cayenne pepper
ghee for deep-frying
¼ tsp paprika
1 tsp finely chopped fresh coriander or parsley leaves

Sift the chickpea flour into a large mixing bowl. Add ½ teaspoon of salt. Slowly pour in the cold water, mixing constantly, until you have a thick, smooth batter. Set aside. Dissolve 2 teaspoons of salt in the warm water and set aside also. Put the yogurt in a bowl with the remaining ½ teaspoon of salt, the ground cumin (reserve a little for garnishing later), and the cayenne pepper. Mix well and refrigerate.

Heat the *ghee* for deep-frying over medium heat. The *ghee* is hot enough when a drop of batter put into it immediately rises to the surface and sizzles. Now hold over the *ghee* a colander with large holes (⅛ inch/3 mm). With the help of a spatula, push several spoonfuls of batter through the holes. Cover the surface of the ghee with droplets. They should cook slowly, for about 2 to 5 minutes, until golden yellow. They should not turn brown. Test to see if the *bundis* are properly cooked by taking one out and pressing it between your fingers. If it is crisp, they are ready. Drop them in the salted water to soak. Transform all the batter into *bundis* and let them soak for 15 minutes.

Just before serving, take the *bundis* out of the water and squeeze them gently between the palms of your hands to remove the excess water. Be careful not to break them. Now mix most of the *bundis* into the yogurt and use the rest as a garnish. Sprinkle with the ground cumin, paprika, and chopped coriander leaves. Serve chilled.

Preparation and cooking time: 20 min
Soaking time: 15 min

Kela raita
Sliced bananas in yogurt sauce

This recipe comes from the monthly magazine of the Hare Kṛṣṇa Movement, Back to Godhead, *which has a section called "Lord Kṛṣṇa's Cuisine." The recipes for this section come from Yamunā dāsī, one of the best cooks in the Hare Kṛṣṇa Movement. This is her favorite* raita *recipe.*

4 small, firm, ripe bananas
2 cups (475 ml) plain yogurt
1 tsp salt
½ tsp sugar
3 tbs chopped fresh mint leaves
2 tbs ghee or vegetable oil
2 tsp black mustard seeds
1 fresh chili, seeded and chopped

Peel the bananas and cut them diagonally to make slices ⅛ inch (3 mm) thick. Set them aside. Whisk the yogurt, salt, sugar, and chopped mint leaves in a mixing bowl. Then add the sliced bananas.

In a small saucepan, heat the *ghee* or vegetable oil over medium heat. When it is hot, add the mustard seeds and cover the pan. Remove the pan from the heat when the seeds stop crackling and popping. Toss in the chili, swirl the pan to mix the ingredients, then pour the seasonings into the yogurt and bananas. Mix well and cover. Refrigerate at least one hour before serving.

Preparation and cooking time: 10 min
Chilling time: 1 hr

Sweets

1 Khir *(Sweet rice)* 251
2 Shrikhand *(Thick flavored yogurt)* 252
3 Burfi *(Milk fudge)* 253
4 Sandesh *(Indian cheese dessert)* 254
5 Kasturi sandesh *(Fancy Indian cheese sweet)* 255
6 Misthi dahi *(Thick sweetened yogurt)* 257
7 Rasagulla *(Cheese balls soaked in rose-flavored syrup)* 258
8 Ras malai *(Cheese balls soaked in cream sauce)* 259
9 Suji ka halava *(Semolina pudding)* 260
10 Bhuni hui chinni ka halava *(Caramel-flavored semolina pudding)* 261
11 Gajar halava *(Carrot pudding)* 262
12 Badam aur pista ka halava *(Hazelnut fudge)* 263
13 Phal ka halava *(Fruit pudding)* 264
14 Khir sevian *(Creamed vermicelli pudding)* 266
15 Kulfi *(Indian ice cream)* 267
16 Besan laddu *(Toasted chick-pea flour confection)* 268
17 Dvaraka burfi *(Toasted chick-pea flour fudge)* 269
18 Luglu *(Chick-pea flour and dried-fruit balls)* 270
19 Jalebi *(Crisp fried spirals in syrup)* 271
20 Mithe samosa *(Fruit turnovers)* 273
21 Phal ka pakora *(Fruit fritters)* 275
22 Kerwai *(Deep-fried stuffed banana balls)* 276
23 Malpura *(Sweet dumplings in flavored yogurt)* 277
24 Gulab jamun *(Deep-fried milk balls in syrup)* 278

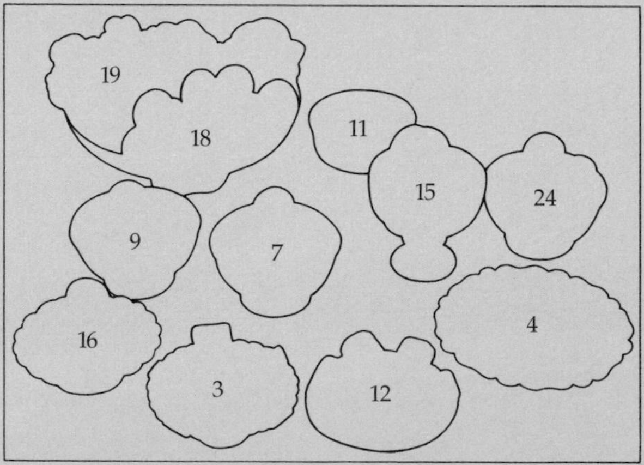

THE recipes in this section represent only a sample of the literally thousands of sweets that originate in India, especially in West Bengal, the "sweets capital of the world." Some transcendentalists avoid sweets at any cost, for fear of agitating their senses and falling down from the spiritual path, but Kṛṣṇa's devotees relish whatever has been offered to Lord Kṛṣṇa, including sweets, and experience the inconceivable mercy of God by doing so. Śrīla Prabhupāda, however, always stressed moderation in whatever one does. Even though devotees have a healthy diet, and Indian sweets are usually made with wholesome ingredients, he advised that for the devotees to keep safe on the "razor's edge" of spiritual life, they should eat very few sweets during the week (better to save them for the temple guests) and wholeheartedly partake of the "love feast" on Sundays.

Indian sweets are generally made from milk products, fresh fruits, whole grains, chickpea flour, and nuts. If you don't want to use granulated sugar, you can substitute unrefined sugar or mild-flavored honey. It's interesting to note that refined sugar was introduced in India during the Mogul period—it didn't exist in Vedic cooking before then. Unrefined sugars, such as *gur* (cane sugar) or *jaggery* (palm sugar), were used instead. Both are excellent sweeteners, and it's worthwhile to buy some to experience their special flavors. The *Āyur-veda* mentions honey as one of the best sweeteners, but says that cooking makes it toxic. So avoid using honey for baking, and don't boil it (instead you can stir it into a liquid that's very hot, but not boiling). Other sweeteners such as rice, sugar, barley malt, and even maple syrup can also be used. You have to experiment when using substitutes because sugars, like flours, are not always interchangeable measure for measure—their sweetening powers vary. Generally, one part of granulated sugar equals one part of firmly packed brown sugar or ½ to ¾ parts honey.

Of all Indian sweets, milk sweets are the most delectable. And with traditional cooking methods you can make them in great variety. Boil down milk over high heat to make *khir* or *burfi*. Cook fresh cheese with sugar to make *sandesh* or *rasgulla*. Flavor thickened yogurt to get a delicious creamy dessert, called *shrikhand*. Or deep-fry powdered-milk balls and soak them in thick syrup to make one of the world's most exquisite sweets, *gulab jamuns*.

Another group of sweets, including *dvaraka burfi, luglu,* and *laddu,* are made from toasted chickpea flour and dried fruits. You can make them in large numbers and keep them for days. There are also various kinds of *halava*. No resemblance to the Turkish variety—these are made from combinations of fresh fruits, hazelnuts, carrots, and semolina.

Khir
Sweet rice

Śrīla Prabhupāda taught us that a feast is not a true feast without sweet rice. So the head cooks of our centers often stay up late Saturday night preparing sweet rice for the Sunday feast. Although there are many different ways to prepare sweet rice, this recipe is the traditional one, and a great favorite.

⅓ cup (50 g) short or medium-grained white rice
10 cups (2.4 l) whole milk
½ tsp ground cardamom seeds
2 bay leaves
½ cup (100 g) sugar
2 tbs sliced almonds, lightly toasted (optional)

Wash the rice and set it aside to drain. In a tall pot that can hold at least twice the volume of the milk, bring the milk to a boil; then adjust the heat so the milk is always rising and frothing, but not bubbling over. To minimize the cooking time, let the milk boil vigorously, uncovered, for the first 15 minutes, while you stir it rhythmically with a wooden spatula to prevent the thick milk on the bottom of the pot from scorching.

Drop the rice into the milk along with the bay leaves. Continue stirring. Keep over medium-high heat and stir very carefully for another 20 minutes until the rice breaks up and rolls with the milk. By now the milk should be reduced to two thirds of its original volume. Stir in the sugar, almonds, and ground cardamom seeds. Cook for 5 more minutes and remove from the heat. Sweet rice should be only slightly thick when removed from the heat, because it will thicken when refrigerated. Chill well before serving—the colder the sweet rice, the better it tastes.

For other classic flavors, replace the ground cardamom seeds with a teaspoon of rose-water and a few pinches of saffron powder, or season with bay leaves only, and add a tiny pinch of natural camphor at the end of cooking.

Preparation and cooking time: 1 hr 15 min
Chilling time: 2 hr

Shrikhand
Thick flavored yogurt

This delicate sweet, an easy-to-prepare guaranteed success, is the perfect dessert with puris, at room temperature or chilled. For an extra treat, put it in dessert bowls and freeze it.

6 cups (1.4 liters) plain yogurt
½ cup (75 g) confectioners' sugar
¼ tsp powdered saffron or 5 saffron strands

Hang the yogurt in two layers of cheesecloth over a bowl to catch the drippings. Allow it to drain overnight, or for at least 5 hours. Then scrape it into a bowl. The drained yogurt should be thick, half its original volume. Add the powdered sugar and saffron to the yogurt. Beat with a whisk. If you are using saffron strands, steep them in a little rose-water before adding to the drained yogurt.

You may also flavor your *shrikhand* with ½ cup (50 g) of crushed red berries, crushed pistachio nuts, a few drops of rose-water or ghee, or a teaspoon of finely grated rind of orange or lemon.

Draining time: overnight or at least 5 hrs
Preparation time: 10 hr

Burfi
Milk fudge

This milk sweet, offered to Lord Kṛṣṇa every morning in our temples, is made by cooking down milk over high heat until it becomes a thick paste. The paste is then sweetened and allowed to set. Burfi *is well worth the time spent making it.*

For a richer burfi, *instead of butter and plain milk, use thick cream or a mixture of two parts thick cream to one part milk.*

8 cups (1.9 l) whole milk
½ cup (100 g) sugar
1 tbs butter

Pour the milk into a wide, heavy-bottomed cast-iron or stainless steel pot and place over high heat. When the milk is about to boil and rise, lower the heat so that the milk boils steadily but without rising. Cooking down the milk requires patience—it may take about one hour (a good opportunity to practice chanting the Hare Kṛṣṇa *mantra*). Stir regularly and uniformly so that the milk does not stick to the bottom of the pan. As the milk thickens, stir faster, using a wide wooden spatula to scrape the bottom of the pot. Either stir carefully on low heat, or vigorously on high heat, but you must stir to prevent it from scorching.

When the milk becomes pastelike and the spatula leaves a momentary trail, add the sugar and butter. Continue cooking, stirring all the time, until the *burfi* becomes very thick and sticky. Cook it until you think it can't cook down any more; then let it cook a few minutes more. *Burfi* is intrinsically tasty, but if you wish to flavor it, now stir in the flavors. Crushed nuts, vanilla extract, toasted coconut, powdered cardamom seeds, ground cinnamon—all are typical flavorings for *burfi.*

Transfer the *burfi* onto a buttered plate. When it is cool enough to handle, shape it into a square cake 1 inch (2.5 cm) thick. Cut it into pieces when it's firm enough to hold its shape.

Preparation and cooking time: 45 min to 10 hr

Sandesh
Indian cheese dessert

On Kṛṣṇa's early-morning plate of milk sweets you'll always find sandesh. *This recipe for basic* sandesh *is tasty by itself. But if you wish to flavor it or decorate it, you can add food coloring or flavorings or mold it into different shapes.*

1¼ lb (550 g) paneer
¾ cup (150 g) sugar

Curdle milk and collect the *paneer,* as described on page 94. Rinse the *paneer* under cold water and squeeze out the excess water by tightening the cheesecloth and firmly squeezing it several times. Leave the paneer to hang for 45 minutes, or put it under a weight for 20 minutes, so that it becomes fairly dry. Turn the paneer onto a clean work surface and knead it vigorously, until its granular texture disappears and you have a soft dough free of lumps. The softer the dough, the better the *sandesh* will be.

Divide the dough in half. Take one half and knead it with the sugar. (The general rule is to knead one half of the dough with sugar one third the original volume of the dough). Cook it slowly in a frying pan on a low heat, stirring constantly with a wooden spoon. The thick *sandesh* will soon become smooth, then thicken again. When it thickens and pulls away from the bottom of the pan (this should take from 4 to 6 minutes), remove it from the heat. Avoid overcooking the *sandesh* because it will become dry and grainy.

Finally, knead the cooked and uncooked *paneer* together (along with a flavoring or coloring agent, if desired), flatten it into a cake 1 inch (2.5 cm) thick, and cut it into squares when it is cool.

Another traditional way of finishing *sandesh* is to knead a few drops of green or red food coloring into the dough and form it into 2 inch (5 cm) oblong shapes. You can coat these with plain or toasted grated coconut.

Preparation and cooking time: 40 min

Kasturi sandesh

Fancy Indian cheese dessert

Our Gītā-nāgarī farm in Port Royal, Pennsylvania, has received several awards from the Dairymen's Association for having the best herd of Brown Swiss cows in the state. At the dairymen's banquet, the Hare Kṛṣṇa display table steals the show with milk confections such as this delicately flavored sandesh, *sometimes called "royal* sandesh."

1¼ lb (550 g) paneer
¾ cup (150 g) sugar
1½ tsp ground cardamom seeds
3 pinches saffron powder
2 tbs grated pistachio nuts
1 tsp rose-water
1 small red rose (optional)

Make basic *sandesh* as described in the previous recipe. Flavor it by kneading in the ground cardamom seeds and powdered saffron. Shape the *sandesh* into a flat cake. Lightly score the surface with a fork, sprinkle the rose-water and ground pistachio nuts over the top, and gently pat the pistachios down.

When it's cool, cut it into squares. If you like, decorate each piece with a rose petal.

Preparation and cooking time: 40 min

Misthi dahi

Thick sweetened yogurt

With its diorama museum, Indian-style temple room, spectacular grounds and architecture, the Bhaktivedanta Cultural Center in Detroit (formerly the Lawrence Fisher Mansion) gives people an introduction to the beauty of Kṛṣṇa consciousness and has become one of Michigan's major tourist attractions. Mukhyā dāsī has overseen the center's cooking for the past ten years. Her misthi dahi *is a favorite at Govinda's, the center's restaurant.*

12 cups (3 l) milk
½ cup (100 g) sugar
or ¼ cup (75 g) honey
½ tsp powdered saffron
or 1 tsp saffron threads, crushed
¼ cup (50 g) plain yogurt

Cook down the milk as described in the recipe for *burfi* until it is about one third its original volume. Then prop a strainer over a small metal bowl or earthenware container and strain the condensed milk to remove any lumps. Allow the milk to stand until the temperature drops to around 115° F (45° C). Mukhyā says she never uses a thermometer when she makes *misthi dahi.* Instead, she knows the milk is ready when she can hold her little finger in it, without scorching it, just long enough to say the Hare Kṛṣṇa mantra, Hare Kṛṣṇa, Hare Kṛṣṇa, Kṛṣṇa Kṛṣṇa, Hare Hare/ Hare Rāma, Hare Rāma, Rāma Rāma, Hare Hare.

Now remove the layer of skin from the surface of the milk. Whisk the sweetener, saffron, and yogurt into the milk. Cover the container and put it in a quiet place close to a source of heat so that the mixture stays very warm. The *misthi dahi* should be firm in 4 to 6 hours. Then refrigerate it.

Serve *misthi dahi* chilled, sprinkled with some grated nutmeg.

Preparation and cooking time: 45 min
Setting time: 4 to 6 hr

Opposite page: *Misthi dahi*

Rasgulla

Cooked cheese balls soaked in rose-flavored syrup

This is one of the milk sweets that gives Bengal its reputation as the sweets capital of the world. Soak the cooked cheese balls in the syrup from four hours to two days. Śrīla Prabhupāda once said that the mark of a well cooked rasgulla *is that it makes a squeaking sound when you bite into it.*

10 oz (275 g) paneer
3 cups (725 ml) water
1½ cups (300 g) sugar
1 tbs rose-water

If you use raw milk to make *paneer,* skim off most of the cream. If the *paneer* is too oily, the cheese balls may fall apart during the cooking. Hang the fresh *paneer* or press it with a weight until it is not quite dry.

Turn the *paneer* onto a work surface and crumble it. Using a pushing motion, knead it vigorously with the heels of your hands until it becomes smooth and your hands feel greasy. Now break off walnut-sized pieces and form them into balls that are perfectly smooth and round, without any cracks.

Make a syrup by boiling the water and sugar for 5 minutes in a medium-sized saucepan. Pour half the syrup into a bowl, flavor it with the rose-water, and set it aside to cool. Put the saucepan with the other half of the syrup back over the heat and gently drop the balls in the syrup. Leave enough room for them to swell they almost double in size. Adjust the heat to keep the water at a gently rolling boil. Cover with a lid and cook for 10 minutes more, until the *paneer* balls are swollen and spongelike. While the *paneer* balls cook, sprinkle some cold water over them once or twice. This makes them spongy and whitish. Now carefully transfer each of the balls with a spoon to the cool syrup. Chill.

Serve each guest 2 or 3 *rasgullas* with a little syrup.

Preparation and cooking time: 45 min
Soaking time: at least 4 hrs

Ras malai

Cheese balls soaked in cream sauce

Ras malai *is the most opulent member of the* rasgulla *family and one of the choicest of Indian sweets. An average serving consists of two or three balls covered with some of the cream sauce.*

10 oz (275 g) paneer
2 cups (400 g) sugar
2 tsp ground pistachio nuts
2 tsp ground almonds
5 cups (1.2 liters) milk
4 tbs thick cream
3 or 4 drops almond essence
2½ cups (600 ml) water

Prepare the cheese balls as directed in the recipe for *rasgulla*. Then make a mixture of 1 teaspoon each of sugar, ground pistachio nuts, and ground almonds. Make a depression in the center of each cheese ball and fill it with a little of the mixture. Pinch the stuffed cheese balls closed and roll them between your hands to make them round. (If you prefer, you can use the cheese balls without the filling).

Cook the milk over high heat, stirring every now and then, until it reduces to two thirds of its original volume. Add the cream and ⅓ cup (75 g) of sugar, bring to a boil. Then set aside.

Mix the water with the remaining sugar in a saucepan. Boil for 15 minutes, and then add a cup of water. Lower the heat to simmering and put the cheese balls into the syrup. Cover the saucepan to keep the syrup at a gently rolling boil. After 10 minutes, remove the cover. Then cook the cheese balls about 10 minutes more. They will swell to almost double their original size.

To see whether the cheese balls are done, tap one with your finger. If it feels soft, they are ready. Remove them from the heat, take them out of the syrup, and put them into the cream sauce to soak. Sprinkle with the almond essence and ground nuts. Serve warm or chilled.

Preparation and cooking time: 1 hr 15 min
Soaking time: 30 min

Suji ka halava
Semolina pudding

When devotees chant the holy names of the Lord on the streets of cities around the world, they often distribute free halava to the public. In France, where we distribute thousands of servings of halava *each week, people often approach devotees to ask for the* "petits gâteaux" *(little cakes) and for the recipe.*

2¾ cups (650 ml) water, or milk, or half of each
1½ cups (300 g) sugar
10 saffron strands (optional)
½ teaspoon grated nutmeg
¼ cup (35 g) raisins
¼ cup (35 g) hazelnuts or walnuts (optional)
1 cup (200 g) butter
1½ cup (225 g) semolina or farina

Combine the water (or milk), sugar, saffron, and nutmeg in a saucepan and boil for 1 minute. Add the raisins, lower the heat and let simmer. Lightly deep-fry the nuts, chop them coarse, and set them aside.

Melt the butter in a saucepan over medium-low heat. Add the semolina and stir-fry with a wooden spoon for about 10 or 15 minutes, until the semolina is golden brown and the butter begins to separate from the grains. Lower the heat. Now slowly pour the sweetened liquid into the grains with one hand while stirring with the other. Be careful! The mixture will sputter as the liquid hits the hot grains. Stir briskly for a moment to break any lumps. Add the chopped nuts. Cover and simmer for 2 or 3 minutes, until all the liquid is absorbed into the grains. Finally, give the *halava* a few quick stirs to fluff it up. Serve *halava* hot or at room temperature.

Preparation and cooking time: 25 min

Bhuni hui chinni ka halava

Caramel-flavored semolina pudding

This opulent, caramel-flavored halava, *made with milk and served steaming hot, is an irresistible dessert. Somehow, no matter how much you've eaten at a meal, there's always room for two helpings of it at the end.*

2¾ cups (650 ml) milk
1½ cups (300 g) sugar
1 cup (200 g) butter
1½ cups (225 g) semolina or farina
¼ cup (35 g) raisins
2 teaspoon grated orange rind and the juice of 1 orange

Put the milk to boil in a saucepan over medium heat. Then melt the sugar slowly in a medium-sized saucepan over medium-low heat, stirring constantly with a wooden spoon to prevent it from burning. As soon as the melted sugar turns light brown, lower the heat and slowly add the hot milk. The sugar will immediately crystallize. Break up some of the crystals, stir, and leave them to dissolve by putting the saucepan on a burner to simmer.

Wash the first saucepan and melt the butter in it over low heat. Fry the semolina gently in the butter, stirring regularly for about 15 minutes until the grains become lightly browned, then turn the heat down to the lowest setting. Add the raisins, grated orange rind, and orange juice to the caramelized milk; then slowly pour the mixture into the semolina. Stir once or twice to break up any lumps. Cover the pan tightly and cook gently over the same low heat for several minutes, until the grains have absorbed all the liquid. Remove the lid and stir the *halava* a few times to fluff it up and to distribute the raisins evenly.

Preparation and cooking time: 30 min

Gajar halava

Carrot pudding

This is a popular sweet in Northern India. It is important to shred the carrots carefully. The shreds should be fine and as long as possible. Gajar halava *can also be made without milk. Just add a little extra butter and cook the* halava *until it takes on the consistency of marmalade.*

2 lbs (900 g) fresh carrots
¾ cup (150 g) butter
2 cups (500 ml) milk
1½ cups (300 g) sugar
3 tbs slivered almonds, lightly fried
3 tbs raisins
½ tsp ground cardamom

Wash the carrots, scrape them, and shred them through the small holes of a metal grater. Melt the butter in a saucepan and put the grated carrots in it. Cook them uncovered over medium heat for 10 minutes, stirring often to ensure even cooking and prevent burning. Add the milk, sugar, almonds, and raisins. Cook for 20 to 30 more minutes, until the *halava* thickens and forms a single mass in the saucepan.

Put the *halava* on a serving dish. As soon as it is cool enough to handle, shape it into a round cake 1 inch (2.5 cm) thick. Garnish it with the ground cardamom. Refrigerate it for 30 minutes. Then cut it into wedges and serve it as a dessert or a snack.

Preparation and cooking time: 50 min
Chilling time: 30 min

Badam aur pista ka halava

Hazelnut fudge

Be sure to cook this halava *to the required consistency so that it stiffens when cooled. To obtain an even richer* halava, *replace the milk with thick cream and use cashew or pistachio nuts.*

1½ cups (225 g) ground hazelnuts or almonds
1½ cups (300 g) brown sugar
1½ cups (370 ml) milk
2 tbs butter

Begin by mixing together all the ingredients in a saucepan over medium heat. Adjust the heat to maintain the mixture at a rolling boil for 15 minutes, stirring occasionally at first, then more frequently as it thickens. You may need to lower the heat as the liquid diminishes.

When the mixture begins to form a single mass and pull away from the bottom of the pot, transfer it onto a buttered plate to cool. (This *halava,* when hot, can also be spread on cakes as a topping). Dampen your fingers and pat the *halava* into a square cake 1 inch (2.5 cm) thick. When it has hardened, cut into pieces and top each piece with half of a fried cashew nut.

Use a thin spatula to lift the cut pieces from the plate and rearrange them on another plate before serving.

Preparation and cooking time: 30 min

Phal ka halava
Fruit pudding

This simple technique of cooking juicy fruits and sugar until the moisture evaporates and the mixture is thick enough to solidify in a mold has been used in India for thousands of years. Phal ka halava *is a delicacy you can make in large quantities. Under refrigeration, it keeps several days. Children love to eat fruit* halava. *You can also make fruit* halava *from ripe pears, mangos, and other juicy fruits.*

10 medium-sized apples, peeled, cored, and cut into chunks
3 tbs butter
1½ cups (300 g) sugar
⅔ cup (100 g) raisins
3 tbs slivered almonds

Heat the butter in a saucepan and fry the apples for 4 or 5 minutes, stirring often. When they are soft and browned, add 2 tablespoons of water, lower the heat, and cook uncovered for 15 minutes, until the apples merge and thicken. Break up the lumps of apples with a spoon and stir often to prevent scorching. Add the sugar. Continue cooking and stirring until the mixture begins to form one mass and pull away from the bottom of the pot. Raise the heat to medium, and stir continuously to increase the evaporation. When it becomes difficult to move the spoon and the mixture becomes translucent around the edges, remove the pan from the heat. Stir in the raisins and nuts. Cook 2 more minutes; then remove from the heat.

Turn the *halava* onto a plate, and form it into a flat cake 1 inch (2.5 cm) thick. When it's cool, cut it into squares.

Preparation and cooking time: 50 min to 1 hr

Opposite page: *Khir sevian (p. 266)*
Bhuni hui chinni ka halava (p. 261)
Phal ka halava

Khir sevian

Creamed vermicelli pudding

This dish comes from the Mogul school of cooking, and its popularity among Vaiṣṇavas shows us that any vegetarian dish, regardless of its origin, can be offered to Lord Kṛṣṇa. Similarly, any person, regardless of his birth, can chant Kṛṣṇa's holy names and become His pure devotee. In fact, some close associates of Śrī Caitanya Mahāprabhu (the incarnation of Kṛṣṇa who came to earth to spread the chanting of Kṛṣṇa's holy names), came from Muslim families.

6 cups (1.4 l) whole milk
1 tbs butter
6 cloves
1 tsp ground cardamom
2 cups (125 g) fine vermicelli
½ cup (100 g) sugar
1 tbs ground pistachio nuts
1 tbs ground almonds
1¾ cups (425 ml) thick cream
1 tsp rose-water

Bring the milk to a boil; then simmer. In another saucepan, melt the butter and quickly fry the cloves and half of the ground cardamom. Add the vermicelli. Stir-fry until it is lightly browned. Pour the milk into the saucepan and boil on medium heat for 5 minutes, stirring often. Stir in the sugar and the nuts. Lower the heat. Cook for 15 minutes (stirring every few minutes to prevent scorching) or as long as needed to allow the mixture to thicken slightly. Remember that it will continue to thicken after it is removed from the heat.

Take the saucepan off the heat, fold in the cream, and add the rose-water. Pour the *khir sevian* into a serving dish, top with the remaining ground cardamom, and serve hot or cold.

Preparation and cooking time: 20 to 25 min

Kulfi
Indian ice cream

Until the advent of refrigeration, kulfi *was made only by* kulfi wallas *(professional* kulfi *makers). Now, however, anyone can make* kulfi *in his own home. In our temples, we often make it as a special treat for Lord Kṛṣṇa.* Kulfi *is the devotee's ice cream because ordinary ice cream often contains eggs.*

Kulfi *is harder than ice cream, so transfer it from the freezer to the refrigerator two or three hours before serving to let it soften.*

2 tbs rice flour
10 cups (2.3 l) whole milk
⅔ cup (125 g) sugar
4 tbs ground pistachio nuts
1 tbs rose-water
½ tsp ground cardamom

Mix the rice flour and 4 tablespoons of the milk in a bowl to make a smooth batter; then set aside. Boil the rest of the milk and cook it down for 45 minutes, stirring every few minutes, until it reduces to no more than two thirds of its original volume. Now stir the rice flour mixture into the milk along with the ground pistachio nuts and sugar. Boil for another 10 minutes. Then remove from the heat.

Flavor the mixture with rose-water and ground cardamom. Cool it to room temperature; then pour it into forms and put it in the freezer. Every 20 to 30 minutes, stir the *kulfi* to break up the crystals that form. When it becomes too thick to stir, leave it to freeze solid. Serve individual portions of *kulfi* on small chilled plates.

For a variation, try flavoring *kulfi* with chicory, carob powder, vanilla, ground hazelnuts or cashews, or crushed berries.

An easy way to make Western ice cream is to combine 6 cups (1.4 l) of well-chilled liquid cream, 1 cup (200 g) of sugar, and some flavoring in an electric blender. Blend for just a few seconds until the mixture thickens to the consistency of whipped cream and the blades run freely. Scrape the mixture into cups and freeze. (If you don't have a blender, you can whip the mixture by hand).

Preparation and cooking time: 1 hr 15 min
Freezing time: 2 hr

Besan laddu

Toasted chickpea-flour confections

Kṛṣṇa had a cowherd friend named Madhumaṅgala, who was so fond of laddus *that he would eat more of them than anyone else, and then ask for more. We may take this as a hint to prepare this sweet in ample quantity, so that no one will be disappointed.*

1¾ cups (350 g) butter
4 cups (400 g) chickpea flour
2 tbs grated coconut
2 tbs walnuts or hazelnuts, chopped coarse
½ tsp freshly ground cardamom seeds or 1 tsp ground cinnamon
2 cups (250 g) powdered sugar

In a thick-bottomed frying pan, melt the butter over low heat. Mix in the chickpea flour with a wooden spoon, always stirring. In about 15 minutes, the flour should be toasted enough to give off a nutty aroma. Stir in the grated coconut, the walnuts, and the ground cardamom. Stir-fry for 2 minutes more, blending the ingredients well. Then take the pan off the heat and add the powdered sugar. Mix thoroughly with a fork to break up lumps and to distribute the ingredients evenly. Set aside to cool for a few minutes.

When the mixture is cool enough to handle, moisten your hands and form it into 12 to 15 walnut-sized balls. Or, if you prefer, mold the mixture into a cake and cut it into small squares or diamonds.

Preparation and cooking time: 30 min

Dvaraka burfi
Toasted chickpea-flour fudge

In Sweden, comparative religion is a required subject for all students, and an occasional field trip is always an integral part of the course. Many students have said that their favorite field trip is the one that goes to the Hare Kṛṣṇa farm just outside Stockholm. Almost every day of the school year, a new busload of children discover the joyful Kṛṣṇa conscious life of chanting, dancing, and feasting. The cook always makes a big plate of dvaraka burfi *for the occasion. It never fails to win the heart of a Swedish student—or anyone else who tries it.*

1¾ cups (400 g) butter
3 cups (300 g) sifted chickpea flour
1 cup (250 ml) milk
1 cup (250 ml) water
1¼ cups (250 g) sugar
¼ cup (35 g) cashew nuts, chopped coarse
2 tbs grated coconut

Melt the butter in a medium-sized saucepan. Stir the chickpea flour into the butter and stir-fry it gently over low heat, taking care not to burn it. After about 15 minutes, when the flour is lightly browned, remove the pan from the heat.

In another saucepan, make the syrup by boiling together the milk, water, and sugar, until a drop of syrup makes one strand between your thumb and forefinger. Stir the nuts and coconut into the syrup, and pour the syrup into the chickpea flour. Cook and stir gently over very low heat until the mixture thickens and becomes less sticky.

After it cools enough to handle, form it into a square cake on a plate. When it becomes firm, cut it into pieces. Top each piece with half a cashew nut or some chopped pistachio nuts.

Preparation and cooking time: 30 min

Luglu

Chickpea-flour–and–dried-fruit balls

Many pilgrims walk hundreds of miles to visit the famous Jagannātha temple in the holy city of Jagannātha Purī, 80 miles south of Calcutta. They come to see the form of Kṛṣṇa known as Lord Jagannātha and relish the prasādam *that has been offered to Him. The resident* pujārīs *(priests) cook* luglus *the size of a fist for Lord Jagannātha. These* luglus *stay fresh for several days and are very popular with the pilgrims, who savor them as they continue their journeys.*

2¼ cups (525 ml) water
1½ cups (300 g) sugar
½ tsp fresh grated nutmeg
¼ tsp ground cloves
⅔ cup (100 g) raisins
1 cup (150 g) chopped dried figs
1 cup (150 g) dried dates, cut in half
1½ cups (150 g) chickpea flour
11 tbs (165 ml) water for bundis
ghee for deep-frying
1 cup (125 g) chopped hazelnuts, almonds or pistachio nuts
1 cup (75 g) grated coconut

Boil together the water, sugar, spices, and the dried fruits, until the dates soften and the mixture resembles a thick sauce. Let simmer.

Now make *bundis* (fried chickpea-flour pearls) by mixing, in a large bowl, the chickpea flour and the water to make a thick, smooth paste, stiff enough to stand in tiny peaks. Heat the *ghee* in a *karhai,* wok, or shallow saucepan over medium heat. Hold a spoon or colander with large holes over the hot *ghee*. With a spatula, push enough batter through the holes to cover the surface of the *ghee* with droplets. Let them cook slowly for about 4 minutes, turning crisp and golden yellow. Don't let them turn brown.

As each batch gets done, remove it from the *ghee,* drain for a moment, then put it in a large mixing bowl. Repeat this process until all the batter is transformed into *bundis,* and put in the bowl. Combine the syrup, chopped nuts and dried coconut with the *bundis* and mix thoroughly. Moisten your hands and form 16 compact balls. Put them on a plate to harden.

Preparation and cooking time: 30 to 40 min

Jalebi

Crisp fried spirals in syrup

Jalebis *are great finger-licking favorites. There are two secrets to making them: deep-fry them in shallow* ghee *(about 2 to 3 inches/ 5 to 7 cm) so that the coils don't droop, and make sure that they soak thoroughly in the syrup yet stay crisp.*

1½ cups (250 g) white flour
1 cup (150 g) rice flour
1 cup (250 ml) plain yogurt
½ tsp powdered saffron
warm water
½ tsp baking powder (optional)
2½ cups (600 ml) water
2½ cups (500 g) sugar
1 tbs rose-water
ghee for deep-frying

In a large bowl, mix together the two kinds of flour, the yogurt, half the saffron, and enough warm water to make a smooth batter. Cover the bowl with a cloth and set it aside in a warm place for 1 to 2 days, giving it time to naturally ferment. (You can accelerate the process by adding ½ teaspoon of baking powder). The batter is ready when bubbles begin to appear on the surface.

Make a syrup by boiling together the water, the sugar, and the rest of the saffron for 10 minutes. Then remove the syrup from the heat and flavor it with the rose-water. Heat the *ghee* in a wok or shallow saucepan. Beat the batter again. It should be the consistency of thick pancake batter. If it is too thin, add some white flour. Using a small-holed cloth icing bag, a small funnel, or even a coconut shell with a hole in it, make coils or loops 5 inches (13 cm) across in the *ghee*. Fry, turning once, until crisp and golden on both sides. Remove with a slotted spoon, drain over the *ghee* for a moment, then transfer to the warm syrup to soak for no more than half a minute, so that they stay crisp.

Pile the *jalebis* on a serving plate and serve them hot, cold, or at room temperature.

Standing time: overnight
Preparation and cooking time: 30 to 40 min

Mithe samosa

Fruit turnovers

It may take a little practice to master the technique of pleating the top of the samosa, *but even if your* samosas *are raggedy-edged, they'll still be delicious.*

For variation, almost any sweet fruit, such as strawberries, peaches, pineapple, mangos, or figs, can be used for the filling. Sweetened paneer *or milk* burfi *can be added to the filling to make it even more delectable.*

½ cup (100 g) melted butter
3 cups (300 g) white flour
¼ tsp salt
⅔ cup (150 ml) cold water
6 medium-sized apples, cored, peeled, and cut into small pieces
1½ tsp ground cinnamon
½ tsp ground cardamom
½ tsp powdered ginger
6 tbs sugar
ghee or vegetable oil for deep-frying
2 tbs confectioners' sugar

In a large mixing bowl, rub half the melted butter into the flour with your fingertips, until the mixture resembles coarse meal. Add the salt. Gradually add the cold water. (Some cooks make a richer dough by substituting yogurt for the water, or by using half cold water and half yogurt). Mix with your hands to form a dough. If the dough is too sticky, coat your hands with flour. Transfer the dough to a floured surface and knead it until it's smooth and firm. Then gather the dough together in a lump, cover with a damp cloth, and set aside for half an hour.

While the dough rests, stir-fry the apples and the other half of the butter over medium heat for 5 minutes. Then add the spices and sugar. Lower the heat and continue to stir until most of the liquid cooks off and the mixture thickens. Then turn it onto a plate to cool.

Knead the dough again and form it into 10 balls. Grease the rolling board and roll out the balls like thick *puris*. Place a tablespoon of filling on half of each round and fold the round in half over the filling. Moisten the dough where the two edges will meet, then press the two layers of dough together along the edge of the fill-

---

Opposite page: *preparation of mithe samosa*

ing and pare away the excess. Now pick up a *samosa* in one hand and use the other to pinch and twist the sealed edge in successive folds to form a pleated top. Each *samosa* should have 10 to 12 pressed-down folds. Make sure there are no holes by which the filling can escape during the deep-frying. Prepare all the *samosas* in this way and arrange them on a plate.

Heat the *ghee* or vegetable oil over medium heat in a vessel for deep-frying. Put in as many *samosas* at a time as will fit without touching one another. Fry them for 10 to 12 minutes, turning them gently with a slotted spoon until they are golden brown on both sides. Remove them and put them in a colander to drain.

You can serve *mithe samosas* either hot or cold. Sprinkle with powdered sugar, or sugar-coat them by dipping them in thick syrup.

Preparation and cooking time: 1 hr 15 min

Phal ka pakora
Fruit fritters

Practically any fruit can be used to make phal ka pakoras. *Bananas can be cut into slices, pineapples into small chunks, apples and pears into wedges. Small fruits like strawberries can be dipped in the batter and deep-fried whole. If you want to leave out the baking powder, the crust will be a little harder but just as tasty.*

2 cups (200 g) white flour
1 tbs milk powder (optional)
½ tsp baking powder (optional)
1 tsp ground cinnamon
1¼ cups (300 ml) warm milk
ghee for deep-frying
1 lb (450 g) fresh fruit, trimmed and cut into uniform pieces
3 tbs powdered sugar

Mix together, in a large bowl, all the ingredients except the fruit, *ghee*, and powdered sugar, to make a batter thick enough to coat the fruit. Place a handful of the cut fruit into the batter. Mix so that each piece is completely covered.

Heat the *ghee* in a *karhai*, wok, or shallow saucepan over medium heat. The *ghee* is ready when a drop of batter bubbles and rises to the surface immediately after being dropped in. Remove the coated pieces of fruit from the batter, one by one, and gently drop them into the hot *ghee*. Cover the surface of the *ghee* with one layer of *pakoras*. Fry for about 3 or 4 minutes until they are golden brown and crisp. Then remove with a slotted spoon and put into a strainer to allow the excess *ghee* to drain. If there is batter left over, cut up enough extra fruit to finish it.

Sprinkle the powdered sugar over them and serve them warm or at room temperature. *Phal ka pakoras* are delicious eaten by themselves or served with milk sweets such as *shrikhand* or *khir*.

Preparation and cooking time: 25 min

Kerwai

Deep-fried stuffed banana balls

10 unripe bananas or plantains
4 tbs ghee or butter
¾ cup (100 g) mixed nuts, chopped
⅓ cup (50 g) raisins
½ tsp ground nutmeg
½ tsp ground cardamom
½ cup (100 g) sugar
3 tbs grated coconut, lightly toasted

Peel the bananas, cut them into chunks, and set them aside. Heat a tablespoon or two of the *ghee* or butter and fry the chopped nuts. When they are browned, add the raisins and fry for a few seconds more. Stir the ground nutmeg and cardamom into the mixture and set it aside to cool.

Heat the remaining *ghee* or butter and fry the bananas until they are soft and brown in spots. Don't be alarmed if a skin forms on the bottom of the pan. Add the sugar and continue stirring until the mixture thickens and forms one mass. This should take about 10 to 15 minutes. Remove and allow to cool.

Divide the banana mixture into 15 parts and mix one part with the nut mixture. Then divide the nut mixture into as many parts as you have of banana mixture. Take each part of banana mixture and form it into a patty. Place one patty into your left hand and make a depression in it with your thumb. Put one part of the nut mixture in the depression and gather the edges of the patty over the mixture. Seal it well. Gently roll it into a smooth ball. Do the same for each patty.

Heat the *ghee* and deep-fry the balls for about 2 minutes until they are browned. Try to prevent the balls from sticking to one another while frying or serving. Sprinkle with the toasted coconut and serve hot.

Preparation and cooking time: 25 min

Malpura

Sweet dumplings in flavored yogurt

Malpuras *should be a little crisp on the surface and cooked thoroughly, so that they soak up the yogurt sauce and become juicy.*

Devotees at our temple in Lima, Peru regularly make malpura *for the guests, including the local motorcycle policemen who often pull up in front of the temple and ask,* "Me guardaron mis tortas?" *(Have you saved me my cakes?)*

2¼ cups (225 g) white flour
1 cup (125 g) confectioners' sugar
½ tsp baking powder
¾ cup (175 ml) milk
clean ghee for deep-frying
2½ cups (600 ml) plain yogurt
¾ cup (150 g) granulated sugar
1 cup (200 g) strawberries or other berries, washed and mashed

Mix together the flour, powdered sugar, baking powder, and milk to make a batter thick enough to cling to a wooden spoon without dripping off. In a *karhai,* wok, or shallow saucepan, heat the *ghee* until it is hot, but not smoking. Scoop up some batter with a tablespoon and push lumps of it into the hot *ghee*. Put in as many balls as will fit without touching one another. Adjust the heat to ensure thorough cooking, so that the interior of the *malpuras* will be cooked as well as the exterior. Fry and turn the *malpuras* for 6 to 8 minutes until they are golden brown and crisp. Remove them with a slotted spoon. Put them in a colander to drain.

In a mixing bowl, beat together the yogurt, granulated sugar, and crushed fruit. Cover the *malpuras* with this sauce and let soak for at least 10 minutes before offering.

Preparation and cooking time: 20 min
Soaking time: at least 10 min

Gulab jamun

Deep-fried milk balls in syrup

Śrīla Prabhupāda's first disciples often speak of the storefront in New York City where the Kṛṣṇa consciousness movement had its beginning in the West. Śrīla Prabhupāda, who took care of his disciples like an affectionate father, would always keep a pot of gulab jamuns *on hand for his charges.*

The devotees fondly refer to gulab jamuns *as "ISKCON Bullets" because they are powerful ammunition in the war against* māyā *(illusion). They're so sweet they make material life seem very sour.*

10 cups (2.4 liters) water
10 cups (2 kg) sugar
1 tbs rose-water or a few drops of rose essence
5 cups (375 g) milk powder
1 cup (100 g) white flour
2 tsp baking soda
1 tsp ground cardamom seeds
¼ cup (50 ml) melted butter or ghee
1 cup (250 ml) whole milk
25 to 30 small pieces rock candy (optional)
clean ghee for deep-frying

Combine the powdered milk, white flour, baking soda, and ground cardamom in a large mixing bowl. Warm the milk over low heat. Rub the *ghee* or butter into the flour with your fingertips, slowly add the warm milk, and mix well to give a firm but pliable dough.

Form the dough into 25 to 30 balls, about 1 inch (2.5 cm) in diameter, in this way: place enough dough for one ball squarely between the palms of your hands. Roll the dough between your palms with a circular motion. Don't cup your hands; use your palms, not your fingers. It is a good sign if some of the dough sticks to your palms.

After 4 or 5 seconds, gradually release the pressure between your hands while simultaneously speeding up the circular motion. If you're doing it right, a ball of dough should form that is perfectly smooth and free from cracks. Roll all the balls like this. If the dough becomes too dry, knead more milk into it. (If you like, insert a small piece of rock candy into each ball and carefully seal the opening. When the milk balls are deep-fried, the rock candy melts).

Heat the *ghee* in a *karhai* or wok over very low heat. The heat must be kept at the lowest setting so that the milk balls cook slowly and thoroughly. Put the milk balls into the *ghee*. They will sink for a minute or two. Keep them from burning on the bottom by turning them with a slotted spoon. As the milk balls rise to the surface and float, spin them in the *ghee* by gently brushing over the top of them every 30 seconds or so with the back of the slotted spoon, to insure that they cook uniformly. Cook them for about 25 minutes, or until they are nicely browned. During this time, you can raise the heat slightly to help them swell.

While the milk balls are cooking, make the syrup. Boil the water and sugar in a pot for about 3 minutes to dissolve the sugar. Then stir in the rose-water and remove the pot from the heat.

Test to see if the milk balls are properly cooked by taking one out and pressing it with your finger to make a dimple. Now release your finger. If the ball immediately springs back to shape, they're ready. Another test is to put one in the syrup; if it doesn't collapse after 3 minutes, the balls are cooked thoroughly. Remove them and put them in a colander to drain. Then transfer the balls to the syrup, where they will become soft and spongy. Soak from 30 minutes to 2 days. *Gulab jamuns* are best served at room temperature, or slightly warm.

Preparation and cooking time: 20 min
Soaking time: at least 10 min

Beverages

1 Nimbu pani *(Lemon or lime drink)* 284
2 Jeera pani *(Cumin and tamarind drink)* 284
3 Adrak chai *(Ginger tea)* 285
4 Gulab sharbet *(Rose-flavored cold drink)* 285
5 Phal ka ras *(Fresh fruit juices)* 286
6 Thandai *(Anise milk with raisins and pistachios)* 287
7 Namkin lassi *(Salty yogurt or buttermilk drink)* 288
8 Mithi lassi *(Sweet yogurt or buttermilk drink)* 289
9 Garam doodh *(Hot milk)* 290
10 Masala doodh *(Hot saffron-flavored milk with pistachios)* 292
11 Narial doodh *(Hot coconut-flavored milk with spices)* 293

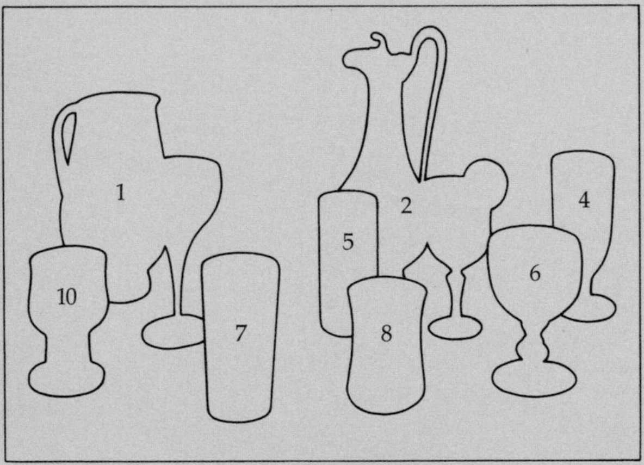

ACCORDING to the *Āyur-veda,* drinking enough liquid to fill a fourth of the stomach during a meal aids digestion. Between meals, drinking can serve not only to quench thirst but also to cool the body when it's hot, or warm it when cool.

Drinks made from yogurt, such as *lassi,* cool the body. So enjoy them during the summer, but avoid them before retiring or when the body is cool, especially in winter. Lemon can be useful any time of year. Ginger tea with lemon and a little honey fortifies the body against colds in the winter. And lemon drinks such as *nimbu pani* and *jeera pani* are refreshing in the summer. When you plan to serve a sweet drink on a hot day, make the drink in advance and use some of the drink to make ice cubes to serve with it. If you are in a hurry, superfine granulated sugar dissolves in just a few seconds.

The best drink for warming the body is piping-hot cow's milk. The *Āyur-veda* says that milk also nourishes the cerebral tissues—but you have to drink it hot for the digestive system to extract its subtle properties. Therefore, always boil milk before serving it, unless it's to be drunk as soon as it comes from the cow.

The *Vedas* say that a comfortable seat, a beverage, and some friendly words are the least one should offer any guest, be he friend or foe. No prepared beverages on hand? Then serve a glass of water to your guest.

Nimbu pani
Lemon or lime drink

⅔ cup (150 ml) lemon or lime juice
5 cups (1.2 l) water
5 tbs sugar
1 tbs rose-water
¼ tsp salt
ice (optional)

Mix all the ingredients well. Serve chilled, with a thin slice of lemon or lime. You can vary the amounts of lemon juice and sugar according to your taste.

Preparation time: 5 min

Jeera pani
Cumin and tamarind drink

6 oz (175 g) tamarind, broken into small pieces
2 cups (475 ml) water
3 tsp finely grated fresh ginger
2 tsp cumin seeds, toasted and ground
½ tsp garam masala
3 tbs brown sugar
1 pinch salt
4 cups (950 ml) ice water
crushed ice, mint leaves and slices of lemon for garnish

Boil the tamarind in the water for 15 minutes. Then extract as much juice and pulp from it as possible by forcing it through a strainer—several times if necessary. Add all the other ingredients to this juice, mix well, and let stand for 15 minutes. Then filter through a piece of cheesecloth. Chill.

Just before serving, dilute the juice with the ice water. Put crushed ice in each serving. Garnish with mint leaves and a slice of lemon or lime.

Preparation and cooking time: 40 min

Adrak chai
Ginger tea

Ginger tea is a good general tonic. If you prefer a more refreshing drink, add ice cubes, extra sugar and lemon juice, and some crushed mint leaves.

5 cups (1.2 liters) water
3 tbs finely grated fresh ginger
6 tbs sugar or 5 tbs honey
1 pinch ground black pepper
4 tbs lemon or orange juice
chopped mint leaves (optional)

Boil the water and ginger rapidly in an uncovered saucepan for about 10 minutes. Stir the sweetener into the mixture until it dissolves. Strain, pressing the ginger against the strainer to extract as much of its essence as possible.

Then add the pepper and the lemon or orange juice. Serve hot.

Preparation and cooking time: 20 min

Gulab sherbet
Rose-flavored cold drink

2¾ cups (550 g) sugar
5 cups (1.2 l) water
1 tbs rose-water
1 tsp red food coloring
iced water and crushed ice
mint leaves

Make a syrup by cooking the sugar and water in a saucepan over gentle heat until the sugar dissolves. Cool. Then add the rose-water and food coloring.

Just before serving put 2 tablespoons of syrup in each glass and fill up with iced water and crushed ice. The amount of syrup can be increased or decreased according to taste.

Preparation and cooking time: 20 min

Phal ka ras
Fresh fruit juices

Kṛṣṇa, the Supreme Lord, has provided many delicious fruits we can make juice from: apples, pears, grapefruits, peaches, apricots, plums, melons, berries, cherries, pineapples, mangos, kiwifruits, and guavas, to name just a few. Either one kind of fruit or combinations of fruits can be blended with just enough water for a smooth drink, then chilled before being served.

ripe fruit
iced water
sweetener
ground sweet spices (optional)
ice cubes or crushed ice

Several points about making fruit juices

• Use ripe fruits to get the most flavor and vitamin content.
• Blend the fruits in a mixer until smooth, adding just enough water to achieve the proper consistency—not too thick, not too thin.
• Strain grape, guava, pineapple, watermelon, or mango juice to eliminate fibrous tissue or seed particles.
• When using citrus fruits such as tangerines, oranges, and grapefruits, separate the pulp from the seeds and add it to the beverage.
• Some fruits go particularly well in pairs: peach and banana, peach and apricot, grapefruit and cranberry, pineapple and orange, kiwifruits and orange, apple and pear, melon and mango.
• To counteract the tendency of banana or apple juice to turn a gray color, add a little lemon or lime juice.
• Apple or pear juice is delicious blended with yogurt, milk, or cream.
• Always serve fruit juices well chilled. If ice is not available, make the fruit juice in advance so it can be refrigerated before serving.
• For a final touch, garnish each serving of fruit juice with a sprig of mint leaves and a slice of fresh fruit.

Preparation time: 15 min
Chilling time: 45 min

Thandai

Anise milk with raisins and pistachios

You don't have to make thandai *with milk. You can use water instead, as is often done, though the milk mellows the taste of the spices.*

⅔ cup (100 g) raisins
2 tbs anise seeds
1¾ cups (425 ml) water
¼ cup (35 g) pistachio nuts
2½ cups (600 ml) whole milk
½ tsp ground cardamom seeds
4 tbs honey or 5 tbs sugar

Cover the raisins with warm water and soak them for 10 minutes. In a saucepan, boil the anise seeds in the water for 5 minutes. Lower the heat and simmer for 10 minutes more.

Blend the pistachio nuts, drained raisins, ground cardamom, and milk in an electric blender and set aside. Strain the anise water and stir the honey into it. Then add it to the mixture, stir well, and chill.

Serve each glass of *thandai* garnished with a sprig of mint leaves.

Preparation and cooking time: 25 min

Namkin lassi
Salty yogurt or buttermilk drink

Lassi *is a most popular drink throughout India, where it is valued for its taste and nutritional value.* Lassi *is a great drink to make for large gatherings. You can prepare it quickly and leave it to chill, well in advance of serving time.*

1 tsp cumin seeds, roasted and ground
4 cups (950 ml) plain yogurt or cultured buttermilk
3 cups (700 ml) water
3 tbs lemon juice
2 tsp salt
crushed ice (optional)

Reserve a pinch of the ground cumin and mix all the other ingredients together with a whisk or electric blender. Pour the mixture into glasses (with or without crushed ice). Garnish with the pinch of ground cumin. Serve chilled or at room temperature.

A tasty variation for *namkin lassi* is made by adding 1 oz (25 g) of fresh mint leaves. Put several mint leaves aside for the garnish. Mix all the other ingredients (except the ice cubes) in an electric blender, until the mint leaves are chopped fine. This should take about 30 seconds. Then add the ice cubes and blend again until the beverage becomes frothy. Pour the mint *lassi* into glasses, each garnished with mint leaves.

To make plain *lassi* combine the yogurt or buttermilk, the ground cumin, and the water. Beat it to a smooth consistency with a whisk or electric blender. Pour this mixture into glasses of crushed ice and serve.

Preparation time: 10 min

Mithi lassi

Sweet yogurt or buttermilk drink

Mithi lassi *is the milkshake of India and the drink most often served at Hare Kṛṣṇa functions. It is easy to prepare and always appreciated. For best results, dissolve the sweetener in a small quantity of hot water before mixing it with the other ingredients.*

4 cups (950 ml) plain yogurt or cultured buttermilk
3 cups (700 ml) ice water
6 tbs sugar or 5 tbs honey
2 tsp rose-water
¼ tsp ground cardamom seeds
crushed ice (optional)

Mix all the ingredients together with a whisk or an electric blender until the surface of the *lassi* becomes frothy. Serve chilled, either by adding crushed ice or by refrigeration.

As an alternative to rose-water and cardamom, try 3 tablespoons of lime or lemon juice, 3 tablespoons of flavored syrup, or ½ cup (50 g) of crushed red berries, ripe banana, or ripe mango.

Preparation time: 10 min

Garam doodh
Hot milk

By Kṛṣṇa's arrangement, the cow eats grass and transforms it into milk, a drink both delicious and rich in all the nutrients needed for good health and spiritual progress. The proteins, fats, and vitamins in milk develop the finer tissues of the brain. Milk is thus the perfect food for one seeking advancement in spiritual life. Śrīla Prabhupāda recommended drinking a cup of hot milk in the morning and one at night.

5 cups (1.2 liters) milk
3 tbs sugar or 2 tbs honey

Either bring the milk to a boil three times, being careful that it doesn't spill over, or maintain it at a gentle rolling boil for 5 minutes. Remove from heat, add the sweetener, and stir until it dissolves.

You may also flavor the milk by adding 3 or 4 bruised cardamom pods, a drop or two of rose-water, 1 tablespoon of chicory or carob powder, a big pinch of ground nutmeg or cinnamon, or a few strands of saffron.

Hot milk can also make a wonderful banana or mango nectar drink. Crush a ripe banana or mango into a pulp and mix it into the sweetened hot milk. Add 1 tablespoon of butter, ¼ teaspoon of ground cinnamon, and ¼ teaspoon of ground nutmeg.

Just before serving any type of hot milk, pour the milk from one cup to another several times. This cools it slightly and aerates it.

Preparation time: 10 min

Opposite page: *Garam doodh*

Masala doodh

Hot saffron-flavored milk with pistachios

Ever since Śrīla Prabhupāda was invited to Moscow by a prominent Russian Sanskrit scholar in 1971, Kṛṣṇa consciousness has spread rapidly in the Soviet Union despite heavy government persecution. Even though there is the constant danger of being detected, the Russian devotees are enthusiastic and determined preachers, and they regularly cook sumptuous feasts for invited guests. From the industrial city of Sverdlovsk, in the Ural Mountains, a devotee reported that Russians are very fond of this recipe for masala doodh.

5 cups (1.2 l) milk
10 saffron strands or ¼ tsp powdered saffron
4 cloves
½ tsp ground cinnamon
3 tbs honey or 4 tbs sugar
1 tbs finely ground pistachio nuts

Bring the milk, saffron, cloves, and cinnamon to boil in a saucepan. Adjust the heat so that the milk maintains a rolling boil for 5 minutes. Then remove from the heat, stir in the honey, and discard the cloves. Sprinkle the ground pistachio nuts over the top. Serve steaming hot.

Preparation time: 10 min

Narial doodh

Hot coconut-flavored milk with spices

1 fresh coconut
5 cups (1.2 l) milk
½ tsp cardamom seeds
4 whole black peppercorns
1 tbs grated ginger
5 tbs sugar or 4 tbs honey

Break the coconut and collect the coconut milk. Heat the shell fragments directly over heat or in an oven until it is easy to pry the pulp from the shell. Pare away any brown skin from the pulp; then dice the pulp. Heat the milk. Dry-roast the cardamom seeds (see page 79) and blend them and the peppercorns until fine. Set aside. Put the diced coconut into a blender, along with 2 cups (475 ml) of milk, and blend for a minute or two, until the coconut is completely smooth.

Prop a strainer over a saucepan large enough to hold 2 quarts (1.9 l) of liquid. Pour the mixture through the strainer, while pressing the coconut against the strainer to extract its essence. Slowly pour the remaining hot milk over the strained coconut and continue to press in the same way. Then squeeze the coconut in your hand to extract the remaining liquid. Discard the strained coconut. Add the coconut milk, ground spices, ginger, and sweetener to the mixture and put over heat until it almost boils. Serve hot.

Preparation time: 10 min

Appendixes

Measurement Conversion Tables

Using Metric Measures

This book gives quantities in both American cup and metric measures. Metric equivalents of American cup measures are shown in parenthesis, like this: 1 cup (175 g) rice. Never change between American cup and metric measures in the same recipe; they are not interchangeable. Exact conversion from American to metric measures does not usually give convenient working quantities, so the metric measures have been rounded off to units of 25 grams. For example, ½ cup of flour, which equals 57 g, is rounded off to 50 g; 1 cup of flour (113 g) is rounded off to 100 g.

The same principle applies to the milliliter measurements. For example, ½ cup, which equals 118 ml, is rounded off to 125 ml; 1 cup, which equals 236.6 ml, is rounded off to 250 ml.

Notes for British Users

Although many American and British units of measure have the same names, not all are identical. In general, the weights are identical but the volumes are not.

The British fl oz is 1.04 times the American fl oz. So the standard Imperial ½-pint measuring cup holds 10 fl oz (10.4 American oz), whereas the standard American ½-pint measuring cup holds 8 American fl oz. To obtain accurate British pint measures, convert American cups into American fl oz using the table given on page 299. Then convert American fl oz into British pints.

• The American standard tablespoon holds 14.2 ml, and the British standard tablespoon holds 17.7 ml. In England use **3/4** tablespoon for every American tablespoon. A teaspoon holds approximately 5 ml in both countries.

Notes for Australian Users

In Australia, metric measures are now used with the standard 250-milliliter measuring cup. The teaspoon is the same in Australia,. New Zealand, Britain, and the United States. The Australian standard tablespoon, however, holds 20 ml, or 4 teaspoons the British tablespoon holds 3½ teaspoons, and the American, Canadian, and New Zealand tablespoon holds only 3.

The following two tables show the metric equivalents of some often used American quantities. The metric measurements are listed both precise and rounded for convenience.

Ounces	Approx. grams	Nearest unit of 25g
1 oz	28 g	25 g
2 oz	57 g	50 g
3 oz	85 g	75 g
4 oz	113 g	100 g
5 oz	142 g	150 g
6 oz	170 g	175 g
7 oz	198 g	200 g
8 oz	227 g	225 g
9 oz	255 g	250 g
10 oz	283 g	275 g
11 oz	312 g	300 g
12 oz	340 g	350 g
13 oz	368 g	375 g
14 oz	396 g	400 g
15 oz	425 g	425 g
16 oz	454 g	450 g

American cups	Approx. ml	Nearest unit of 25 ml
¼ cup	59.15 ml	50 ml
½ cup	118.3 ml	125 ml
1 cup	236.6 ml	250 ml
2 cups	473.2 ml	475 ml
4 cups	946.4 ml	950 ml

The next table compares American cups, American fl oz, and British pints. The last table compares American, British, and Australian tablespoons.

American cups	American fl oz	Nearest ¼ British pint unit
¾ cup	5.2 fl oz	pint
1¼ cup	10.4 fl oz	pint
2 cups	15.6 fl oz	pint
2½ cups	20.8 fl oz	1 pint
3¼ cups	26 fl oz	pints
4 cups	31.2 fl oz	pints
4½ cups	36.4 fl oz	pints
5¼ cups	41.6 fl oz	2 pints

American	British	Australian
1 tablespoon	1 scant tablespoon	½ tablespoon
2 tablespoon	1¾ tablespoon	1½ tablespoon
3 tablespoon	2½ tablespoon	2½ tablespoon
4 tablespoon	3½ tablespoon	3 tablespoon

PORTEE M

Where to Get Essential Ingredients

MOST of the ingredients mentioned in this book should be easy to find. Ethnic grocery stores and health food shops of all descriptions are opening in cities all over the map, and as the public's interest in better health increases, a wide selection of wholesome products is appearing on the shelves of ordinary supermarkets.

Asafoetida, black mustard seeds, black cumin seeds, curry leaves, tamarind, and other hard-to-find spices and seasonings are available in Indian or Pakistani grocery stores. Most of these shops also carry a variety of Indian utensils and cooking tools. If the nearest Indian grocery store is too far, try to find one who will supply spices and other items by post. You can also find whole grains, dal, chickpea flour, and unrefined sugars at Asian grocery stores and most health food shops. Check around for the best prices. You can save money by buying goods in large quantities or from wholesalers.

For information about where to get essential ingredients at good prices, you are always welcome to contact the Hare Kṛṣṇa temple nearest you. If you can, drop by to meet the devotees and taste their cooking. You'll find a list of our temples, farm communities, and our restaurants in the next appendix.

The Author

In 1972, after receiving his masters degree in biology from Long Island University, Ādirāja Dāsa felt compelled to drop everything and travel for as long as he needed to find the answers to some questions that deeply concerned him. He had a feeling that the solution to solving the world's problems involved the human race's attaining a higher state of consciousness.

But, in his words, "I had no idea it would have anything to do with whether we killed animals or ate some of them. At that time, I was an amateur taxidermist, and I thought it was normal and necessary for humans to eat domesticated species of 'food animals.'"

Ādirāja bicycled cross-country, spent several months in Hawaii, where he met Hare Kṛṣṇa devotees for the first time, and then backpacked around the world for the next two years, practicing and comparing Eastern and Western religions. By the time he reached India he decided to stop eating meat and fish. "Within days I felt as if a shroud was lifted from my consciousness. My sense of compassion and connectedness with the world around me was heightened, and my desire to grow spiritually became stronger. After I realized how my choice not to eat animals unveiled a deeper and more loving part of myself, I began to wonder if other people who eat flesh were depriving themselves of this sense of love and harmony."

Several months later, in 1975, he joined the Hare Kṛṣṇa movement in Geneva, Switzerland. His spiritual master, His Divine Grace A. C. Bhaktivedanta Swami Prabhupāda, wanted as many people as possible to experience *prasādam.* He insisted that by eating *prasādam* people would get a higher taste for spiritual life and lose their taste for meat. This concept appealed to Ādirāja, so for the next seventeen years he directed free *prasādam* distribution programs in Geneva, Paris, and Detroit. In 1983 he published a cookbook in French, *Un Goût Supérieur.* The royalties from this book helped him support *Nourriture sans Frontières,* an association he created that worked in cooperation with the government of France to feed needy people.

Ādirāja now lives near the Hare Kṛṣṇa center in Detroit. Over the past twelve years he has often given presentations to share his insights about the inseparable connection between spirituality and vegetarianism. At present Ādirāja is writing a book called *The Hare Krishna Book of Vegan Food Preparation,* which is expected to be published in early 2007. If you would like to correspond with him, write: Ādirāja Dāsa, c/o ISKCON Detroit, 383 Lennox Ave., Detroit, Michigan 48215, or e-mail him at tommilano108@yahoo.com.

Glossary

Asafoetida: a strong-smelling spice used in small quantities to flavor savories, soups, and vegetable dishes.

Āyur-veda: Vedic scriptures dealing with preventive and curative medicine.

Bhagavad-gītā: the sacred dialogue spoken five thousand years ago between Lord Kṛṣṇa and His devotee Arjuna on the Battlefield of Kurukṣetra, in India. It has five main topics: the Absolute Truth, the living entities, material nature, time, and *karma. Bhagavad-gītā* is the essence of Vedic knowledge.

Bhakti-yoga: devotional service to the Supreme Lord.

Caitanya-caritāmṛta: the biography of Lord Caitanya Mahāprabhu written over four hundred years ago by Kṛṣṇadāsa Kavirāja Gosvāmī.

Caitanya Mahāprabhu: the incarnation of Kṛṣṇa who came five centuries ago, in the role of His own devotee, to teach the process of devotional service by chanting the holy names of God.

Chapati: flat, round whole-wheat bread, cooked on a griddle and held over a flame until it inflates like a balloon.

Dal: husked and split lentils used to make savories, sweets, and soups; the soup made from such lentils.

Dosa: a sort of Indian pancake, sometimes stuffed with spiced potatoes.

Ekādaśī: the eleventh day of both the waxing and waning moon. On Ekādaśī, devotees of Kṛṣṇa simplify their diet by abstaining from grains, beans, and peas, and increase their remembrance of Kṛṣṇa by intensifying their chanting of the Hare Kṛṣṇa mantra and other devotional activities.

Garam masala: (literally, "hot spices") a blend of powdered spices added to a dish at the end of the cooking.

Ghee: clarified butter. Its delicate flavor and special qualities make it the best of all cooking mediums.

Gulab jamun: a sweet made of deep-fried powdered milk balls, soaked in rose-flavored syrup.

Halava: a dessert made from toasted grains, butter, and sugar.

Hare Kṛṣṇa mantra: a sixteen-word prayer composed of the names *Hare, Kṛṣṇa,* and *Rāma:* Hare Kṛṣṇa, Hare Kṛṣṇa, Kṛṣṇa Kṛṣṇa, Hare Hare/ Hare Rāma, Hare Rāma, Rāma Rāma, Hare Hare. Hare *(ha ray')* is the personal form of God's own happiness, His eternal consort, Śrīmatī Rādhārāṇī. Kṛṣṇa, "the all-attractive one," and Rāma, "the all-pleasing one," are names of God. This prayer means "My dear Rādhārāṇī and Kṛṣṇa, please engage me in Your devotional service." The *Vedas* recommend the chanting of the Hare Kṛṣṇa mantra as the easiest and most sublime method of awakening one's dormant love of God.

ISKCON: the abbreviation for the International Society for Krishna Consciousness; the Hare Kṛṣṇa Movement.

Karhai: a deep, rounded pan with handles on both sides, used for deep-frying or pan-frying.

Karma: fruitive action, which always produces a reaction, good or bad.

Kṛṣṇa: a name for the Supreme Personality of Godhead, meaning "infinitely attractive."

Masala: a blend of spices.

Panch masala: a mixture of five whole spices used in preparing vegetable dishes.

Paneer: a fresh cheese with many uses in Indian cooking.

Prasādam: "the mercy of Lord Kṛṣṇa." Food prepared for the pleasure of Kṛṣṇa and offered to Him with love and devotion. Because Kṛṣṇa tastes the offering, the food becomes spiritualized and purifies anyone who eats it.

Puri: a small deep-fried flat bread made from white flour, whole-wheat flour, or a mixture of both.

Raita: fruits or semicooked vegetables in lightly seasoned yogurt.

Sabji: vegetable or vegetable dish.

Samosa: a deep-fried turnover, stuffed with cooked fruits or spiced vegetables.

Śrīla Prabhupāda (1896–1977): the founder and spiritual master of the International Society for Krishna Consciousness. Śrīla Prabhupāda was a fully God conscious saint who had perfect realization of the Vedic scriptures. He worked incessantly to spread Kṛṣṇa consciousness all over the world.

Śrīmad-Bhāgavatam: the scripture composed by Śrīla Vyāsadeva (the literary incarnation of Lord Kṛṣṇa) to describe and explain Lord Kṛṣṇa's pastimes.

Tava: a slightly concave cast-iron frying pan used for cooking *chapatis* and other flat Indian breads.

Thali: a low-rimmed metal plate.

Vaiṣṇava: a devotee of Lord Kṛṣṇa, the Supreme Personality of Godhead.

Vedas (Vedic literatures): scriptures compiled five thousand years ago in India by Śrīla Vyāsadeva, an incarnation of Lord Kṛṣṇa. The Vedas conclude that the ultimate goal of human life is to reestablish our eternal loving relationship with Kṛṣṇa (God).

Vṛndāvana: the village in North India where Lord Kṛṣṇa lived as a child; the supreme transcendental abode of the Supreme Lord in the spiritual universe.

Yogi: a transcendentalist, one who strives to attain the Supreme.

Sanskrit Pronunciation Guide

The system of transliteration used in this book conforms to a system that scholars have accepted to indicate the pronunciation of each sound in the Sanskrit language.

The short vowel **a** is pronounced like the **u** in b**u**t, long **ā** like the **a** in f**a**r. Short **i** is pronounced as in p**i**n, long **ī** as in p**i**que, short **u** as in p**u**ll, and long **ū** as in r**u**le. The vowel **ṛ** is pronounced like the **ri** in **ri**m, **e** like the **ey** in th**ey**, **o** like the **o** in g**o**, **ai** like the **ai** in **ai**sle, and **au** like the **ow** in h**ow**. The *anusvāra* (**ṁ**) is pronounced like the **n** in the French word *bo***n**, and *visarga* (**ḥ**) is pronounced as a final **h** sound. At the end of a couplet, **aḥ** is pronounced **aha**, and **iḥ** is pronounced **ihi**.

The guttural consonants—**k, kh, g, gh,** and **ṅ**—are pronounced from the throat in much the same manner as in English. **K** is pronounced as in **k**ite, **kh** as in Ec**kh**art, **g** as in **g**ive, **gh** as in di**g h**ard, and **ṅ** as in si**ng.**

The palatal consonants—**c, ch, j, jh,** and **ñ**—are pronounced with the tongue touching the firm ridge behind the teeth. **C** is pronounced as in **ch**air, **ch** as in staun**ch-h**eart, **j** as in **j**oy, **jh** as in he**dgeh**og, and **ñ** as in ca**ny**on.

The cerebral consonants—**ṭ, ṭh, ḍ, ḍh,** and **ṇ**—are pronounced with the tip of the tongue turned up and drawn back against the dome of the palate. **Ṭ** is pronounced as in **t**ub, **ṭh** as in ligh**t-h**eart, **ḍ** as in **d**ove, **ḍh** as in re**d-h**ot, and **ṇ** as in **n**ut. The dental consonants—**t, th, d, dh,** and **n**—are pronounced in the same manner as the cerebrals, but with the forepart of the tongue against the teeth.

The labial consonants—**p, ph, b, bh,** and **m**—are pronounced with the lips. **P** is pronounced as in **p**ine, **ph** as in u**ph**ill, **b** as in **b**ird, **bh** as in ru**b-h**ard, and **m** as in **m**other.

The semivowels—**y, r, l,** and **v**—are pronounced as in **y**es, **r**un, **l**ight, and **v**ine respectively. The sibilants—**ś, ṣ,** and **s**—are pronounced, respectively, as in the German word **s***prechen* and the English words **sh**ine and **s**un. The letter **h** is pronounced as in **h**ome.

Index

Hazelnut fudge 263

Indian crackers 157
Indian ice cream 267
ISKCON, founded by Śrīla
Prabhupāda 45–6
See also: Hare Kṛṣṇa movement

Jalebi 271

Karhai 58
Karma, defined 26–7
Khir 251
Khichri 133–36
Kofta 194–201
Kṛṣṇa, chanting names of 45, 47,
meaning of name 14
offering food to 39-43
Kulfi 267

Laddu 268
Lassi 288–9
Lemon or lime drink 284
Lemon rice 106
Luglu 270

Mango chutney 239
Mango powder 83
Masala dosa 158
Masala puri 151
Masalas, how to make 76–7
Meat-eating, disease linked with 20–1
Milk fudge 253
Milk, hot 290-3
Milk, importance of 89–90
Milk products, about 89–91
Mint chutney 237
Mint leaves 83
Misthi dahi 257
Mixed vegetable rice 114
Mung beans in yogurt sauce 132
Mung dal and vegetable stew 131
Mustard seeds, black 83

Nutmeg 83

Pakora, fruit 275
vegetable 209
Pancakes, chickpea flour 161
filled with spiced potatoes 158–9
whole-wheat 160
Panch masala 77
Paneer, making of 94–5
see also Cheese
Pan-fried seasoned cheese 208
Papadam 206
Peas and cheese in tomato sauce 175
rice with cheese and 111
Peppers, fried chickpeas and 139
Pineapple chutney 234
Plain white rice 104-5
Potato
and cauliflower balls, deep-fried 194-5
and coconut salad 240
cabbage and, fried 171
curried cauliflower, and 168
flat-bread filled with 155
au gratin 169
pancakes filled with spices 158–9
patties, fried 216
swirls, fried spicy 215
with fried cauliflower and cheese 167
Potato-stuffed pancakes 158
Prabhupāda, as founder of ISKCON 45–6
distributes *prasādam* 46
quoted
on animal-killers 31
on cleanliness 66
on offering food to Kṛṣṇa 32
on *prasādam* distribution 47
on sinful activity 30
Prasādam
as spiritual nourishment 32–5
distribution of important 46–8
effect of eating 15
mentality for eating 42–3
Prabhupāda stressed importance
of 46–7
praised by Śrī Caitanya 32
sharing of 53
Puri 151

Raita 231
banana 245
chickpea flour pearls in seasoned
yogurt 244

The International Society for Krishna Consciousness

CENTERS AROUND THE WORLD

Founder-*Ācārya:* His Divine Grace A. C. Bhaktivedanta Swami Prabhupāda

CANADA

Brampton-Mississauga, Ontario — Unit 20, 1030 Kamato Dr., L4W 4B6/ Tel. (416) 840-6587 or (905) 826-1290/ iskconbrampton@gmail.com

Calgary, Alberta — 313 Fourth St. N.E., T2E 3S3/ Tel. (403) 265-3302/ vamanstones@shaw.ca

Edmonton, Alberta — 9353 35th Ave. NW, T6E 5R5/ Tel. (780) 439-9999/ edmonton@harekrishnatemple.com

Montreal, Quebec — 1626 Pie IX Boulevard, H1V 2C5/ Tel. & fax: (514) 521-1301/ iskconmontreal@gmail.com

◆ **Ottawa, Ontario** — 212 Somerset St. E., K1N 6V4/ Tel. (613) 565-6544/ radha_damodara@yahoo.com

Regina, Saskatchewan — 1279 Retallack St., S4T 2H8/ Tel. (306) 525-0002 0r -6461/ jagadishadas@yahoo.com

Scarborough, Ontario — 3500 McNicoll Avenue, Unit #3, M1V 4C7/ Tel. (416) 300 7101/ iskconscarborough@hotmail.com

◆ **Toronto, Ontario** — 243 Avenue Rd., M5R 2J6/ Tel. (416) 922-5415/ toronto@iskcon.net

◆ **Vancouver, B.C.** — 5462 S.E. Marine Dr., Burnaby V5J 3G8/ Tel. (604) 433-9728/ akrura@krishna.com/ Govinda's Bookstore & Cafe: (604) 433-7100 or (888) 433-8722

RURAL COMMUNITY

Ashcroft, B.C. — Saranagati Dhama (mail: P.O. Box 99, V0K 1A0)/ Tel. (250) 457-7438/ iskconsaranagati@hotmail.com

U.S.A.

Atlanta, Georgia — 1287 South Ponce de Leon Ave., N.E., 30306/ Tel. & fax: (404) 377-8680/ admin@atlantaharekrishnas.com

Austin, Texas — 10700 Jonwood Way, 78753/ Tel. (512) 835-2121/ sda@backtohome.com

Baltimore, Maryland — 200 Bloomsbury Ave., Catonsville, 21228/ Tel. (410) 744-1624/ contact@iskconbaltimore.org

Berkeley, California — 2334 Stuart Street, 94705/ Tel. (510) 540-9215/ info@iskconberkeley.net

Boise, Idaho — 1615 Martha St., 83706/ Tel. (208) 344-4274/ boise_temple@yahoo.com

Boston, Massachusetts — 72 Commonwealth Ave., 02116/ Tel. (617) 247-8611/ info@iskconboston.org

◆ **Chicago, Illinois** — 1716 W. Lunt Ave., 60626/ Tel. (773) 973-0900/ chicagoiskcon@yahoo.com

Columbus, Ohio — 379 W. Eighth Ave., 43201/ Tel. (614) 421-1661/ premvilasdas.rns@gmail.com

◆ **Dallas, Texas** — 5430 Gurley Ave., 75223/ Tel. (214) 827-6330/ info@radhakalachandji.com

◆ **Denver, Colorado** — 1400 Cherry St., 80220/ Tel. (303) 333-5461/ info@krishnadenver.com

Detroit, Michigan — 383 Lenox Ave., 48215/ Tel. (313) 824-6000/ gaurangi108@hotmail.com

Gainesville, Florida — 214 N.W. 14th St., 32603/ Tel. (352) 336-4183/ kalakantha.acbsp@pamho.net

Hartford, Connecticut — 1683 Main St., E. Hartford, 06108/ Tel. & fax: (860) 289-7252/ pyari108@gmail.com

◆ **Honolulu, Hawaii** — 51 Coelho Way, 96817/ Tel. (808) 595-4913/ narahari@hawaiiweddings.com

Houston, Texas — 1320 W. 34th St., 77018/ Tel. (713) 686-4482/ management@iskconhouston.org

Kansas City, Missouri — Rupanuga Vedic College, 5201 Paseo Blvd., 64110/ Tel. (816) 924-5640/ rvc@rvc.edu

Laguna Beach, California — 285 Legion St., 92651/ Tel. (949) 494-7029/ info@lagunatemple.com

Las Vegas, Nevada — Govinda's enter of Vedic India, 7181 Dean Martin Dr., 89118/ Tel. (702) 434-8332/ info@govindascenter.com

◆ **Los Angeles, California** — 3764 Watseka Ave., 90034/ Tel. (310) 836-2676/ membership@harekrishnala.com

◆ **Miami, Florida** — 3220 Virginia St., 33133 (mail: 3109 Grand Ave., #491, Coconut Grove, FL 33133/ Tel. (305) 442-7218/ devotionalservice@iskcon-miami.org

Mountain View, California — 1965 Latham St., 94040/ Tel. (650) 336 7993 / isvtemple108@gmail.com

New Orleans, Louisiana — 2936 Esplanade Ave., 70119/ Tel. (504) 304-0032 (office) or (504) 638-1944 (temple)/ gopal211@aol.com

New York, New York — 305 Schermerhorn St., Brooklyn, 11217/ Tel. (718) 855-6714/ ramabhadra@aol.com

New York, New York — The Bhakti Center, 25 First Ave., 10003/ Tel. (212) 253-6182

Orlando, Florida — 2651 Rouse Rd., 32817/ Tel. (407) 257-3865/ info@iskconorlando.com

Philadelphia, Pennsylvania — 41 West Allens Lane, 19119/ Tel. (215) 247-4600/ info@iskconphiladelphia.com

Philadelphia, Pennsylvania — 1408 South St., 19146/ Tel. (215) 985-9303/ govindasvegetarian.gmailcom

Phoenix, Arizona — 100 S. Weber Dr., Chandler, 85226/ Tel. (480) 705-4900/ premadhatridd@gmail.com

Portland, Oregon — 2095 NW Aloclek Dr., Suites 1107 & 1109, Hillsboro 97124/ Tel. (503) 675-5000/ info@iskconportland.com

◆ **St. Louis, Missouri** — 3926 Lindell Blvd., 63108/ Tel. (314) 535-8085 or 255-2207/ root@iskconstlouis.org

Salt Lake City, Utah — 965 E. 3370 South, 84106/ Tel. (801) 487-4005/ utahkrishnas@gmail.com

San Diego, California — 1030 Grand Ave., Pacific Beach, 92109/ Tel. (858) 483-2500/ krishna.sandiego@gmail.com

Seattle, Washington — 1420 228th Ave. S.E., Sammamish, 98075/ Tel. (425) 246-8436/ info@vediccculturalcenter.org

◆ **Spanish Fork, Utah** — Krishna Temple Project & KHQN Radio, 8628 S. State Road, 84660/ Tel. (801) 798-3559/ utahkrishnas@gmail.com

Tallahassee, Florida — 1323 Nylic St., 32304/ Tel. & fax: (850) 224-3803/ tallahassee.iskcon@gmail.com

Towaco, New Jersey — 100 Jacksonville Rd. (mail: P.O. Box

109), 07082/ Tel. & fax: (973) 299-0970/ madhupati.jas@pamho.net

◆**Tucson, Arizona** — 711 E. Blacklidge Dr., 85719/ Tel. (520) 792-0630/ sandaminidd@cs.com

Washington, D.C. — 10310 Oaklyn Dr., Potomac, Maryland 20854/ Tel. (301) 299-2100/ info@iskconofdc.org

RURAL COMMUNITIES

Alachua, Florida (New Raman Reti) — 17306 N.W. 112th Blvd., 32615 (mail: P.O. Box 819, 32616)/ Tel. (386) 462-2017/ alachuatemple@gmail.com

Carriere, Mississippi (New Talavan) — 31492 Anner Road, 39426/ Tel. (601) 749-9460 or 799-1354/ talavan@hughes.net

Gurabo, Puerto Rico (New Govardhana Hill) — Carr. 181, Km. 16.3, Bo. Santa Rita, Gurabo (mail: HC-01, Box 8440, Gurabo, PR 00778)/ Tel. & fax: (787) 767-3530 or 737-1722/ manoratha@gmail.com

Hillsborough, North Carolina (New Goloka) — 1032 Dimmocks Mill Rd., 27278/ Tel. (919) 732-6492/ bkgoswami@earthlink.net

◆ **Moundsville, West Virginia (New Vrindaban)** — 3759 McCrearys Ridge Rd., 26041/ Tel. (304) 843-1600 (Guesthouse extension: 111)/ mail@newvrindaban.com

Mulberry, Tennessee (Murari-sevaka) — 532 Murari Lane, 37359 Tel. (931) 759-6888/ murari_sevaka@yahoo.com

Port Royal, Pennsylvania (Gita Nagari) — 534 Gita Nagari Rd., 17082/ Tel. (717) 527-4101/ dhruva.bts@pamho.net

Sandy Ridge, North Carolina (Prabhupada Village) — 1283 Prabhupada Rd., 27046/ Tel. (336) 593-2322/ prabhupadavillage@gmail.com

ADDITIONAL RESTAURANTS

Hato Rey, Puerto Rico — Tamal Krishna's Veggie Garden, 131 Eleanor Roosevelt, 00918/ Tel. (787) 754-6959/ tkveggiegarden@aol.com

UNITED KINGDOM AND IRELAND

Belfast, Northern Ireland — Brooklands, 140 Upper Dunmurray Lane, BT17 OHE/ Tel. +44 (028) 9062 0530/ hk.temple108@gmail.com

Birmingham, England — 84 Stanmore Rd., Edgbaston B16 9TB/ Tel. +44 (121) 420 4999/ iskconbirmingham@gmail.com

Cardiff, Wales — The Soul Centre, 116 Cowbridge Rd., Canton/ Tel. +44 (29) 2039 0391/ the.soul.centre@pamho.net

Coventry, England — Kingfield Rd., Coventry (mail: 19 Gloucester St., Coventry CV1 3BZ)/ Tel. +44 (24) 7655 2822 or 5420/ haridas.kds@pamho.net

Dublin, Ireland — 83 Middle Abbey St., Dublin 1/ Tel. +353 (1) 661 5095/ dublin@krishna.ie; Govinda's: info@govindas.ie

Leicester, England — 21 Thoresby St., North Evington, LE5 4GU/ Tel. +44 (116) 276 2587/ pradyumna.jas@pamho.net

Lesmahagow, Scotland — Karuna Bhavan, Bankhouse Rd., Lesmahagow, Lanarkshire, ML11 0ES/ Tel. +44 (1555) 894790/ karunabhavan@aol.com

◆ **London, England (city)** — 10 Soho St., W1D 3DL/ Tel. +44 (20) 7437-3662; residential /pujaris, 7439-3606; shop, 7287-0269; Govinda's Restaurant, 7437-4928/ london@pamho.net

◆ **London, England (country)** — Bhaktivedanta Manor, Dharam Marg, Hilfield Lane, Watford, Herts, WD25 8EZ/ Tel. +44 (1923) 851000/ info@krishnatemple.com; (for accommodations:) bmguesthouse@krishna.com

London, England (south) — 42 Enmore Road, South Norwood, SE25 5NG/ Tel. +44 7988857530/ krishnaprema89@hotmail.com

London, England (Kings Cross) — 102 Caledonian Rd., Kings Cross, Islington, N1 9DN/ Tel. +44 (20) 7168 5732/ foodforalluk@aol.com

Manchester, England — 20 Mayfield Rd., Whalley Range, M16 8FT/ Tel. +44 (161) 226-4416/ contact@iskconmanchester.com

Newcastle-upon-Tyne, England — 304 Westgate Rd., NE4 6AR/ Tel. +44 (191) 272 1911

◆ **Swansea, Wales** — 8 Craddock St., SA1 3EN/ Tel. +44 (1792) 468469/ iskcon.swansea@pamho.net; restaurant: govin-das@hotmail.com

RURAL COMMUNITIES

London, England — (contact Bhaktivedanta Manor)

Upper Lough Erne, Northern Ireland — Govindadwipa Dhama, Inisrath Island, Derrylin, Co. Fermanagh, BT92 9GN/ Tel. +44 (28) 6772 1512/ iskconbirmingham@gmail.com

ADDITIONAL RESTAURANTS

Dublin, Ireland — Govinda's, 4 Aungier St., Dublin 2/ Tel. +353 (1) 475 0309/ info@govindas.ie

Dublin, Ireland — Govinda's, 83 Middle Abbey St., Dublin 1/ Tel. +353 (1) 661 5095/ info@govindas.ie

Dublin, Ireland — Govinda's, 18 Merrion Row, Dublin 2/ Tel. +353 (1) 661 5095/ praghosa.sdg@pamho.net

AUSTRALASIA

AUSTRALIA

Adelaide — 25 Le Hunte St. (mail: P.O. Box 114, Kilburn, SA 5084)/ Tel. & fax: +61 (8) 8359-5120/ iskconsa@tpg.com.au

Brisbane — 32 Jennifer St., Seventten Mile Rocks, QLD 4073 (mail: PO Box 525, Sherwood, QLD 4075)/ Tel. =61 (7) 3376 2388/ info@
iskcon.org.au

Canberra — 44 Limestone Ave., Ainslie, ACT 2602 (mail: P.O. Box 1411, Canberra, ACT 2601)/ Tel. & fax: +61 (2) 6262-6208

Melbourne — 197 Danks St. (mail: P.O. Box 125), Albert Park , VIC 3206/ Tel. +61 (3) 9699-5122/ melbourne@pamho.net

Perth — 155–159 Canning Rd., Kalamunda (mail: P.O. Box 201 Kalamunda 6076)/ Tel. +61 (8) 6293-1519/ perth@pamho.net

Sydney — 180 Falcon St., North Sydney, NSW 2060 (mail: P.O. Box 459, Cammeray, NSW 2062)/ Tel. +61 (2) 9959-4558/ admin@iskcon.com.au

Sydney — Govinda's Yoga and Meditation Centre, 112 Darlinghurst Rd., Darlinghurst NSW 2010 (mail: P.O. Box 174, Kings Cross 1340)/ Tel. +61 (2) 9380-5162/ sita@govindas.com.au

RURAL COMMUNITIES

Bambra, VIC (New Nandagram) — 50 Seaches Outlet, off 1265 Winchelsea Deans Marsh Rd., Bambra VIC 3241/ Tel. +61 (3) 5288-7383

Cessnock, NSW (New Gokula) — Lewis Lane (off Mount View Rd., Millfield, near Cessnock (mail: P.O. Box 399, Cessnock, NSW 2325)/ Tel. +61 (2) 4998-1800/

Murwillumbah, NSW (New Govardhana) — Tyalgum Rd., Eungella (mail: P.O. Box 687), NSW 2484/ Tel. +61 (2) 6672-6579/ ajita@in.com.au

RESTAURANTS

Brisbane — Govinda's, 99 Elizabeth St., 1st floor, QLD 4000/

Tel. +61 (7) 3210-0255
Brisbane — Krishna's Cafe, 1st Floor, 82 Vulture St., West End, QLD 4000/ brisbane@pamho.net
Burleigh Heads — Govindas, 20 James St., Burleigh Heads, QLD 4220/ Tel. +61 (7) 5607-0782/ ajita@in.com.au
Maroochydore — Govinda's Vegetarian Cafe, 2/7 First Avenue, QLD 4558/ Tel. +61 (7) 5451-0299
Melbourne — Crossways, 1st Floor, 123 Swanston St., VIC 3000/ Tel. +61 (3) 9650-2939
Melbourne — Gopal's, 139 Swanston St., VIC 3000/ Tel. +61 (3) 9650-1578
Newcastle — 110 King Street, NSW 2300/ Tel. +61 (02) 4929-6900/ info@govindascafe.com.au
Perth — Govinda's Restaurant, 194 William St., Northbridge, W.A. 6003/ Tel. +61 (8) 9227-1648/ perth@pamho.net
Perth — Hare Krishna Food for Life, NSW 2300/ Tel. +61 (02) 4929-6900/ info@govindascafe.com.au

NEW ZEALAND AND FIJI
Christchurch, NZ — 83 Bealey Ave. (mail: P.O. Box 25-190)/ Tel. +64 (3) 366-5174/ iskconchch@clear.net.nz
Hamilton, NZ — 188 Maui St., RD 8, Te Rapa/ Tel. +64 (7) 850-5108/ rmaster@wave.co.nz
Labasa, Fiji — Delailabasa (mail: P.O. Box 133)/ Tel. +679 812912
Lautoka, Fiji — 5 Tavewa Ave. (mail: P.O. Box 125)/ Tel. +679 6664112/ regprakash@excite.com
Nausori, Fiji — Hare Krishna Cultural Centre, 2nd Floor, Shop & Save Building, 11 Gulam Nadi St., Nausori Town (mail: P.O. Box 2183, Govt. Bldgs., Suva)/ Tel. +679 9969748 or 3475097/ vdas@frca.org.fj
Rakiraki, Fiji — Rewasa (mail: P.O. Box 204)/ Tel. +679 694243
Sigatoka, Fiji — Sri Sri Radha Damodar Temple, Off Mission St., Sigatoka Town/ Tel. +679 9373703/ drgsmarna@connect.com.fj
Suva, Fiji — 166 Brewster St. (mail: P.O. Box 4299, Samabula)/ Tel. +679 3318441/ iskconsuva@connect.com.fj
Wellington, NZ — 105 Newlands Rd., Newlands/ Tel. +64 (4) 478-4108/ info@iskconwellington.org.nz
Wellington, NZ — Gaura Yoga Centre, 1st Floor, 175 Vivian St. (mail: P.O. Box 6271, Marion Square)/ Tel. +64 (4) 801-5500/ yoga@gaurayoga.co.nz

RURAL COMMUNITY
Auckland, NZ (New Varshan) — Hwy. 28, Riverhead, next to Huapai Golf Course (mail: R.D. 2, Kumeu)/ Tel. +64 (9) 412-8075/

RESTAURANT
Wellington, NZ — Higher Taste Hare Krishna Restaurant, Old Bank Arcade, Ground Flr., Corner Customhouse, Quay & Hunter St., Wellington/ Tel. +64 (4) 472-2233

INDIA (partial list)*
Ahmedabad, Gujarat — Satellite Rd., Gandhinagar Highway Crossing, 380 054/ Tel. (79) 686-1945, -1645, or -2350/ iskcon.ahmedabad@pamho.net (Guesthouse: guesthouse.ahmedabad@pamho.net)
Allahabad, UP — Hare Krishna Dham, 161 Kashi Raj Nagar, Baluaghat 211 003/ Tel. (532) 2416718/ iskcon.allahabad@pamho.net
Amritsar, Punjab — Chowk Moni Bazar, Laxmansar, 143 001/ Tel. (183) 2540177
Amravati, Maharashtra — Saraswati Colony, Rathi Nagar 444 603/ Tel. (721) 2666849 or 9421805105/ iskconamravati@ymail.com
Aravade, Maharashtra — Hare Krishna Gram, Tal. Tagaon, Dist. Sangli/ Tel. (2346) 255-766
Bangalore, Karnataka — ISKCON Sri Jagannath Mandir, No.5 Sripuram, 1st cross, Sheshadripuram, 560 020/ Tel. 9901060738 or 9886709603/ varada.krsna.jps@pamho.net
Baroda, Gujarat — Hare Krishna Land, Gotri Rd., 390 021/ Tel. (265) 2310630 or 2331012/ iskcon.baroda@pamho.net
◆ **Bhubaneswar, Odisha** — N.H. No. 5, IRC Village, 751 015/ Tel. (674) 2553517, 2553475, or 2554283/ gm.iskconbbsr.ggs@pamho.net
Chandigarh, Punjab — Hare Krishna Dham, Sector 36-B, 160 036/ Tel. (172) 2601590 or 2603232/ iskcon.chandigarh@pamho.net
Chennai (Madras), TN — Hare Krishna Land, off ECR, Akkarai, Sholinganallur, Chennai 600 119/ Tel. (44) 24530921 or 24530923/ iskconchennai@gmail.com
◆ **Coimbatore, TN** — Jagannath Mandir, Hare Krishna Land, Aerodrome P.O., Opp. CIT, 641 014/ Tel. (422) 2626509 or 2626508/ info@iskcon-coimbatore.org
Dwarka, Gujarat — Bharatiya Bhavan, Devi Bhavan Rd., 361 335/ Tel. (2892) 34606
Guwahati, Assam — Ulubari Chariali, South Sarania, 781 007/ Tel. (361) 2525963/ iskcon.guwahati@pamho.net
Haridwar, Uttaranchal — Srila Prabhupada Ashram, G. House, Nai Basti, Mahadev Nagar, Bhimgoda, 249 401/ Tel. (1334) 260818
Hyderabad, AP — Hare Krishna Land, Nampally Station Rd., 500 001/ Tel. 8106130279 or (40) 24744969/ iskcon.hyderabad@pamho.net; Guesthouse: guesthouse.iskconhyd@pamho.net
Imphal, Manipur — Hare Krishna Land, Airport Rd., 795 001/ Tel. (385) 2455693/ manimandir@sancharnet.in
Indore, MP — ISKCON, Nipania, Indore/ Tel. 9300474043/ mahaman.acbsp@pamho.net
Jaipur, Rajasthan — ISKCON Road, Opp. Vijay Path, Mansarovar, Jaipur 302 020 (mail: ISKCON, 84/230, Sant Namdev Marg, Opp. K.V. No. 5, Mansarovar, Jaipur 302 020)/ Tel. (414) 2782765 or 2781860/ jaipur@pamho.net
Jammu, J&K — Srila Prabhupada Ashram, c/o Shankar Charitable Trust, Shakti Nagar, Near AG Office/ Tel. (191) 2582306
Kolkata (Calcutta), WB — 3C Albert Rd. (behind Minto Park, opp. Birla High School), 700 017/ Tel. (33) 3028-9258 or -9280/ iskcon.calcutta@pamho.net
◆ **Kurukshetra, Haryana** — ISKCON, Main Bazaar, 136 118/ Tel. (1744) 234806 or 235529
Lucknow, UP — 1 Ashok Nagar, Guru Govind Singh Marg, 226 018/ Tel. (522) 2635000, 2630026; or 9415235050/ iskcon.lucknow@pamho.net
◆ **Mayapur, WB** — ISKCON, Shree Mayapur Chandrodaya Mandir, Mayapur Dham, Dist. Nadia, 741313/ Tel. (3472) 245620, 245240 or 245355/ mayapur.chandrodaya@pamho.net
◆ **Mumbai (Bombay), Maharashtra** — Hare Krishna Land, Juhu 400 049/ Tel. (22) 26206860/ info@iskconmumbai.com; guesthouse.mumbai@pamho.net
◆ **Mumbai, Maharashtra** — 7 K. M. Munshi Marg, Chowpatty 400 007/ Tel. (22) 23665500/ info@radhagopinath.com

Mumbai, Maharashtra — Shristhi Complex, Mira Rd. (E), opposite Royal College, Dist. Thane, 401 107/ Tel. (22) 28454667 or 28454672/ jagjivan.gkg@pamho.net
Mysore, Karnataka — #31, 18th Cross, Jayanagar, 570 014/ Tel. (821) 2500582 or 6567333/ mysore.iskcon@gmail.com
Nellore, AP — ISKCON City, Hare Krishna Rd., 524 004/ Tel. (861) 2314577 or (92155) 36589/ sukadevaswami@gmail.com
◆ **New Delhi, UP** — Hare Krishna Hill, Sant Nagar Main Road, East of Kailash, 110 065/ Tel. (11) 2623-5133, 4, 5, 6, 7/ delhi@pamho.net; (Guesthouse) guest.house.new.delhi@pamho.net
◆ **New Delhi, UP** — 41/77, Punjabi Bagh (West), 110 026/ Tel. (11) 25222851 or 25227478 Noida, UP — A-5, Sector 33, opp. NTPC office, Noida 201 301/ Tel. (120) 2506211/ iskcon.punjabi.bagh@pamho.net
Patna, Bihar — Sri Sri Banke Bihariji Mandir, Golok Dham, Budha Marg, Patna-1/ Tel. (612) 2220794, 2687637, or 2685081; or 09431021881/ krishna.kripa.jps@pamho.net
Pune, Maharashtra — 4 Tarapoor Rd., Camp, 411 001/ Tel. (20) 41033222 or 41033223/ nvcc@iskconpune.in
Puri, Odisha — Bhakti Kuti, Swargadwar, 752 001/ Tel. (6752) 231440
Secunderabad, AP — 27 St. John's Rd., 500 026/ Tel. (40) 780-5232
Silchar, Assam — Ambikapatti, Silchar, Dist. Cachar, 788 004/ Tel. (3842) 34615
Srirangam, TN — 103 Amma Mandapam Rd., Srirangam, Trichy 620 006/ Tel. (431) 2433945/ iskcon_srirangam@yahoo.co.in
Surat, Gujarat — Ashram Rd., Jahangirpura, 395 005/ Tel. (261) 276-5891 or 276-5516/ surat@pamho.net
◆ **Thiruvananthapuram (Trivandrum), Kerala** — Hospital Rd., Thycaud, 695 014/ Tel. (471) 2328197/ jsdasa@yahoo.co.in
◆ **Tirupati, AP** — K.T. Rd., Vinayaka Nagar, 517 507/ Tel. (877) 2231760 or 2230009/ revati.raman.jps@pamho.net; Guestouse: guesthouse.tirupati@pamho.net
Udhampur, J&K — Srila Prabhupada Ashram, Srila Prabhupada Marg, Srila Prabhupada Nagar 182 101/ Tel. (1992) 270298/ info@iskconudhampur.com
Ujjain, MP — 35–37 Hare Krishna Land, Bharatpuri, 456 010/ Tel. (734) 2535000 or 2531000, or 9300969016/ iskcon.ujjain@pamho.net
Varanasi, UP — ISKCON, B 27/80 Durgakund Rd., Near Durgakund Police Station, Varanasi 221 010/ Tel. (542) 246422 or 222617
◆ **Vrindavan, UP** — Krishna-Balaram Mandir, Bhaktivedanta Swami Marg, Raman Reti, Mathura Dist., 281 124/ Tel. & Fax: (565) 2540728/ iskcon.vrindavan@pamho.net; (Guesthouse:) Tel. (565) 2540022; ramamani@sancharnet.in

ADDITIONAL RESTAURANT

Kolkata, WB — Govinda's, ISKCON House, 22 Gurusaday Rd., 700 019/ Tel. (33) 24866922, 24866009

EUROPE (partial list)*

Amsterdam — Van Hilligaertstraat 17, 1072 JX/ Tel. +31 (20) 675-1404 or -1694/ amsterdam@pamho.net
Bergamo, Italy — Villaggio Hare Krishna (da Medolago strada per Terno d'Isola), 24040 Chignolo d'Isola (BG)/ Tel. +39 (035) 4940705/ villagio.hare.krsna@hare.krsna.it
Budapest — III. Lehel Street 15–17 (Csillaghedy), 1039 Budapest/ Tel. +36 (1) 391-0435 or 397-5219/ budapest@pamho.net
Copenhagen — Skjulhøj Alle 44, 2720 Vanløse, Copenhagen/ Tel. +45 4828 6446/ iskcon.denmark@pamho.net
Grödinge, Sweden — Radha-Krishna Temple, Korsnäs Gård, 14792 Grödinge, Tel. +46 (8) 53025062/ bmd@pamho.net
Helsinki — Ruoholahdenkatu 24 D (III krs) 00180/ Tel. +358 (9) 694-9879 or -9837/ harekrishna@harekrishna.fi
◆ **Lisbon** — Rua Dona Estefãnia, 91 R/C 1000 Lisboa/ Tel. & fax: +351(1) 314-0314 or 352-0038
Madrid — Espíritu Santo 19, 28004 Madrid/ Tel. +34 91 521-3096
Paris — 230 Avenue de la Division Leclerc, 95200 Sarcelles Village/ Tel. +33 682590079/ paris@pamho.net
◆ **Radhadesh, Belgium** — Chateau de Petite Somme, 6940 Septon-Durbuy/ Tel. +32 (86) 322926 (restaurant: 321421)/ radhadesh@pamho.net
◆ **Rome** — Govinda Centro Hare Krsna, via Santa Maria del Pianto, 16, 00186/ Tel. +39 (06) 68891540/ govinda.roma@harekrsna.it
◆ **Stockholm** — Fridhemsgatan 22, 11240/ Tel. +46 (8) 654-9002/ Restaurant: Tel. & fax: +46 (8) 654-9004/ lokanatha@hotmail.com
Zürich — Mohini, Weinbergstr, 15, 8011/ Tel. +41 (44) 252-5211/ info@mohini.ch

RURAL COMMUNITIES

France (La Nouvelle Mayapura) — Domaine d'Oublaisse, 36360, Lucay le Mâle/ Tel. +33 (2) 5440-2395/ oublaise@free.fr
Germany (Simhachalam) — Zielberg 20, 94118 Jandelsbrunn/ Tel. +49 (8583) 316/ info@simhachalam.de
Hungary (New Vraja-dhama) — Krisna-völgy, 8699 Somogyvamos, Fö u, 38/ Tel. & fax: +36 (85) 540-002 or 340-185/ info@krisnavolgy.hu
Italy (Villa Vrindavan) — Via Scopeti 108, 50026 San Casciano in Val di Pesa (FL)/ Tel. +39 (55) 820054/ isvaripriya@libero.it
Spain (New Vraja Mandala) — (Santa Clara) Brihuega, Guadalajara/ Tel. +34 949 280436

ADDITIONAL RESTAURANTS

Barcelona — Restaurante Govinda, Plaza de la Villa de Madrid 4–5, 08002/ Tel. +34 (93) 318-7729
Copenhagen — Govinda's, Nørre Farimagsgade 82, DK-1364 Kbh K/ Tel. +45 3333 7444
Milan — Govinda's, Via Valpetrosa 5, 20123/ Tel. +39 (2) 862417
Oslo — Krishna's Cuisine, Kirkeveien 59B, 0364/ Tel. +47 (2) 260-6250

COMMONWEALTH OF INDEPENDENT STATES
(partial list)*

Kiev — 16, Zoryany pereulok. 04078/ Tel. +380 (44) 4338312, or 4347028, or 4345533
Moscow — Leningradsky Prospect, Vladenie 39 (mail: Begovaya str., 13, OPS 284, a/ya 17, 125284 Moscow)/ Tel. +7 (495) 7394377/ temple@veda.ru

ASIA (partial list)*

Bangkok, Thailand — Soi3, Tanon Itsarapap, Toonburi/ Tel. +66 (2) 9445346 or (81) 4455401 or (89) 7810623/ swami.

bvv.narasimha@pamho.net

Dhaka, Bangladesh — 79 Swamibag, Dhaka-11/ Tel. +880 (2) 7122747 or 7122448/ info@iskconbd.org

Hong Kong, China — 6/F Oceanview Court, 27 Chatham Road South (mail:P.O.Box 98919)/ Tel.+852 (2) 739-6818/ iskconhk@iskconhk.org

Jakarta, Indonesia — Yayasan Radha-Govinda, P.O. Box 2694, Jakarta Pusat 10001/ Tel. +62 (21) 489-9646/ matsyads@bogor.wasantara.net.id

Kathmandu, Nepal — Budhanilkantha (mail: GPO Box 3520)/ Tel. +977 (1) 4373790 or 4373786/ iskconkathmandu@gmail.com

Kuala Lumpur, Malaysia — Lot 9901, Jalan Awan Jawa, Taman Yarl, 58200 Kuala Lumpur/ Tel. +60 (3) 7980-7355/ president@iskconkl.com

Manila, Philippines — Radha-Madhava Center, #9105 Banuyo St., San Antonio village, Makati City/ Tel. +63 (2) 8963357/ iskconmanila@yahoo.com

Myitkyina, Myanmar — ISKCON Sri Jagannath Temple, Bogyoke Street, Shansu Taung, Myitkyina, Kachin State/ mahanadi@mptmail.net.mm

Tai Pei City Taiwan, China — Zhong Xiao East Rd. Section 2, Lane 39, Alley 2, No. 3, 2F/ Tel. +886 (2) 2395-6010 or 2395-6715/ bhavna@ms22.hinet.net

Tokyo, Japan — 2-23-4 Funabori, Edogawa-ku, Tokyo 134-0091/ Tel. +81 (3) 3877-3000/ iskcon.new.gaya.japan@gmail.com

LATIN AMERICA (partial list)*

Buenos Aires, Argentina — Ciudad de la Paz 394, Colegiales, Buenos Aires 1426/ Tel. +54 4555-5654/ nat.div@gmail.com

Caracas, Venezuela — Av. Los Proceres (con Calle Marquez del Toro), San Bernardino/ Tel. +58 (212) 550-1818

Guayaquil, Ecuador — 6 de Marzo 226 and V. M. Rendon/ Tel. +593 (4) 308412 or 309420

◆ **Lima, Peru** — Schell 634 Miraflores/ Tel. +51 (14) 444-2871

Mexico City, Mexico — Tiburcio Montiel 45, Colonia San Miguel, Chapultepec D.F., 11850/ Tel. and fax: +52 (55) 5272-5944/ iskcon@krishnamexico.com

Rio de Janeiro, Brazil — Estrada da Barra da Tijuca, 1990, Itanhangá, Rio de Janeiro, RJ/ Tel. +55 (21) 3563-1627/ contato@harekrishnarj.com.br

San Salvador, El Salvador — 8a Avenida Norte, Casa No. 2–4, Santa Tecla, La Libertad/ Tel. +503 2288-2900/ mail@harekrishnaelsalvador.com

São Paulo, Brazil — Rua Tomas Goncalves 70, Butanta, 05590-030/ Tel. +55 (11) 8496-3158/ comunicacao@harekrishnasp.com.br

West Coast Demerara, Guyana — Sri Gaura Nitai Ashirvad Mandir, Lot "B," Nauville Flanders (Crane Old Road), West Coast Demerara/ Tel. +592 254 0494

AFRICA (partial list)*

Accra, Ghana — Samsam Rd., Off Accra-Nsawam Hwy., Medie, Accra North (mail: P.O. Box 11686)/ Tel. & fax +233 (21) 229988/ srivas_bts@yahoo.co.in

Cape Town, South Africa — 17 St. Andrews Rd., Rondebosch 7700/ Tel. +27 (21) 6861179

◆ **Durban, South Africa** — 50 Bhaktivedanta Swami Circle, Unit 5 (mail: P.O. Box 56003), Chatsworth, 4030/ Tel. +27 (31) 403-3328/ iskcon.durban@pamho.net

Johannesburg, South Africa — 7971 Capricorn Ave. (entrance on Nirvana Drive East), Ext. 9, Lenasia (mail: P.O. Box 926, Lenasia 1820)/ Tel. +27 (11) 854-1975 or 7969/ iskconjh@iafrica.com

Lagos, Nigeria — No. 23 Egbeyemi St., Off Coker Rd., Illupeju, Lagos (mail: P. O. Box 8793, Marina)/ Tel. +234 8069245577 or 7066011800

Mombasa, Kenya — Hare Krishna House, Sauti Ya Kenya and Kisumu Rds. (mail: P.O. Box 82224, Mombasa)/ Tel. +254 (11) 312248

Nairobi, Kenya — Hare Krishna Close, Off West Nagara Rd., Nairobi 0100 (mail: P.O. Box 28946)/ Tel. +254 (20) 3744365/ iskcon_nairobi@yahoo.com

◆ **Phoenix, Mauritius** — Hare Krishna Land, Srila Prabhupada St., Pont Fer/ Tel. +230 6965804/ iskcon.phoenix@intnet.mu

Port Harcourt, Nigeria — Umuebule 11, 2nd tarred road, Etche (mail: P.O. Box 4429, Trans Amadi)/ Tel. +234 8033215096

Pretoria, South Africa — 1189 Church St., Hatfield, 0083 (mail: P.O. Box 14077, Hatfield, 0028)/ Tel. & fax: +27 (12) 342-6216/ iskconpt@global.co.za

RURAL COMMUNITY

Mauritius (ISKCON Vedic Farm) — Hare Krishna Rd., Vrindaban/ Tel. +230 418-3185 or 418-3955

To save space, we've skipped the codes for North America (1) and India (91). ◆ Temples with restaurants or dining

*The full list is always available at Krishna.com, where it also includes Krishna conscious gatherings.

Far from a center?
Contact us on the Internet.

http://www.krishna.com • E-mail: bbt.usa@krishna.com